A Very Special Journey of Grief, Grace, and Gratitude

No, They Are Not Okay…but It's Okay!
Raising Special Needs Kids

Julie Clark Ames

NEWMAN SPRINGS PUBLISHING
320 Broad Street
Red Bank, NJ 07701

First originally published by Newman Springs Publishing 2019

Cover Photo: Christina (7 years old), Maria (9 years old),
and Anna (4 years old)

ISBN 978-1-64531-695-4 (Paperback)
ISBN 978-1-64531-696-1 (Digital)

Printed in the United States of America

Book Endorsements

"Julie's story of parenting special needs children is personal, powerful, and intensely practical. She writes about every aspect of the special needs journey. Her book is real. Honest. Heartbreaking. And, best of all, inspirational. Julie is living this experience and she will help you live it."

—David E. Clarke, Ph.D.
Christian psychologist, author, and speaker

"If you want to be immersed in another's life, so deeply, that you feel and encounter the complete range of emotions from joy to sorrow, through the days and nights, and the caldron of the other's life, then this book will lead you on a journey you're not likely to encounter elsewhere. For my part, as a Franciscan Friar and Catholic priest, it was a journey into an amazing story of grace lived out in the life of the Ames family as they raise special needs kids. I read the book on the Feast of the Holy Family on which one of the scripture readings was from St. Paul: *"Put on, as God's chosen ones, holy and beloved, heartfelt compassion, kindness, humility, gentleness, and patience, bearing with one another and forgiving one another."* (Col 3:12-13). If you want to see this passage lived out, not perfectly, but faithfully; if you want to see what holiness looks like, then this book is a must read."

—Fr. George Corrigan, OFM
Pastor of Sacred Heart Catholic Church

"Rarely does a book provide such an extraordinarily compelling story along with essential resources for families and professionals. Julie's insightful narrative provides a unique, insider's perspective on the joys and struggles of everyday life for families of individuals with disabilities as well as thoughtful reflection on critical lifespan questions. While packed with current, useful information for parents and siblings navigating their own family journeys, the book also contains valuable information for professionals in diverse fields including education, health care, counseling, and business. As a special educator and sibling of a person with a disability, I greatly appreciate the authenticity, practicality, and significance of this important work."

—**Ann Cranston-Gingras, PhD**
Professor and Associate Dean for Academic Affairs
University of South Florida

"Julie Ames is a special person and gifted writer in the way she humbly and generously shares her experiences and insights for other caregivers' benefit. What a gift this book is for anyone seeking compassion and direction in advocating for special needs loved ones!"

—**Debbie Lundberg, Author, MBA**
Founder & CEO, Presenting Powerfully

"Julie takes readers on a personal journey sharing her experiences raising two children with special needs. Her raw emotions are openly displayed shedding light on the silent emotional struggles that will resound with parents who share similar paths. Julie includes beneficial information to help readers navigate challenges related to medical needs, education, and family. I would highly recommend this book for every parent raising a child with special needs."

—**Loresa Stansell, MA, LPC, NCC**
Counselor, Author, and Speaker

Disclaimers

This book is based on the author's memories of past events, locations, and conversations. Some names and descriptive characteristics have been changed. Dates and events may not be in the exact ordered that they occurred. Some license has been taken for storytelling purposes. My opinions in this book are not meant to replace professional medical or legal advice. The author shall not be held liable or responsible for any loss or damage allegedly arising from any information or suggestions in this book.

To my dearest Jeffrey,

The man who believed in my ability to write this book even when I didn't think I could. Thank you for all the love, laughter, endless discussions, and editing; and thank you for truly being there for better or for worse.

To our wonderful girls Maria, Christina, and Anna, they were each an answer to our prayers.

To Mom and Dad for being there for me. Mom, for always cheering me on and having faith even when I didn't think things would be fine. Dad, for being steadfast with his support and love.

Thank you.

A special thank-you to Andrea Lehner for her dedication, thoughtfulness, and skill as a writer that helped bring my story to life.

Contents

Introduction

Dear reader,

Since you've picked up this book, chances are you're already familiar with the terms *autism* and *autism spectrum disorder*, but have you heard of a genetic condition called *chromosomal transloca-tion*? No? Nor had I prior to a geneticist informing me that my two oldest of three daughters have this rare genetic condition. Nor did I know until that day that I, too, have a similar translocation. The only difference between mine and the translocation my daughters inherited from me is that my translocation is balanced, meaning the tips of my chromosomes 3 and 5 are evenly exchanged. With my daughters, the tip of chromosome 3 was deleted, while the genetic code from the tip of chromosome 5 was duplicated on both. The result is that while I'm unaffected, an unknowing carrier, my two oldest daughters, Maria and Christina, have significant developmental delays and learning disabilities that eventually led them to being classified as autistic.

While not completely unheard of in the medical community, chromosomal translocations are rare enough that our daughters went undiagnosed for several years. In fact, it was not until I was pregnant with our fourth child that I simultaneously learned of their diagnoses and discovered that I was the cause and could quite possibly give birth to another child with the same condition. Our youngest daughter, Anna, did not inherit the translocation, so there was also a chance the new baby would be fine. But just four months into the pregnancy, the little heartbeat was gone. I was devastated. And I knew, I just knew, that the genetic translocation was to blame. I also realized, for the first time, what a miracle it was that my first two survived childbirth.

Many translocation babies do not survive, and those that do are often severely disabled or may not live beyond a few months, depending on the unique pairing of the chromosomes affected. In fact, if the deletion were reversed and it were the tip of chromosome 5 rather than 3 that was missing, the result would have been a rare but well-documented condition known as cri du chat syndrome.[1] Different pairings, or even the location on the strand where the duplication deletion occurs, determine the severity of the outcome. In this regard, our daughters' conditions are so unique that none of the doctors or specialists we've seen have been able to adequately predict what the future holds, medically, for either of them.

The genetic cause of our daughters' developmental delays is very technical and complex, but this book is not about the cause; it's about our journey of accepting and learning to live with the reality of their condition. This is a story—our very personal story—of how my husband and I adapted to the daily challenges; survived emotional and physical crises; found ways to laugh through our tears; navigated the special education system; fought to protect our rights when false allegations of abuse dragged our daughters into the middle of a gut-wrenching investigation; and, through it all, stayed grounded to our faith, our relationship, and our family.

This is not a one-size-fits-all "how-to" book on living with autism. Nor is it a dry book of facts about the condition, its causes,

---

[1] Cri-du-chat (cat's cry) syndrome, also known as 5p- (5p minus) syndrome, is a chromosomal condition that results when a piece of chromosome 5 is missing. Infants with this condition often have a high-pitched cry that sounds like that of a cat. The disorder is characterized by intellectual disability and delayed development, small head size (microcephaly), low birth weight, and weak muscle tone (hypotonia) in infancy. Affected individuals also have distinctive facial features, including widely set eyes (hypertelorism), low-set ears, a small jaw, and a rounded face. Some children with cri-du-chat syndrome are born with a heart defect. The size of the deletion varies among affected individuals; studies suggest that larger deletions tend to result in more severe intellectual disability and developmental delay than smaller deletions.

or hope-filled promises for remedies. I'm not a medical expert, nor am I a child development specialist. I am, however, a mother, just like any other mother of the one in fifty-nine children in the US currently diagnosed with some degree of autism.[2] And this is a very real, sometimes raw, look at the struggles—and rewards—of raising two special needs children.

While the circumstances in every special needs home are different, it is my hope that my story will resonate with all readers—parents, grandparents, siblings, and caretakers of special needs children, as well as special education professionals, teachers, and even those in the medical community. By sharing my story and lessons learned along the way in as honest and open a manner as possible, I hope to help families find the courage to get through their darker days, to inspire them to find the presence of God's grace in their homes, and to provide tips for making transitions to different stages of development easier (and safer!). Additionally, for those who so nobly decide to make helping special needs children their life's work, I hope to provide insight to the emotional roller coaster that these parents spend a lifetime enduring. Let me start by acknowledging the obvious: parents do not anticipate this path. No one plans to give birth to a child with developmental disabilities. No parents wish this for their children. We love our children unconditionally, but this journey is about more than love. It's about reconciling all those prechildbirth fantasies of raising the perfect child with the down-and-dirty reality of daily life with a special needs child. At first, there's nothing but fear and anguish, because there's no road map for this journey. The unknown is terrifying, especially when it involves the health and well-being of our children. Selfishly, we mourn for the loss of all those usual milestones—driving, graduation, college, marriage, grandchildren— that we know other parents will get to experience with their kids. In reality, we are mourning the loss of a life we once thought we would have. But ever so slowly, we create new milestones, new goals, and a

---

[2] Source: AutismSpeaks.org 2013. Other sources in 2018 suggest the frequency may have risen to one in forty.

new vision of life that includes finding happiness in the gifts we have received through our children.

For me, the journey began when I met my husband, Jeffrey. We were both ambitious, highly educated, and career-minded engineers. I graduated with a degree in industrial engineering from the Georgia Institute of Technology; Jeff graduated from West Point with a mechanical engineering degree. We met at Georgia Tech during my senior year. Jeff had just completed five years at Fort Bragg, North Carolina, to include a command assignment with the 82nd Airborne. And he had been selected for advanced schooling. He chose Georgia Tech for its top-rated engineering program. Within a year we were married, Jeff had his master's, I had my bachelor's, and we moved to Washington, DC, for his next assignment at the Pentagon.

For nearly ten years, we pursued our career goals, with little thought of children. I was a cost analyst with a *secret* clearance working on challenging projects such as the construction of the aircraft carrier USS *Ronald Reagan* and the creation of the USS *Missouri* Battleship Museum. This was my life prior to having Maria and deciding to become a stay-at-home mom. I can't say that I ever pictured being at home full-time for the rest of my life—my professional side was deeply rooted, and still is in many regards. But with the birth of Maria, I hung up my fitted suits and began my new role as Mom. Little did I know then that my vision of a life fulfilled by world travel, a prestigious title, and advanced degrees would devolve into a life filled with hospital emergencies, countless doctor visits, encounters with social services, a crash course in the special education system, numerous moments of public embarrassment, and cleaning up more vomit than I care to remember. As each day passed, the glory and glamour of my former life faded further and further from view. Travel, nannies, expensive cars, and designer clothes are not a part of my life; but that's okay.

This life is different *but* not less. Progress is slow, and victories small, but each is greeted with tearful gratitude. Never would I have imagined, one day, the thrill and excitement of experiencing our first trip away with all our children, a paltry ninety miles from home for a two-day vacation. Today, my home is filled with love, joy, and occasionally, order. Most importantly, I have learned to accept the disappointments, rebound from discouragement, and find peace in the midst of chaos. I sincerely hope that by reading my story, your special journey, however similar or different, will be just a little easier.

Julie

Part 1

From Realization to Acceptance

Genesis

When the World Stopped Spinning
Discovering the Genetic Disorder

April 8, 2003. I remember the day vividly. I remember sitting in a white IKEA chair in our study as I read the four-page letter from the geneticist. I guess I should've been more prepared for the results after having gone through the testing, but the simple fact was I was not ready to see it in print. But there it was in black-and-white—Maria and Christina had a confirmed genetic anomaly, which meant their conditions were permanent. As if that wasn't enough, this was the letter that informed me that I was the one who had given it to them.

I can't begin to describe the weight and, oddly, the relief that came with that letter. Up until that point, Jeff and I had accepted that our girls were a bit behind in their development, but we were hopeful that at some point they'd outgrow it. When the geneticist nonchalantly told us not to worry about the fact that our six-year-old might still be drinking out of a sippy cup into adulthood, that she had a teenage patient who still used a bottle, I was annoyed at how she could speak about something so serious in such a cavalier, dismissive manner. I was looking for answers and trying to find ways to help our girls catch up; I wasn't expecting to learn that not only were they going to be facing challenges their entire lives but that if I had more children they would likely have the same—or worse—problems.

Sitting there in that white chair, my world seemed to stop. Everything I thought I knew about my life and my future just changed. The guilt of knowing I passed this condition to my babies was unbelievable. Yet between the shock and grief, there was the relief of having a diagnosis. After all the years of doctors, all the struggles of trying to get the girls to learn, of making excuses and hiding the severity of their developmental delays, I finally had a concrete reason that would allow me to get them the help they needed.

Over the next few days, the guilt weighed heavily on me. Jeff didn't seem to understand why I was so upset, which only added to my frustration. For him, we simply had more information than we had a day earlier, but the new information didn't change anything. He took a much more pragmatic view of the situation. "Why agonize over it?" he would say. "We just need to deal with it."

Dealing with it wasn't quite as clear-cut and simple for me, however. Realizing that two of my three children weren't normal and never would be was tantamount to grieving a death. I was losing everything. My hopes and dreams for my children, my visions for normalcy, and any joy at the prospect of having another baby were instantly destroyed. It was like a bomb exploded when I opened that letter; everything was changing. If only it wasn't my fault. If only there was something that could fix it all.

Eventually, I would learn to accept our changed reality the same way Jeff did. I would move out of the grief-guilt cycle. I would recover from my shock and return to focusing on getting the girls the right doctors, therapists, and schools. Yes, I would get there, but I wouldn't get there for some time. Little did I know that I had more hurdles looming in my immediate future that would punctuate this period of my life as one of the darkest I've endured. In what can only be described as the epitome of bad timing, it turned out that I had conceived just a day before receiving my genetic test results. So as I grieved about the idea of future babies being at risk, I had no idea I was already pregnant with our fourth child. I would soon have to answer questions that would test the limits of my moral fiber and fortitude.

Maria's Birth	1996
Christina's Birth	1998
Anna's Birth	2000
Genetic Diagnosis	2003

Leading Up to Genetic Testing

Not long before we sought genetic testing, we moved from Virginia to Florida to be closer to family. Moving meant new doctors, which I knew would take time to set up. Just before the move, I took Maria for her annual physical and discovered that she hadn't grown at all during the previous year, and she had developed a heart murmur. This raised a red flag for our pediatrician, so he sent us to an endocrinologist who ran some initial blood tests to check for Turner's syndrome.[3] The tests were negative for Turner's, but an unspecified genetic anomaly was detected. Maria was six at the time.

As soon as we settled in Florida, we found a geneticist to follow up with the endocrinologist's discovery. Because Maria and Christina displayed some developmental similarities, the geneticist first recommended testing Christina and soon decided Jeff and I needed to be tested as well. It was soon confirmed Maria and Christina both had the same anomaly, an unbalanced chromosomal rearrangement—a small deletion on the tip of chromosome 3 that was replaced with a duplication of chromosome 5, also referred to as deletion-duplication or chromosomal translocation. *Cri du chat* is caused by the same chromosomal translocation only in reverse. A deletion of chromosome 5 is replaced by a duplication of chromosome 3. The reason I'm okay is the tips of my chromosomes 3 and 5 are perfectly switched

---

[3] Turner syndrome is a chromosomal condition that affects development in females. The most common feature of Turner syndrome is short stature, which becomes evident by about age 5. An early loss of ovarian function (ovarian hypofunction or premature ovarian failure) is also very common. Most girls and women with Turner syndrome have normal intelligence. Developmental delays, nonverbal learning disabilities, and behavioral problems are possible, although these characteristics vary among affected individuals.

without the deletion-duplication that occurred with Maria's and Christina's. I'm considered a "balanced translocation." Fortunately, Anna is unaffected.

The geneticist was not as helpful as she could have been. She simply told us the condition would mean the girls would be shorter and learn more slowly than normal children. Even though she down-played the effects, the geneticist did give us what we needed—a clear physiological reason for their challenges. Now we knew. Now we had a piece of paper with test results that enabled us to seek appro-priate help in addressing each of the girls' unique challenges. Later, after pursuing psychiatric care for the girls' anxiety issues, we were further advised that they were *autistic* as a result of the chromosomal translocation.

Like most parents, I initially dreaded having my girls receive any kind of label. Unlike other parents, however, I had already been struggling with my ability to teach them normal childhood mile-stones. A label meant I wasn't a failure. Now I knew why they still weren't potty-trained at ages six and four. The diagnosis explained why Christina needed speech therapy and why Maria couldn't eat solid food. Now we knew why the girls were so far behind others of the same age. But knowing all these things didn't make the per-manency of their conditions any easier to accept. I continued resist-ing the idea of publicly announcing their genetic anomalies. While I grasped to the relief that came from knowing there was an actual reason for their challenges, I was still not prepared to accept that they would not pass for normal girls.

Before the testing, they were just two little girls who were delayed in some areas. When Maria had first entered kindergarten the previous fall, it was obvious she wasn't ready for school. After three weeks, I decided to try homeschooling. Throughout the win-ter, I tried and tried to teach both Maria and Christina very simple concepts, like above and below, front or behind, over and under; but neither could grasp them. This, combined with their physical difficulties of only eating soft foods and still wearing training pants, put an incredible strain on my self-esteem. What kind of mother couldn't even teach her children basic concepts? I had given up a respected career as an industrial engineer with the navy, with a secret-level security clearance, and yet I couldn't even get my kids to chew solid food. Going to social events was humiliating. I tried to hide their limitations from my family. I was embarrassed, and I felt more and more like a failure every day. The diagnosis, at least, gave me a sense of relief. It was not my fault I couldn't teach them after all. There was a legitimate reason Maria and Christina were delayed. The feeling of guilt for failing as a mother abated somewhat, only to be replaced with a stronger sense of guilt for being the source of the genetic condition that caused their autism.

I remember, too, how denial helped fill me with false hope during those days. After we settled in our new home in Florida, I enrolled Maria in our local school to start kindergarten once again. It didn't take long to notice that she was still struggling. The teacher did not want to be the one to tell me Maria might need a lower-functioning class, but I knew something wasn't right. I wanted so badly for Maria to print her name. I worked and worked with her. It's funny how you can fixate your hopes on one small thing like that. In my mind, if she could do that one thing, just that one, it would prove she was capable of staying in the regular-education class.

Denial is a powerful thing. Even with the letter from the geneticist, part of me did not accept the truth. Then came the day that Maria's teacher selected a different parent for homeroom mom. I had volunteered, and she had seemed eager enough to have me help out. Not being chosen was not what upset me. When the teacher announced someone else as homeroom mom, I received a very loud and clear message that she knew Maria was not going to make it in her class. Why would she choose me when she knew Maria would have to be moved to a different classroom? It was an indirect message with a direct reality. I couldn't pretend or fool the outside world any longer.

I recall talking with Jeff about being thankful that I didn't get this news when I was younger. I would not have been able to handle it without the inner strength that only comes with maturity and having developed a stronger sense of identity. I think back to my mind-set in my youth and know that a blow like this one would have psychologically devastated me at that time. We also found strength and gratitude for not knowing about my genetic condition before having our three girls. If we had known at any point prior to conceiving any one of the girls, chances are strong that we would not have had them. Today, I can't imagine my life without these three blessings. Despite the sadness, I found comfort in the fact that God had graced us with a wonderful, albeit imperfect, family. God had made the decisions about their births for me; I hadn't had to test my faith—yet.

Not knowing I was pregnant again and that I would have to face the decisions that come with consciously bearing a child that could be autistic or suffer from severe mental retardation gave me a respite for what was to come. For those few short weeks between conception and receiving positive results on a pregnancy test, I had a brief glimpse of peace. However, that peace would not last long.

Another Baby?

When I learned the genetic testing results, I didn't tell anyone, not even my parents. When I learned that I was pregnant, I still didn't want to voice the truth about Maria and Christina, about myself, and about the uncertain future of the life growing in my womb. I can't say exactly why, other than that I knew I needed the information to be private, at least for the time being. Perhaps there was a part of me that didn't want to be judged by others. I already felt like I was being judged for having a fourth child, and if people knew the oldest two had a genetic condition that caused developmental delays, I could just imagine their scorn.

As Catholics, whether or not to keep the baby wasn't even a question, we knew we would have it. Jeff has so much patience and love in his heart; every baby God chose to provide would be a welcome gift. That is one of the traits I deeply admire in him. I, however, was a little more daunted at the prospect of having another special needs child. Yet when the nurse at my prenatal visit asked me if I wanted cystic fibrosis testing done, I declined. Although this pregnancy was unplanned, I saw no benefit in exposing the baby to potentially harmful tests. The results of the test would not have mattered anyhow; there wasn't anything we could do except love the baby just as we loved Maria, Christina, and Anna. Abortion was never considered an option.

Throughout the first trimester, I remained silent about the genetic anomaly. I still hadn't told my family. Among my friends, I expressed concern about the health of the baby, but I attributed it to being over forty. All I would say was, "I have two special needs children, and there is a likelihood that the baby will be too." Of course, there was the glimmer of hope that it wouldn't. We had had Anna—a perfectly healthy and bright little girl. What if this baby was our perfect son? It was a pregnancy riddled with mixed emotions.

To make matters even more difficult, Christina suddenly began hyperventilating constantly. This was new. We took her to a neurologist who began testing her for Rett syndrome, a degenerative nerve disease that could potentially take her from us at a very young age. Most expectant mothers are filled with joy; I wanted so badly to be happy, but the uncertainty of the baby and the new situation with Christina was heart-wrenching. I remember going through my day, doing a routine, mundane task and breaking down in tears as I tried to figure out what a little girl should do before she dies. The Rett test was negative, but I will never forget the rawness of the pain that came with that thought.

Finding a prolife doctor proved to be very important during this pregnancy. I first went to an obstetrician who wasn't; the entire visit was rife with negativity. The doctor made me very uncomfortable with a rude and callous attitude. When I voiced my concerns over the cystic fibrosis testing her nurse was recommending, the doctor said flatly, "Well, cystic fibrosis is no reason to kill a baby." I was shocked and at a complete loss for words. Was she suggesting that there *is* a good reason to kill a baby? She had already read my genetic report and knew the probability for a chromosomal translocation in this baby. Was she implying I was wrong to be having this baby? I couldn't help but think, *What about me? What qualified me for life? What if some doctor had recommended aborting me because of the risk?*

I was so appalled by her demeanor I got my files and never went back. I was already upset enough about the situation without adding an unsympathetic doctor to the mix. Thankfully, I found a new obstetrician with a different philosophy. He was a parent of a boy with Down syndrome, and he knew that despite the challenges, our special needs children are blessings to be treasured. I found peace in his office. By the time I left, I had a sonogram showing a healthy pregnancy with an egg in the right place. Everything began looking brighter.

In the weeks that followed, I began to feel better than I had in a very long time. We heard the heartbeat for the first time at twelve weeks. Besides some spotting and Braxton Hicks contractions that the doctor assured me were fine, I felt great. It was summer in Florida. The sun was shining. The girls were happy. Everything looked beautiful.

I was amazed at how great I felt during this pregnancy in contrast to Anna's. My pregnancy with Anna was by far the most difficult of my first three. Ironically, the hardest pregnancy was with my healthiest child. This time, I didn't have the morning sickness and exhaustion that usually rendered me immobile for most of the first trimester. Physically, I felt great.

On the morning of my sixteen-week prenatal exam, the girls and I enjoyed a lovely swim. I can still remember the way the sun was casting shadows on the bottom of the pool. I did a bit of housework, got the girls dressed, and waited for my mom to arrive. She was coming with us to keep an eye on the girls while I was in the exam room. Afterward, we were all going to the library as a treat for the girls. They love the library, and giving them something to look forward to helps them get through boring moments in a waiting room.

I signed in, made sure Mom and the girls were settled, and waited for my name to be called, thinking once again about how much energy I had for being four months pregnant. When I was in the exam room, I even joked with the nurse while she was taking my vitals. "There's either something wrong, or I'm finally getting my boy," I said. She smiled with me, hopeful that this great pregnancy was indicative of carrying a boy. I had to think of it that way because the alternative—what my gut was telling me—was too heartbreaking to be true.

That would be the last joke I'd attempt for a very long time.

There was no heartbeat.

A sonogram confirmed it.

I came out of the exam room in a stunned daze. The girls were acting up from waiting too long, nearly two hours compared to the half hour we expected. My mother was agitated from trying to deal with them. Her patience had worn thin. "What took so long?" she demanded in her exasperation. She didn't know. I was too dumbfounded to think clearly. "The baby is dead!" I blurted out, right there in the middle of the waiting room.

The rest of the afternoon was a blur. Children with autism become fixated on plans; they don't adapt to changes or disappointment easily. So even though my mother and I were both struggling to breathe from the crushing weight of the grief, we had to go through the motions of taking the girls to the library. We were bereft with the news of a lost baby. I was already struggling with the fact that I had two days to wait for a D&C (dilation and curettage). The doctor said the baby was too large to miscarry on my own at home, so there was a certain element of risk if my body tried to deliver within the next forty-eight hours.

The things you remember from life-changing days are like a vignette. I remember the shadows cast on the bottom of the pool as I swam that morning. I remember making a prophetic statement guised as a joke to the nurse. I remember being embarrassed by how loud and wound up the girls were that afternoon at the library. I remember one of my mother's friends from a Christian women's group showing up at the library and feeling annoyed that my mother was talking to her at a time when I was suffering a quiet despair. But I don't remember telling Jeff about the baby.

We were both wracked with an incredible grief for the loss of not only this baby but also for the normalcy we had only recently learned was no longer part of our future. It's often said that God works in mysterious ways. Later, I was able to receive comfort from my mother's untimely run-in at the library. Her friend was from the

Christian Women's Group, and she encouraged me to join them at one of their luncheons, which I did. And I found a great deal of solace over the next few weeks in their companionship.

I never did find out if the baby was a boy or if it was chromosomally normal, nor did I want to. I suspect, however, that it was not. In my heart, I believe it was a cri du chat baby, which is why God took it into his arms early.

Following the loss of my baby, I sank into a deep depression. I blamed Natural Family Planning (NFP) for giving me a baby I hadn't planned on and then taking it away. I blamed NFP for the pain I was suffering and the fullness of the loss I felt. I knew that would be my last pregnancy. In full knowledge of my genetic condition, I could never purposefully plan to have another child regardless of how much *I* wanted one. Neither Jeff nor I really knew what challenges Maria and Christina had awaiting them, so even adopting a baby was no longer a smart solution for us. That baby was my last chance, and it was gone. It was taken the same way my dreams for Maria and Christina were taken. In a few short months, I had lost my two "normal" children and a new baby. It was more than I could bear.

In the weeks that followed the D&C, I was on a precipice. I was a shell of my former self, going through the motions of feeding, bathing, and dressing the kids. The grief was so consuming; I didn't know if I'd recover from it. Jeff tried to counsel me as best he could, but his words couldn't find their way into my head or heart. He seemed to realize I needed more than words, so he bought me a bicycle. I rode and rode. Riding that bike became more than an outlet for energy; it became a tool for healing. On my bike, I was temporarily freed from the pressures of caretaking. I was free to sob silently as I pedaled myself into physical and emotional exhaustion. The bicycle was an instrumental tool for finding the road back to myself, but it wasn't the bike alone that saved me.

Finding a Future

The idea of continuing with Natural Family Planning was unreasonable. I refused to put myself at risk for enduring that kind of pain again for the remainder of my childbearing years, but I couldn't reconcile any other options with my faith. Jeff and I discussed many alternatives. I felt desperate for a solution. I was even tempted by resorting to "the morning after" pill as a safety net, but that contradicted our beliefs about when life begins. Jeff was adamantly opposed. I was, too, but I was in such despair about the entire situation. I had at least ten years before natural menopause set in. The idea of losing the intimacy in my marriage was devastating. If we continued following the NFP doctrine, that is essentially what I felt would happen. We knew we needed to do something. We simply couldn't take any more chances.

During a follow up visit with my OB-GYN, he asked me when I was planning my next pregnancy. Did he know I was struggling with finding a solid means of prevention? Maybe. Maybe it was a routine question that he asked all his patients after a miscarriage or D&C. I don't know, but I do know that as I answered, "I'm not planning any more pregnancies," I broke down in tears there in his office. I don't normally lose my composure, but saying it aloud pushed me over the brink. And it opened the door for the conversation he probably knew I needed to have. I was able to ask questions forbidden among staunch NFP advocates: *What are my alternatives? What can I do to make sure I don't get pregnant again?*

I mentioned earlier what a blessing it was to have found a pro-life doctor. He understood the choices and the conflict. We were able to have a philosophical discussion about when life begins. He was very proud of the fact that he'd never performed an abortion. His recommendation was that either Jeff have a vasectomy or I have a tubal ligation.

As I searched for answers, both physical and spiritual, I found myself seeking guidance from our priest. He was an older man with a calmness that I found reassuring as we discussed the idea of life and conception. He extended an open palm and said, "I once held a baby this size." That made me tremble to my core because that was the size of the baby I had just lost. He had a firm but kindly way about him as he counseled me. He gave me a book I had tried to read once without success years earlier. The author talks extensively about Job and why bad things happen to good people. I almost didn't take the book, because it hadn't made sense to me years earlier, but my priest was insistent. That book gave me so much comfort as I read it over the following days. I understand now why he was adamant that I try reading it again.

What sticks with me most from that meeting, however, is when my priest point-blank said, "You are depressed."

"No," I argued. "I'm not." I couldn't even acknowledge that to myself at the time.

"Yes," he said. "You are." Then he added with a depth of voice that still rings in my ears, "Julie, you've done enough. You've done enough." He was freeing me from the constraints of NFP, in contradiction to traditional Catholic doctrine.

In September, just five months after opening the letter from the geneticist, I had a tubal ligation. Just like everything else from that year, it didn't go smoothly. Immediately after the procedure, the doctor advised us of the results. He informed us that he was able to see that one tube was clearly cut, but the other was out of position, and he was unable to see where he had cut it. He could not tell me if this procedure I had agonized over—a procedure that in my mind was equal to self-mutilation of the body God designed—had succeeded or not. Are you kidding! I went through all that just to end up back where we were? No! This absolutely could not be happening to us on top of everything else we had endured. Jeff told me not to worry; I wouldn't have to repeat the procedure. He'd get a vasectomy. But that only compounded my frustration. Not only was I mutilated, but now he would be too.

At my follow-up exam, the doctor scheduled me for a more comprehensive dye test at the hospital to find out for sure. "Please," I pleaded to the doctor, to God, "I just want my life back!"

This time, among many others, God listened to my prayer and answered. The test at the hospital proved the procedure had indeed been a success. The book was now closed on my genetic condition.

After a time, I would heal from the loss and re-envision my life and my girls' futures. When a parent learns they have a special needs child, it feels as if the world has taken everything away. Parents have babies with grand hopes and dreams for all the happiness, success, and opportunity that their children will have throughout life. Learning that a child will always face challenges and won't have a "normal" life can be devastating. In time, we accept and learn to make new dreams, to have new hopes for our children. We begin to redefine dreams based on the gifts our Creator has bestowed upon them. We let go of the rest. In the end, every parent wants their child to have a contented life. In that regard, special needs children are no different than any others. Maria and Christina are happy, vibrant girls. As a mother, I am complete.

Symptoms

Ignoring the Signs
Early Indications and Misdiagnoses

The first time I heard the term "special needs" in reference to Maria and Christina was, ironically, not at their pediatrician's appointment but during a well-baby checkup for my youngest, Anna. The doctor made a general comment about how well I was handling homeschooling two special needs children along with a new baby. *That's odd,* I thought. No one, not even their doctors, had mentioned special needs to me before. The closest any doctor previously came to telling me that one of my children might have a problem was when one pediatrician asked if Maria was bothered by tags in her clothes. "Kids like that don't like them," he said. That was it. Nothing else. Tags did not bother Maria, and I never thought to ask, "What kids like that?"

At that point in my life, I didn't know about autism. I don't think it was being discussed quite as openly then as it is today, or maybe I just didn't know to look for something like that in my child. Either way, I didn't realize that a group of characteristics can come together and result in a diagnosis of autism. Of course, I knew the girls had some unique issues: Christina was in speech therapy, they both had eating and weight issues, and I was homeschooling Maria because she wasn't able to keep up in kindergarten. Each problem was being handled as its own issue rather than a symptom of a greater problem. Our girls were just kids who were not developing at the same rate as others. They would catch up in their own time; we were sure of it.

Knowing what I now know, I can look back and see where there were early indicators that we missed, and more importantly, that the medical community missed. We saw several doctors and specialists along the way, each meant to address a related problem, but none went so far as to find the underlying cause of the various surface issues that were showing up. Ironically, it was the same doctor who first casually mentioned special needs who ended up referring Maria to an endocrinologist when she had failed to grow at all during an entire year.

Maria and Christina have been under the fifth percentile on the growth charts since birth. In fact, they each had their own individualized charts created to monitor their growth. They developed slowly, but as long as they were showing some growth, the doctors weren't overly alarmed. However, when Maria's growth stagnated between her fifth and sixth year, the doctor finally realized we needed to start looking for a reason. He sent us to the endocrinologist, who then recommended the genetic testing that finally brought the answer so many of us—including medical specialists—had missed for so many years.

Maria
Baby Makes Three

When Maria was born, we were overjoyed with our baby girl and starting our journey as parents. In many ways, I was like any new mom: reading every baby book I could get my hands on, nervous and excited about caring for my baby, and only prepared in theory for the challenges of living with a newborn. In other ways, I see where I was at a disadvantage going into this new stage of life. I had never been around babies. I didn't have friends with babies. Jeff and I weren't "kid" people. And even though we came from large families with plenty of experience and children, they lived hundreds of miles away. It was just me, Jeff, the baby, and all my books—books Jeff later threatened to throw away if I didn't stop obsessing over the content within them that was making me crazy with worry. We were learning how to be parents through our daughter and each other, not through the advice or wisdom of others. For the most part, that was okay. But it did mean that I missed some signs because I simply didn't know any better.

A good example of this is when I tried to transition Maria to solids. She was such a messy eater! I would put her in her car seat and spoon food into her mouth, just like the book said to do. It went everywhere! I thought this was normal enough. After all, aren't babies known for being messy? I'd never been around other babies during meals. Even when I went out with mommy groups, it was typically at a time between feedings. At mealtime, I'd sit patiently spooning and spooning baby food into Maria's mouth, thinking that she was swallowing at least part of what was going in. She pushed so much out it was hard to tell.

As I mentioned, Maria's weight had always been a concern. Even at birth, she failed to thrive and had to be evaluated every two days. She didn't nurse well, which delayed my ability to produce milk for nearly a week. This difficulty was an early indicator of the many feeding issues we would encounter with her over the years. With formula, she did put on some weight, albeit very little; but we were assured by the doctors that as long as she was gaining something, she was okay. Looking back at her newborn photos years later, we were shocked to see just how frail she looked.

At the time, it was our reality, and we did everything we could to keep her healthy. Getting her to gain weight was such a perpetual struggle that when she finally reached ten pounds—at four months old—it felt like we had crossed a huge milestone. So when the pediatrician asked me if I was feeding her, I was taken aback. "Of course, I'm feeding her!" I replied. I spent hours feeding her. I didn't think to tell him what an ordeal feeding was or how much of a mess she made. In my mind, these were normal parts of parenting.

Today, after years of struggling with her low weight and feeding therapy to teach her to eat solid foods, I know that during all those tedious feeding sessions, baby Maria was tongue thrusting. The sensation of food on her tongue caused her to push it out. This has nothing to do with hunger or taste or a parent's ability to feed their child.

It is a physical response to stimuli no different than retracting your hand when you touch something hot. Many years later, we learned that she simply did not have the ability to control or manipulate her tongue in a way that allowed her to chew and swallow solid food.

Besides her low birth weight (the doctors were monitoring that), tongue thrusting was the first sign that we, as parents, missed. Even if I had known what it was and brought it to the doctor's attention, I don't know that he would have gone so far as initiating genetic testing. But had we understood early on that Maria's eating difficulties were caused by physical limitations, we would have been spared a lot of mental anguish down the road.

While it does help to have a diagnosis or reason that our children have special needs, words on a piece of paper don't solve anything. The symptoms and daily challenges are still present and need to be dealt with. At six months old, it wasn't necessary for us to know that Maria had a chromosomal translocation, but we did need to know that she had a tangible feeding issue. It would take thirteen years and professional evaluations before anyone was able to help us. Amazingly, many of these professionals told us she was fine, even when we were seeking specific help with feeding.

At one point when Maria was four, a friend suggested that we take her for an eating evaluation because she still would not eat solid food. We were living in Virginia at the time, so I made an appointment at a highly respected hospital in Washington, D.C., thinking they would be the best. Before the appointment, I painstakingly listed every drop Maria consumed. Her diet consisted of nutrition shakes, milk, very thin oatmeal, and rice cereal with mashed fruit in it. We counted calories, proteins, carbohydrates—everything she took in during the course of a day. The evaluator looked over the nutritional statistics and determined that Maria had a healthy diet and was getting everything she needed. Theoretically, a person can live on just nutrition shakes, at least according to the nutritionist. While we were glad to hear her nutritional needs were being met, the therapist's declaration that there was nothing she could do to help Maria eat was not the outcome we were hoping for. The nutritionist couldn't even provide us with a referral to anyone who could help. Essentially, we learned nothing except that we were on our own.

That experience left us feeling so helpless and alone that we resorted to a variety of tactics to try to get Maria eating new, solid foods. Remember, we still did not know about her genetic condition or the resulting motor skills challenges. We approached the problem head-on, just like many parents of a stubborn eater who are desperate to see their child eat. First, we tried withholding the tummy-filling shakes and only giving her oatmeal for an entire weekend, thinking if she got hungry enough, she would eat it. That was a dismal failure. By Sunday evening, she was lethargic and still not eating. We knew we had to scrap that plan, regroup, and start fresh.

We tried a variety of positive and negative reward techniques, each to no avail. Maria was very stubborn in her refusal to eat. I remember watching a Helen Keller movie at one point during this time and thinking how much they must have left out about Annie Sullivan's struggle to make those initial breakthroughs. In a way, I felt like that was what we were dealing with in trying to get Maria to eat. It became a battle of the wills. We finally resorted to taking a more heavy-handed approach and saw some moderate success. She began eating oatmeal and yogurt, but that was as much as we were able to accomplish on our own.

It took nearly two years after our experience with the nutritionist at the highly respected hospital in Washington, DC before the pediatrician referred us to have another eating evaluation conducted. This one was scheduled at a highly respected hospital with the same name in Virginia, and the focus was going to be more on her physical ability to eat rather than her nutritional intake. We were told to bring Maria in for the appointment hungry so the therapist could watch her eat. During the evaluation session, the therapist watched Maria eat her yogurt and proclaimed that she was fine. That was that. She did not offer Maria any food that required chewing or any food Maria wasn't familiar with. There was no discussion about tactile defensiveness or sensory integration problems. These are terms I would later discover on my own when I stumbled across a book on feeding issues in a friend's occupational therapy catalog. Once again, we were sent home with a professional diagnosis of "she's fine."

Maria's inability to eat weighed heavily on me for several years. I was acutely aware that there was a problem, but I did not know how to get help. One of the books I bought that focused on problem eaters had a self-evaluative rating scale; anything over a 35 meant the child was a difficult eater. Maria and Christina (Christina had similar eating difficulties) both rated near 70 when I tested them in 2011. We weren't sure how much merit to put in the test, however, because we were aware of other kids who were normal eaters who also scored well above the authors' threshold. This was just another instance of no one having any clear answers and learning that there were no tried-and-true reliable means to evaluate "normal."

After moving to Florida, we were eventually referred to a feeding therapist who was able to help Maria progress with her eating. Maria is sixteen years old as of this writing; her eating has improved beyond shakes and oatmeal, but she still is not able to eat or enjoy food like you or I can. Feeding therapy is an ongoing process that we need to revisit regularly.

While we lived in Virginia, the girls' medical appointments were at a fairly large pediatric group. This meant that they weren't always seen by the same doctor, which had some pros and cons. The downside was that none of the doctors ever really got to know either of the girls well enough to pick up on minute changes. If I didn't think to mention something, like Maria's messy eating, it might go by without notice. On the upside, however, seeing several different doctors meant we had several opportunities for different input.

When Maria was just nine months old, I saw her pediatrician for her well check-up. Her eyes did not seem to be working together with one eye slightly turning in. Shortly after the visit, the pediatrician called me to follow up. I was surprised to discover he was calling about her weight rather than the eye problem. At that point, we were deeply concerned about her eye, so he recommended an eye doctor. The pediatrician didn't seem as concerned about the eye issue or Maria's other developmental issues as he was about her low weight, but at least we got the referral.

When Maria was just under a year old, we saw an ophthalmologist, who observed that her eyes bounced. It was such a minor movement that I had never noticed it before. Once he pointed it out, I was able to look and see her eyeballs twitching slightly.

The condition, we learned from the eye specialist, was called nystagmus, which causes the eyes to move vertically or horizontally, or to oscillate. It's sometimes referred to as "dancing eyes." Nystagmus is not typically a serious condition, and most children outgrow it without treatment. Just to be safe, however, the eye doctor referred us to a neurologist for an MRI to rule out the possibility of a brain tumor. This would be our first of many visits to a neurologist. Fortunately, this early experience turned out to be fairly routine. Besides the normal parental worry of watching your baby being sedated and strapped to the board for the MRI, the result was a relief. The clear MRI proved the eye movement was a simple nystagmus, not a tumor.

Conversely, a clear MRI typically gives patients a sense that everything is okay. It's essentially proving the child has normal brain activity. We weren't thinking in terms of genetic problems at that stage, and neither were the doctors. We took solace in the clear MRI when other developmental symptoms presented during the following months, so in a way, the MRI created a false sense of security and delayed our diagnosis.

While Maria was being checked for the nystagmus, we learned she had another eye condition called strabismus. This causes the eye to turn in and does require treatment before the brain stops trying to use the affected eye. Essentially, the brain compensates for the weak eye by learning to use only the strong eye. Without correction to encourage use of the weak eye, the person will eventually lose their ability to see out of or control the weak eye. The result can be what is commonly known as "lazy eye." In Maria's case, surgery was needed to help straighten the eye. This, of course, created quite a bit of anxiety for me.

Unlike the MRI, which was a simple, relatively risk-free procedure, our tiny little girl was now going in for eye surgery. I can still remember seeing her lying there in her little green union suit. She seemed so small and frail. The nurses kept assuring me she would be fine and that it was okay to cry. I was so close but fought off the tears. When it was time to begin the surgery, they let me give her a kiss and say goodbye before putting her to sleep and having me leave the room. After the surgery, Maria looked really bad. Luckily, the staff prepared me by warning that she wouldn't feel nearly as bad as she would look.

The surgery was a success, and she was fine. We breathed a sigh of relief, not realizing the real challenge was yet to come. In the following weeks, it would be up to us to persist in some very unpleasant tasks of forcing Maria to start reusing her weaker eye. We wanted to avoid glasses if possible, so we started with patching. She absolutely hated wearing the eye patch. The only way I could get her to leave it alone was to distract her with Duplo's (large Lego blocks). I sat with her playing Duplo's for hours every day. It was possibly the most boring, monotonous thing I've ever done; but if we could retrain the eye muscles without resorting to glasses, the boredom would be a small sacrifice.

Despite our best efforts, glasses became inevitable. Our little toddler had a vicious stubborn streak, and she did not like the glasses. Every time I put them on her, she would tear them off and glare at me. Finally, after a year of using an eye patch, Jeff made it his mission over the long Thanksgiving weekend to get her to wear her glasses. He spent the entire weekend patiently putting them back on whenever she pulled them off. His persistence eventually wore her down until she stopped fighting. We even enlisted help of friends by asking them to comment on her "beautiful pink glasses" whenever they saw her. Eventually, Maria accepted wearing the glasses, and it became a nonissue. All the stress and worry of the year eventually ebbed away with the successful surgery, a clear MRI, and pretty pink glasses.

When Maria hadn't started walking by twenty months, one of the pediatricians voiced concern about the delay and referred us to an occupational therapist. Maria was pulling herself up and standing, but she wasn't walking yet. During a routine follow-up visit with the neurologist, I mentioned this. His response was, "Well, she's just cautious." He also mentioned that one of his associates, another neurologist, didn't start walking until two years old. He told me this to prove that being slow to walk doesn't necessarily mean the child has cognitive or developmental deficiencies. This was one example of someone who grew up to be very successful despite missing an early childhood milestone. For a nervous mother, this was comforting to hear.

Nevertheless, as dutiful parents, we scheduled an appointment with the recommended occupational therapist. I remember noticing how the exam room was filled with toys, undoubtedly used for coordination and muscle training. The therapist evaluated Maria and said she wanted to see her twice a week for walking classes. As a mom wanting to follow professional recommendations, I felt I was obligated to start her on walking classes. But as a woman in the midst of a difficult second pregnancy, I was not overjoyed at the prospect of carting her to therapy twice a week.

Jeff was the voice of reason. "Walking lessons? What kind of baby needs walking lessons?" he asked. Jeff's stance has always been that as long as the girls are moving forward with their development, they are fine. We only need to worry if they backslide. He was not in favor of walking therapy, and with the peace of mind that the neurologist had recently told us Maria was normal and would make progress in her own time, we decided against moving forward with walking lessons.

I'm glad we made that decision because Maria began walking on her own within the same timetable the therapist had proposed. While walking therapy probably would not have been harmful, if we had gone, I would have thought the therapist was the greatest thing since sliced bread because she got my daughter to walk when, in fact, that would not have been true. Soon enough, Maria was walking without any special intervention or therapy, and it wasn't long before she was following Jeff everywhere around the house and backyard, excited to be Daddy's little helper.

This experience did two things for us. First, it reaffirmed our position that each child develops at his or her own pace, which really came into play when we were faced with making parental choices regarding recommendations from the school (prior to genetic testing). Second, it made us skeptical of "soft sciences," like counseling and occupational therapy. They are considered "professional sciences" that have to be evidence based but are not always exact. Someone will always be there to promise a magical outcome, so we must be very careful what concepts and therapeutic treatments we decide to buy into.

The Little Moments

One of the most memorable moments I had as a young mother was right after Christina was born. We were going to a doctor's appointment. I was carrying newborn Christina while Maria walked next to me holding my hand. She was two years old, and it was the very first time we were able to share this quintessential mother-child moment. I was overwhelmed with happiness; my little girl and I were actually walking hand in hand.

Christina
Our Growing Family

Christina was also born small (five pounds and fourteen ounces), even smaller than Maria (6 lbs. .08 ozs.). Because of Maria's history, our doctors immediately recommended supplemental feeding for Christina. I nursed her enough to pass the protective antibodies that only mother's milk can provide, but I did not lose any time getting her started with formula. Like Maria, Christina has had challenges with eating and gaining weight, but her genetic-related challenges have manifested in somewhat different ways. Maria has trouble with her gross motor skills, but Christina struggles with fine motor coordination. While this includes challenges with eating, it also means tasks like writing have been harder for her. Conversely, where Maria's walking was delayed, Christina was on her feet and moving full-steam ahead by eighteen months.

Because of Christina's lack of hand coordination, she was not able to hold her own bottle until she was a year and a half. Transitioning from the bottle to a sippy cup presented a challenge similar to getting Maria to wear glasses. We had to dedicate months to it and remain vigilant to our mission. It was heartbreaking at times. Christina would stand at the fridge, nonverbally begging for a bottle. I felt so guilty because I knew she was hungry despite the many bowls of rice cereal I was feeding her throughout the day. Without the bottle, her tummy was never full enough. I even called the doctor at one point with fears of malnourishment as her skin began taking on a sallow quality. They reassured me we were doing the right thing. She was two, after all, and it was time to get her off the bottle. None of us knew she lacked the physical coordination to drink from the spouted lid. Thankfully, she finally discovered the technique, and we were able to move forward once again.

One of Christina's earliest symptoms was something we later realized was part of her personality combined with a common trait for autistic children. Christina seemed to have no threshold for pain, and being strong-willed, she would release her frustration or anger by throwing herself over backwards. It wasn't the same as a tantrum; being nonverbal, it was her only way of communicating her frustration. This behavior became acute during the terrible twos. Whenever I told her no, she would fling herself onto her back. Once she threw herself down so hard in her crib that she chipped off a piece of her front tooth. She did not seem to feel anything, not even the chipped tooth. I recall watching her and thinking, "Doesn't she know that hurts?" I couldn't understand why she didn't connect the behavior to the pain. Now I think that her sensory issues prevented her from feeling it. As the girls got older, we noticed that Maria had the same high tolerance for pain. We would jokingly say they were coated in Teflon, both emotionally and physically.

One of Christina's favorite things to do during this time was flipping backwards. She would come to me to hold her in my lap in a way where she could flip backward without injuring herself. She loved this activity. I believe she was working on her vestibular and proprioceptive systems. These are known as the sixth and seventh sense. Both of these systems are related to body movement. The vestibular system gives feedback to the brain about the body's position in relation to gravity, movement, and balance, such as what direction you are facing or how close to you are to an object. The proprioceptive system gives feedback to the brain about the amount of effort being used to move the body. It regulates both emotional responses and sensory input.

Around the same time, Christina also developed an aversion to bubbles in the bath, even if they were just the residual suds from baby shampoo. One evening when I was bathing her, she began screaming inconsolably. I was pregnant with Anna and was not physically able to get close enough to handle her during this phase. Jeff had to take over baths; she threw such fits that even he had a hard time managing this tiny little child. We believe that this was the age where her nervous system was coming alive and triggering extreme sensory issues that, fortunately, only lasted a few months.

The most challenging issue we've faced with Christina has been speech. When she was an infant, the pediatrician asked if she was babbling yet. "No," I said. "But neither did the first one by this age." I wasn't trying to be rude. I didn't understand the implication. All I had to compare Christina to was Maria. Since Maria developed more slowly, and that was all I had to base my parental experience on, it didn't set off any alarms that Christina was delayed.

By the time Christina was four, however, her inability to speak was something we were worrying about. Maria's speech came slowly, but it did come. The only setback we had with her speech was when she went from saying a few single-syllable words to none at all for a couple of months. Then she started talking again as suddenly as she had stopped. Christina was different in this regard. Even when she really wanted something, she could not verbally articulate it. She learned to communicate in other ways, but by four, we were seeking outside help.

We started by going to Child Find where they put Christina through a battery of tests. Christina hated going there, but our pediatrician encouraged us to stick with the process so we could get the therapy she needed. In the end, we managed to get her about a month of personalized speech therapy before we moved from Virginia to Florida. It wasn't very long after the move that we discovered the chromosomal translocation. With that diagnosis came the Individualized Education Plan (IEP), and that was her ticket for receiving ongoing speech therapy.

Anna
So This Is What Normal Is Like?

Watching Anna develop through her first year was like switching on a light. I saw so many differences in her development from that of her sisters. The differences made Maria's and Christina's delays much more apparent. Not only did she reach milestones "according to the book," she explored the world around her differently. It was little things like walking barefoot on the grass or the feel of sand under her feet that Anna didn't mind but the other two could not tolerate. Developmentally, she was catching up to them and doing things like brushing her teeth and potty training at the same time they were even though they were nearly two and four years older. Once when she was about a year old, a mosquito landed on her face. I saw that she noticed it and was trying to get it off. I thought, "Wow. She is different." Neither Maria nor Christina would notice something so small on their skin.

There were other milestones that Anna reached that were so remarkably different that we wanted to shout and rejoice. My moment with Anna came when she was six months old. I had her in her high chair, and just like the book said, I took out a jar of baby food to start introducing her to solids. I spooned a little into her mouth, and to my great joy, she swallowed it. I was in shock. I ran out to where Jeff was working in the backyard and yelled to him, "You'll never believe what happened! I just fed Anna, and she ate it! I can't believe other parents have it this easy." Compared to what I'd been through trying to get Maria and Christina to eat, this was more than a dream come true. It was so much easier than anything I had experienced with the other two. "So this is what normal is like," I thought.

Over the next few months, Anna continued eating new foods. I could cut up pieces of food and put them in front of her, and she'd eat them. We had struggled so long to get Maria to eat we were hopeful that when baby number two, Christina, came along, Maria would mimic her and learn to eat. That did not happen. Now with baby number three, we hoped that both of the older girls would watch her eat and follow suit. Anna did her part. She ate. The other two would watch her with great curiosity, but never once did either of them try it themselves.

More Clues, More Mistakes

Before doctors ever uttered the words *autism* or *special needs*, we knew on some level that something wasn't right. Most parents beam with pride when strangers compliment their children. I remember when a kindly couple at church stopped to tell me how adorable Maria was. I forced a smile and thanked them to acknowledge their compliment. Of course, I agreed that my little girl was cute and sweet, but I also knew something was wrong, something that these well-meaning strangers couldn't see or realize. That was a very sad moment of awareness for me, and those were thoughts that I could not reconcile until I had a diagnosis several years later. Even though I couldn't put my finger on any precise reason, my mother's intuition must have been trying to prepare me to accept the forthcoming diagnosis.

That brief flickering of awareness may have been inside me, but it was not strong enough to make me pursue a special education evaluation when Maria started school. I will talk about schools in more detail later. Here it is important to note that Maria started school just like any other child. Her teacher made a few comments about how sweet and special Maria was, but she stopped short of making any serious insinuations about Maria's abilities even though she clearly saw the signs that Maria was going to need help. Once it became clear that Maria was not keeping up, I made the decision to homeschool her until she was ready to reenter the school system. We knew we were moving to a new state during the middle of the school year, so it really wasn't a drastic decision. Maria was not ready; giving her a few more months at home would not hurt.

Trying to teach Maria and Christina at home was very challenging. They had difficulty grasping the most basic concepts, which made me constantly second-guess myself. Selecting the right materials to use was a daunting task. I felt like there was so much at stake. Jeff has always been more pragmatic when faced with such decisions. He reminded me that Maria was only five—there wasn't too much that could go wrong. So I kept trying. Recently, I looked back at some of their workbooks. It is amazing how much they did not understand.

If we hadn't received the genetic testing when we did, I think the academic delays would have soon become obvious to all of us. At the time, however, the girls were still so young that they fell into that gray area where no one wants to make drastic or premature decisions about special education. Other than being behind schedule in certain aspects of their development, both girls acted like most other kids their age. They did not acquire some of the typical autistic behaviors, such as Maria's stimming[4] (rubbing her hands together and making shushing sounds with the saliva in her mouth) and Christina's repeating words, until they were around ten years old. There weren't any tell-tale signs. Our friends and family were just as surprised to learn they were autistic as we were, especially after we had been to so many doctors and specialists over the years. If all of these professionals missed the diagnosis, how were we as parents supposed to suspect anything to the contrary?

Of all the missed opportunities to receive a proper diagnosis, there is one that stands out above the rest as completely irresponsible on the part of the medical provider. When Maria was two, just after Christina was born, we took her for a full evaluation at a Prestigious Medical Academic Institution in Washington, DC. I have several things to say about the experience at the prestigious institution; none are positive. The entire process was riddled with

---

[4] Stimming is a self-stimulatory behavior. In a person with autism, stimming usually refers to specific behaviors such as hand-flapping, rocking, spinning, or echolalia, the repetition of words and phrases.

errors and ineptitude from beginning to end. I remember being so incredibly frustrated during our meeting with this panel of specialists who had supposedly conducted a complete, comprehensive evaluation of Maria's development. They would not tell us what, if anything, was wrong. All we received was a determination of her developmental age and a referral for occupational therapy. At one point, I asked about her inability to eat solid food. She was only drinking nutri-

> Missing milestones might be a sign of underlying problems, but the developmental range is so great there is no reason to panic. Each child, whether special needs or not, will develop at his or her own pace. It is important to be observant but not obsessive.

tional shakes at the time. "What is she going to do when she's a teenager?" I asked. "When she goes to McDonald's with friends, is she just going to order a shake?" The specialists laughed and shrugged off what was a very real, very important worry for us. Were we just supposed to accept that she would survive her entire life on shakes alone?

Their lack of concern and seriousness was just one measure of their incompetence. The report we received was littered with errors. A good portion of the basic statistical information about Maria's development was incorrect. We were even sent portions of the report that were clearly marked "not to be given to the parents." And the most egregious error of all? A geneticist who never personally examined Maria signed off on the evaluation. The one thing—genetic testing—that would have given us an answer was missed due to their negligence. Instead, we had to struggle with feeding issues, speech delays, sensory issues, and schooling on our own, for another four years, before receiving the genetic testing that should have happened when Maria was two and Christina was a newborn.

Secrets

Don't Rob Me of My Joy
Secrets and Comparisons

Christmas Eve
A Night to Forget

I ran through the checklist in my mind one more time to make sure I had everything: pull-ups for Maria and Christina, diapers for Anna, food the older two could eat, baby food for Anna, milk (because you can't count on people having milk on hand), and all the necessary backup toys and changes of clothes. I really hoped we wouldn't need a change of clothes. It was Christmas Eve, and all three girls were wearing beautiful velvet and lace holiday dresses. They looked absolutely adorable. I wanted them to stay that way. I wanted the night to be perfect; it was our first Christmas in Florida and the first one I would be spending with my relatives since we had started our own family in Virginia, six years prior.

Yes, I was sure I had everything. Now all I could do was hope and pray to make it through the evening without anybody else noticing that my oldest two were still wearing training pants. "It wouldn't be that unusual to have to help them in the bathroom, right? Not with tights. Don't all five- and seven-year-olds need help going to the bathroom when they're wearing tights and fancy dresses?" I thought, trying to assuage my apprehension. Driving forty-five minutes at night in a bad rainstorm wasn't helping an already stressful situation, either.

At this point, we had not yet learned about chromosomal translocations, but I had already become adept at hiding some of their developmental delays from everyone, including family. I honed ways of hiding training pants and eating problems to avoid the awkwardness that can occur in social situations like church gatherings or playdates. I had never really felt like I was hiding their delays out of embarrassment; it was just easier, especially since I didn't actually have an answer or a reason for those delays. Nor did I feel like I needed to explain anything to anyone. However, preparing for the big family holiday dinner at my dad's house was different. This was the first time I remember being acutely aware and ashamed of their inability to eat normal food or use the toilet on their own.

Driving conditions were horrible on the way to my dad's house. I looked over at Jeff; his attention was focused on the road, so I decided not to say anything. I could tell he was as tense as I was— probably more so considering that he and my dad were still trying to establish their relationship now that Jeff was not only his son-in-law but also his employee. When my father approached Jeff to come to Florida and work for him, we made the decision with some clear ground rules in mind. First, our relationship was still ours. Jeff and I have always maintained a unified front when it comes to our marriage and our children. My relationship with my father was to remain exclusive of their working relationship; likewise, business issues were to stay between them. We didn't want any lines crossed that would compromise our family solidarity. Jeff and I talked and prayed about it for a long time before Jeff agreed to take the position.

So far, everyone had done a great job about respecting boundaries, but the situation was new, and their relationship needed time to mature. Jeff was still in the process of learning the business, which meant two apprentice years of long, hot, dirty days in the shop. While we knew this was necessary training for the upper-level position he was brought in to eventually fill, those were exhausting days for him. Packing the kids up and going out at night for a big, family gathering probably wasn't high on his list of things to do at that point in time. But he knew how glad I was for the chance to be with my family at Christmas, so he put on his game face and agreed to go.

51

My dad was so happy to have us there. He anxiously watched for our arrival and met us in the driveway with an umbrella. We unloaded the car and shuttled the girls and all our paraphernalia into the house as quickly as we could, trying not to get soaked in the process. The house was packed with relatives I hadn't seen in years at Christmas. In we came with our three little girls, each looking sweet and adorable, grabbing up all of the attention. At one point, Christina climbed up on the piano bench and looked like a little doll sitting there with her holiday dress fanned out around her. It was such a sweet, heartwarming moment for me. I could tell how much it meant to my dad to have us there too. We'd been away so long that it was good to be back among family again.

I enjoyed seeing everyone, but the night was still an ordeal. Being a large family, we commonly have a main table for the adults and a separate table set up for the kids during holiday meals. Because Maria and Christina required constant assistance, Jeff and I ended up eating at the children's table. That was fine, but it made visiting with the other adults nearly impossible. Then there were the frequent trips to the bathroom, each requiring my help. Being girls, bathroom duty falls to me when we are in public. Bathroom trips are always long and tedious because the girls need to follow a very specific process to handle the transition of undressing and redressing. That night, however, the process was exacerbated by those adorable holiday dresses: take the shoes and tights off, take the training pants off, clean them up, put new training pants on, put the tights and shoes back on, straighten up the dress, wash and dry hands, and then repeat the cycle with the next child.

Anna was still in diapers, so between feeding and changing the three girls all night, I barely had a moment to relax or enjoy a bite of the fantastic-looking dinner. Most people associate holidays meals with leaving so full they can't even think of food; I left starving. I missed dinner and dessert while tending to the girls. I remember really wanting to go to the kitchen for a taste of the dessert I had heard everyone raving about before we had to leave. By that point, it was late, and we'd been guests in a crowded home for several hours. Jeff was thinking of the long drive home in bad weather and wanted to get started. He didn't want to wait for me to eat dessert. The frustration was overwhelming. I'd been excluded from all of the evening's festivities because the girls needed my constant assistance, and my first experience with trying to hide the girls' delays from my family had taken its toll. By the time we left, I was embarrassed, aggravated, hungry, and exhausted. Needless to say, the ride home was long and miserable.

Adapting to the Differences

During college, I became accustomed to having distance from my family. Then Jeff and I began our life together in Virginia, hundreds of miles from either of our families. Sure, we saw our relatives now and again during special events or vacations, but those visits were usually short and with one side of the family or the other. Since my parents were divorced, there was never really a way to see the entire family during my brief visits before moving back to Florida. Had my parents been married, it would've been easy to have all of the extended family in one place for a reunion party. As it was, seeing my many aunts and uncles (seven on my mother's side and four on my dad's) became increasingly difficult. When we did visit, we usually only had time to see my parents and grandparents. The family was just too big to see everyone, so it was easy to drift apart during the years we lived out of state.

The distance made it easy to keep the challenges I was experiencing with my first two babies to myself. No one from either family was there in Virginia with us to notice Maria's or Christina's delays. Since I didn't really realize there was a problem for a long time, I never thought to mention some of the issues we were encountering to my parents. Jeff's conversations with his family never broached subjects like child development. Living far away from relatives makes it surprisingly easy to keep things to yourself. Jeff and I have always valued our privacy, so neither of us were the type to volunteer information about the girls' development to anyone. When I talked to my mother, I would mention some of Maria's weight issues or going to various doctors, but those were normal conversations. I never said anything to trigger alarm or to give any of my relatives a reason to think Maria and Christina weren't perfectly normal, healthy little girls.

The first time we had family members visit us in Virginia, after Maria's birth, was for her baptism. She was about three months old at the time. My father and stepmother traveled up, along with my brother, his wife, and their six-month-old daughter. The contrast between the two babies was astounding. My niece seemed to be a bionic baby in the ninetieth percentile on the growth charts and already doing everything on or ahead of schedule. Then there was my little Maria, barely even on the growth charts at under the fifth percentile. She was, in fact, teetering on the brink of having to have a special growth chart developed, a process that is only used for children who fall too far below the norm to remain on the standardized bell curve growth chart.

That was the first time I ever looked at another child and wished mine was as healthy. We were doing everything we could to get weight on Maria, but nothing was working. My father made an offhanded comment when he saw how sickly Maria looked that only heightened my despair at the time. "Get her off the damn breast milk," he said, mistakenly concluding that she was malnourished from being inadequately breastfed.[5] He clearly didn't know that we were already bottle-feeding her with specialized supplements, fighting for every ounce of weight gain. But still, the comment stung and made me even more sensitive to Maria's weight challenges. Between that and the side-by-side comparison to my niece, the stage was set for me to start subtly covering up those missed milestones and developmental delays.

The first time I consciously tried to hide a problem from my family was when Christina was born. My pregnancy had been terribly difficult. I had been having a rough time getting around, especially

---

[5]   Author's note: While I didn't pursue the pros or cons of breastfeeding with my father in response to his comment, I believe his sentiment was based on thinking I wasn't producing an adequate milk supply to nourish Maria and was not intended to question the benefits of breastfeeding in general.

since Maria was nearing two and not yet walking. We knew by that point that she wasn't keeping up. That made us even more anxious about the health of the baby I was carrying, so much so that when my father offered to fly me and Maria to Florida for Christmas, we decided not to go for fear the trip would stress the developing baby. For the first time, we came to terms with how precarious Maria's first weeks had been. We felt very lucky not to have lost her, and we didn't want to take that chance with the second baby.

Our instincts were right. Christina was also born small at 5 pounds and 14 ounces. This was her true weight as it was recorded in the nursery. The scale in the delivery room had her at 6 pounds and 3.8 ounces. The nurse explained that the delivery room scale was off, resulting in the discrepancy. Even though I knew the lower weight was the accurate one, I thought back to everything we went through with Maria's weight, and I decided to use the inaccurate but healthier-sounding weight on Christina's birth announcements. I just wasn't ready to share her real weight with the world. I doubt that anyone was paying that much attention, but those few ounces were a really big deal to us at the time.

When the girls were younger, it was fairly easy to hide developmental differences from others, especially with some of the smaller issues that only a mother would notice. For instance, whenever we went on playdates or to the church social hour, other mothers would give their babies and toddlers Cheerios to snack on. My girls wouldn't dream of putting those hard, crunchy little circles into their mouths. They liked to play with them, but they never ate them. Well-intentioned moms would offer my girls Cheerios. I found it was easier just to politely accept and let them play with the cereal than to decline and have to provide an explanation. It was a situation that always felt awkward, but I learned to minimize those moments without drawing additional attention to the girls' delays.

I handled their delayed potty training in a similar manner. For a while, pull-ups helped me get around the issue that they weren't potty-trained yet, at least while they were still young enough to need the same parental help in the bathroom as did their potty-trained peers. No one knew that when we went into the stall we were changing pull-ups without even attempting to use the toilet. For the most part, it was just easier to avoid those situations whenever possible. By only scheduling playgroups at certain times or making trips to the bathroom behind other excuses, I subconsciously kept finding new ways to adapt to being around acquaintances during those early childhood years. Moving back to Florida changed that. Being around family more often heightened my awareness of how I had been quietly compensating for these developmental delays.

As my parents had increased access to the girls following our move, they naturally became more involved in their daily lives. This included the usual observations and suggestions grandparents will often give parents regarding child-raising. In our case, almost immediately after our arrival in Florida, my mother began pressuring me to enroll the girls in dance. Dance was an important part of her life; as such, she started me in dance very young and kept me involved well into my teens. She couldn't understand why I was not doing the same with my daughters. But my goals at that time were getting them to eat and to learn to write their names; dance was the furthest thing from my mind. Physically, they were not ready for dance. Bone-age testing provided a ready excuse: it showed them both to be between two and three years delayed. While I did eventually get them involved with dance, at the time I had to be assertive with my mother and explain the bone-age test results. This helped her understand it wasn't a matter of whether or not I wanted them to be in dance classes—they truly were not yet ready.

Letting Others In

As I explained earlier in my story, shortly after moving to Florida, my world turned in on itself. While I was pregnant with our fourth baby, the one that I would later miscarry and believe to be my cri du chat baby, I learned about the genetic anomaly affecting Maria and Christina, the same anomaly that I was carrying and possibly passing to the new baby. To say that I was having a difficult time coming to terms with the news is an understatement. Between the diagnosis and the pregnancy, it was as if all the elements came together to create the perfect storm of denial.

I didn't want to deal with anyone else's reaction to the truth about our genetics, so I didn't tell them. Instead, I matter-of-factly told people that I knew there was a good chance this baby would have developmental delays similar to two of my three children. Genetics were never mentioned. The phrase "special needs" was never mentioned and wouldn't be until the schools became involved. As it was, only those very close to the girls knew they were delayed. I didn't see a need to broadcast the reason when nobody could do anything to change it or do anything except possibly make me feel even guiltier than I already did at that time.

If anyone did happen to ask if Maria and Christina were delayed, we simply responded that we'd had testing done but no syndromes were diagnosed; we never mentioned the specific nature of the tests. Nor did I tell anyone about the tubal ligation I had following my miscarriage. In our opinion, it was a private decision based on a private situation. The funny part is that years later, when I eventually told my mother I had had the surgery, she wasn't surprised at all. In fact, she suspected it at the time but also respected my privacy enough not to pry. Thinking back, I could have been more open with my parents about what we were going through. Those who love us are more accepting than we sometimes expect. By keeping them blocked from the discussion, we don't allow them a chance to support us and to show that unconditional love.

Following Maria's first Individualized Education Plan (IEP) meeting at her school (details I will share in the next chapter), I finally realized I could no longer keep the girls' genetic condition secret. I would need to tell the rest of the family and I needed to tell them right away. I didn't want them hearing it "through the grapevine" stemming from the schools. I did wait to tell most of my family, however, until after our large Easter celebration gathering. I didn't want our news to be the focus of the discussion that day. I had so many reservations about telling the world about the girls' genetic condition. Keeping the devastating diagnosis to myself wasn't easy, but I rationalized that if no one knew about it, the girls wouldn't be treated differently. I wanted so much for everyone to treat them like any other children. I wanted people's expectations to be the same. As a mother, the last thing I wanted was for this diagnosis to change the way people saw and treated my girls. I didn't want them isolated or alienated from other people. I wanted them to have a normal, full life. Until that fateful meeting with the school, I didn't want to accept that my definition of a normal, full life would have to change to meet their needs, not my original expectations.

Even if the IEP meeting hadn't been the catalyst for telling the world about their conditions, I'm sure it would only have been a matter of time until I would've had to cross that bridge. Both girls were developing idiosyncratic behaviors that are common on the autism spectrum, some more severe and potentially dangerous than others (Christina's hyperventilation, for example). I realized that having people know would make life easier rather than harder. Others could better understand their differences if given a reason. By telling the school about the genetic anomaly, we were able to get the educational support and help they needed. Of course, not having a syndrome with defined characteristics was a stumbling block at first, but once it was understood that the translocation didn't have a specific syndrome (it's not prevalent enough to have been associated with a syndrome), they were able to qualify for special needs programs.

In the end, it was just easier to tell everyone—family, friends, teachers. People knew something was wrong; so by giving them a reason, it all made sense. By telling my dad, it made him realize the finality of the situation. It wasn't a problem that he could fix. As engineers, the need to solve problems is a characteristic we share. Having that discussion actually opened up new understanding, acceptance, and support between us. And as it turned out, my mother had been silently wondering for years what was wrong with the kids. She'd been harboring misguided suspicions that Jeff must've done drugs before I met him. We can laugh now at the improbable suspicion; Jeff carried a "top secret" and I had a "secret-level" security clearance for our defense work, and neither of us would have ever risked losing that clearance level to do drugs. Neither he nor I have ever participated in anything like that. She says now that I misunderstood that she was concerned about the possibility of the adverse effects prescribed pharmaceuticals can later have on chromosomal development in fetuses; but either way, the answer was that genetics, not drugs, were to blame.

My point is, without giving people a reason—the truth—they will make up their own reasons. Some may never say anything while they speculate. No, it's much better to be open and forthcoming with the loved ones in your life. They are your support system, and they will surprise you with their acceptance. However, they may need a bit of time to adjust to the news. Everyone needs time to process news of this magnitude. All those who love your children will experience a range of emotions similar to yours after learning about a special needs diagnosis.

I had kept it a secret for so long that by the time I told my family, I was already, slowly, beginning to move past the shock stage. In an odd way, I felt like I was the one doing the consoling at first. Being the griever and the consoler is not an easy role; and the suddenness of the diagnosis, at least in terms of sharing it with my relatives, created a vacuum that could only be filled with time, patience, and acceptance. Everyone had questions that only Jeff and I could answer based on what we were slowly learning ourselves. For me, it would take a while to recover from the grief of losing my perceived life and the future I had anticipated for both myself and my girls.

Path to Acceptance

Perhaps one of the hardest parts of the diagnosis was acceptance. I had to redefine my perception of normal based on this new reality. I had to let go of the expectations for the usual milestones and achievements most parents foresee for their children: driving, college, marriage. Instead, Jeff and I had to sit down and think about what our new expectations were going to be for Maria and Christina. We had to ask ourselves, "What are the basics needed to function in society and to have a good life?" Since intelligence was no longer part of the equation and education was going to be difficult, we had to let go of expectations for high academic and career achievements. But what other parts of this "life balance" could we work on? The number one trait we discovered we could still develop within our special needs children was *character*.

Even though we had to accept that our girls would grow up with certain limitations, we knew we could still strive to raise happy girls with good character. We could still raise them to have goals that were attainable. We could provide them with the best special needs education we could find. We could teach them to have love and compassion for others; to understand certain social graces, such as manners and appropriate hygiene and dress; to have the life skills to care for themselves; and to have discipline in their actions. Most importantly, we would make sure, beyond any doubt, that they would always feel love and parental acceptance.

Being a mother comes with a responsibility to do your absolute best to provide a loving, nurturing environment for your child, regardless of his or her abilities or limitations. Sometimes, this can be more challenging than expected. I remember listening to our priest talk about carrying crosses during a sermon one Sunday when I was still adjusting to the girls' diagnosis. He said that it's common to look around and think that someone else's problems are easier or lesser than our own. Then he said, "But if you have someone else's cross, it wouldn't be the right size for you. Your cross is the one you are meant to have." This statement really impacted me and helped me move beyond comparing my burden to that of others, and it helped me let go of my sense of loss. I gradually came to accept that raising two special needs daughters is part of my role and my journey through life.

God gifted me with Maria, Christina, and Anna because I was meant to be their mother. I, like everyone else, will be judged by how well I've fulfilled my station in life, which includes being their mother. No child is perfect, and it is okay to want to see our children as being whole. But dwelling on these issues is not constructive parenting. In fact, it can be quite damaging to the child. Every child longs to please, and if the parent (especially the mother) is only focused on the child's shortcomings instead of his or her strengths, the child will suffer from a diminished sense of self-worth. We need to remember to pray for the unconditional love and strength to do what needs to be done so that we can fulfill our obligations to our children and our roles as mothers. It's also important that we remember to enjoy our children on a daily basis. This may sound obvious, but I honestly believe that many parents forget to cherish and enjoy their children for who they are, especially under the strain of certain behaviors and challenges that come with special needs.

Acceptance doesn't happen overnight, however. I was fortunate to have had several people come into my life at just the right time to help me move from grief to acceptance. Blessings often came through the kindness of strangers who happened to say the right thing or smile the right way when I felt especially burdened or stressed. I will always remember a special cashier at a favorite fast-food restaurant. I often took the girls there to play in the tunnels, and she was always so friendly and had such a positive attitude that she brightened some of my darkest days.

Another time, I recall feeling so embarrassed because I had to bring their own food to the restaurant. They could barely contain their excitement as I ordered the kids meals, with the special toys. But it was always the same: play with the toys and ignore the food. I found myself apologizing to the cashier for the fact that my kids didn't eat like other kids. She smiled and said, "All you can do is your part, and God has to do the rest." I still think about that now and then. I am sure she was some kind of angel sent to help me at that moment. She was just so positive.

During the depths of my depression, I came across another mother who was homeschooling her two teenage sons. Both boys had severe mental retardation and were still unable to do many autonomous tasks such as cutting their own food. I talked to her at length as she explained how she handled her reality. I wanted her to tell me my problems would go away and that the life I wanted for myself would come back to me. Of course, she didn't, but I've always remembered how happy she was and how dedicated she was to her children. Her positive attitude was healing and helped me to accept my new reality.

Letting Go

When coming to terms with a diagnosis, it's really important not to place blame. For some reason, people have a tendency to want to assign blame for things that are wrong. Yes, in our case, we know the genetic anomaly came from me. But how did I get it? That opens entirely new issues. Those thoughts, especially in situations where a family may not know the cause of their child's problems, will serve no purpose other than to create additional stress and trauma for a special needs family. Blame has no place in raising special needs children. Creating an environment of love, patience, acceptance, gratitude, and stability is much more important than attaching blame.

I struggled with blaming myself for so long. I felt myself becoming bitter, and that was something that terrified me. I didn't want to be that type of person, filled with negativity, driving people away. I struggled not just to accept the girls' diagnosis but also to accept that it was my fault, that I was the reason for their challenges. Through it all, Jeff was amazing. His love and steadfastness helped pull me through. His unwavering love for the girls helped me turn my focus away from self-blame and back to their needs. I have a vivid memory of one remarkable moment when he and I were discussing the challenges we were facing. Jeff gazed out at the girls playing in the backyard and said what was in his heart: "I wouldn't trade them for anything in the world." He couldn't have realized how much the tenderness and love in his statement would help me come back to them from my dark, downward emotional spiral.

After that, I realized that there's joy to be had no matter what age they are or what stage they are going through. I stopped believing that my best days were limited to those rare occasions when I felt a twinge of hope for their progress. I realized that I would feel true joy again, which was something I had once thought to be lost for good. The idea that it was okay to develop new dreams was helpful, so that's what I did. Instead of allowing myself to be devastated by their inability to learn, I started looking for evidence of slow learners who had become successful. Trying to teach the girls even simple tasks was such a struggle, for a while I wanted to stop fighting and just have fun with them instead. I rationalized that since the genetic anomaly might shorten their lifespan, why should I waste our days in a constant fight to teach them? But I realized that these thoughts were not helpful. They needed to learn, for their own sense of accomplishment, worth, and purpose. To stop trying would be taking an easier but less fulfilling road.

I didn't truly let go of my grief and sadness over losing "normal children" until I let go of my need to compare my girls with other children. I didn't realize how I'd been subconsciously comparing Maria and Christina to other children, even all the way back to infancy when Maria was side by side with my healthy niece. I never felt negativity or jealousy toward the healthy child or parents, but I remember feeling an inexplicable ache inside, a painful longing. This happened both before and after the diagnosis but with more acuity after.

While this unfortunate tendency was certainly causing me unneeded pain, I didn't realize how much it was wearing on Jeff until one poignant moment after a Sunday Mass. The social hour afterwards was always a bit difficult for me because of our daughters' feeding issues. We would sit at our little table with our special food packed from home while other kids happily played and devoured doughnuts. Often, we'd be there when the local Brownie troop would come through for their meeting dressed in their cute little uniforms. Something about knowing our girls couldn't participate in scouts always stung a bit more than some of their other limitations. I wanted that for them. I wanted to see them dressed up in the adorable uniforms, eagerly heading to a troop meeting.

That day, I didn't realize that I was comparing Maria and Christina to the other kids in church. I pointed out something cute that one little girl, close in age to Maria, was doing. In my mind, I was making a complimentary observation. But Jeff heard something different. He heard that pang of longing lacing my voice. And apparently, he had heard it many times before, because on that particular day he had had enough. "Don't rob me of my joy," he snapped. "Stop comparing her."

That's when I realized that as much as I loved my girls, I was hurting all of us by wishing for even one second that they were capable of things they weren't. Jeff has never done this (or at least he has never let on). He has always cherished them for exactly who they are. His comment that day opened my eyes. I was not enjoying them as I could have been. He didn't want to spend his life looking at what they weren't. He simply wanted to enjoy and love his daughters as any father should be allowed to. And that was when I finally was able to let go of comparisons and false expectations once and for all.

We have gone to many large holiday dinners with my family since that first one; we even hosted one a couple of years ago. The holidays are very enjoyable, and they've gotten easier every year. I still pack food for Maria. I bring some things for Christina, but it's not as critical with her as it is with Maria. And I still bring milk. Last year, we took a portable DVD player along to help keep the girls more relaxed, which allowed me to relax and enjoy the evening as well.

It is a relief not needing to hide anything now, but we still have some moments that probably catch others off guard. For example, one year I was in the bathroom helping Christina when she started huffing and hyperventilating. She almost knocked a decorative Christmas tree off the back of the toilet. Her head was about to hit the picture on the wall. I was struggling to calm her down while keeping her from breaking anything in the tight space. I remember thinking about how odd all those noises we were making must have sounded to others outside of the bathroom. I laughed a little imagining what they must've thought was going on in that bathroom.

Once in a while, I still experience a twinge of wishing they were normal. Sometimes these moments are expected, such as when the Girl Scouts, who are the same age as Christina, rang the doorbell selling cookies or when I realized my friend's child who is Maria's age was learning to drive. Other times, they snuck up on me, as during one of our holiday dinners when I was chatting with a couple of our relatives. Christina was standing behind us hyperventilating and huffing. I had to get up to stop her. When I sat back down, one of the people I had been talking with was gone. Christina's behavior was just a little too uncomfortable for him. My feelings weren't hurt. I know this person loves Christina, but some people just have a different comfort level with special needs behaviors. Like everything else, I've learned to accept that over the years.

Being around other people, seeing the decisions they make and how they choose to live, whether in a family setting or just out in public, we are always reminded of how the lack of normalcy has become our norm. What we've adjusted to and have learned to accept doesn't change around others; it just becomes more readily apparent. Once when driving home from a social event, Jeff turned to me and said, "I wouldn't trade places with anyone there." I laughed and said, "Well, I can assure you that they wouldn't want to trade places with us either." We both smiled. We are happy with our girls.

Boundaries

We need the emotional support of others when going through something as traumatic as learning of a special needs diagnosis. As important as it is to have an external support system, setting boundaries is equally important. This is true with any family dynamic, but it's particularly true with special needs families. Raising special needs children involves allowing numerous medical and education experts into the family. Parents who've never before thought about certain disorders or syndromes are suddenly thrust into a realm of new issues, vocabulary, and decisions. Having the support of family is very helpful; however, if those relatives are too overbearing and opinionated, parents will have a much harder time making good, informed decisions. For this reason, it's strongly advisable when sharing information with family to take an approach of having a clear stance that you are doing so to include them, not to solicit advice or have them try to "fix" anything for you.

When you open the door to family, friends, schools, or whomever, they will come in. Special needs parents must be unified in their decisions and draw clear lines on how closely those outside the home are allowed to become involved. Be cautious on whom you choose to share sensitive information with; exercise your parental rights and discretion based on the personalities of individual family members and friends. It's okay to ask for support, but for the sake of the child, you always want to appear strong and sure about the information or developments you share. It's okay to let them know what you are up against, but you don't want anyone overstepping and adding strife to an already trying situation.

In our case, it was a good thing we decided to tell everyone about the girls' diagnosis when we did, because Christina began having seizures not long afterward. That was an extraordinarily difficult and frightening time; I can't imagine how much more difficult it would've been without the support and understanding of my family. Yet because Jeff and I had already been clear in how we were going to handle the diagnosis and that the choices about how we would raise our girls would remain ours alone, the support we received from family was exactly what we needed. No one tried to step in and take over when we were dealing with this new development. They provided emotional support yet allowed us the appropriate space to face new decisions as parents unified in the desire to do what we thought was best for our daughter.

Part 2

Outside Agencies

Schooling

It Really Is Rocket Science
Surviving and Excelling in Special Ed

When a child is diagnosed with a developmental or learning disability, the school system suddenly becomes more involved in that child's—and that family's—life. In some ways, the services offered through special education are invaluable. Without these resources and the truly dedicated, caring teachers who have committed their careers to helping disabled children, special needs children and their families would have a much more difficult road to travel. However, despite all the positives, public schools are government-funded agencies, which inherently means there is plenty of bureaucracy and red tape involved in every aspect, especially when it comes to highly individualized and expensive special education programs. Every decision requires administrative collaboration, written summaries, and signatures of all parties involved (except the actual student, that is). The meetings, reports, and IEPs are overwhelming for parents new to special education. But with a little guidance and experience, the waters that are special education become easier to navigate. In fact, when parents know how to communicate with the schools, they can ensure that their children not only survive in the system but thrive within it.

Resources offered by the schools can be tremendously helpful for both parent and child, as long as parents are diligent about staying involved in their child's education. As parents, we have to know when the school is helping and when a line is being crossed. We have to decide what is ultimately right for our child's development, health, and happiness. Even well-intentioned teachers, therapists, and administrators can overstep. While they may be experts in the field of special education, as parents, we must never forget that we are the experts in the field of our own children.

There is a way to find a happy balance between familial privacy and the often-intrusive always-paperwork-laden system that is special education. Of course, finding this balance is easier when parents already know their children will need these services. In my case, the schools essentially "broke the news" to me that my children would need to be placed in the special education program. We learned this for both Maria and Christina over the span of one very painful, emotionally devastating year. In one case, I was completely blindsided by a formal meeting; in another, the message came unspoken yet crystal clear—my girls were never going to succeed in a regular academic setting.

Christina

Overview

It was because of Christina's more obvious speech delays that we took our first steps toward special education with her, rather than Maria. At our pediatrician's urging, we took Christina to Child Find in Virginia when she was four. [In Virginia, children who may be in need of special education or related services are referred to Child Find for information, developmental screenings, and possible referral for additional comprehensive evaluations to determine eligibility for services.] Our intent was to qualify her to receive speech therapy services. Child Find was not a good experience for us. Christina became overstressed and refused to cooperate during the hearing test. Then the staff tried to pressure us into enrolling her in their school. Finally, emotionally exhausted, we finished the examination and left. We had what we really needed—an appointment for Christina with a speech therapist. Christina received speech therapy at home for one month. Although we moved from Virginia to Florida soon after, we were able to take the results of the evaluations to the schools in Florida and access services there without any further tests being required.

Christina's speech sessions in Florida, at the local elementary school, were much more stressful for her than the few in-home therapy sessions she had received in Virginia. During our first sessions in Florida, she became very agitated by the ordeal. Even though she was potty-trained, she regularly had accidents during her sessions. Worse yet, in the midst of her speech therapy, we saw the onset of her hyperventilation problem that has led to many other traumatic and frightening health issues over the years.

Getting to the sessions was no easy task, either. I had to take all three children with me since they could not be left alone, and finding a babysitter available during school hours was not practical. Normal errands with all three girls were challenging enough, given that Anna was still too young to walk. But the speech sessions were nearly impossible, since Christina would throw such fits about going that she needed to be carried as well as Anna. I remember one time having Christina scream so loud that people came out from their offices all over the school to see what was going on. I felt terrible, but I also thought I was doing what was ultimately in her best interest. I did not yet realize she was such a high-anxiety child. At each session, just when I would think I couldn't take it anymore, that I couldn't put her through the trauma any longer, she would finally calm down, and I would think she will be okay for the next visit. This lasted for just a few months, and then the sessions were over for the summer. The next fall, the school administrators insisted she was too old (five) to reenroll in her prior setting, and she would have to transition to a more advanced class. Envisioning the disastrous effects of even more pressure on her highly anxious mental and emotional state, we refused and kept her home for that year to recover and mature.

Looking back, I probably should've done things differently. I always wonder if we had held off and waited until she was older before putting her in school for the sole benefit of getting speech therapy, would she have been spared some of the anxiety-induced health issues she has today? But there was at that time, and is today, so much emphasis on "early intervention." The pressure on parents to submit their children to therapy at the earliest indication of issues is overwhelming. Hindsight tells me that we could have avoided many of these problems if we hadn't put her through those early stressors. Her psychiatrist assures me this is not the case. He says Christina most likely would've started hyperventilating sooner or later, but I don't know that I agree. When she finally did start school two years later, when she was ready, she performed so much better. However, more than a decade later, she is still plagued with recurring episodes of hyperventilation. Unfortunately, we can't redo the past; we can only learn and move forward.

The Details

Because we moved to Florida in the middle of a school year, both girls only attended the last half of the academic year. Initially, I sought just speech support services from the school district. Christina's speech therapist first recommended placing her in the Early Exceptional Learning Program (EELP) to provide her with additional support. EELP serviced pre-K special and regular education children who weren't quite ready to move into kindergarten. Some of the school's teachers also utilized EELP as a day care for their younger children. The developmental range was a good fit for Christina at that time. Maria was attending a regular education kindergarten class at the same school, and they both seemed happy, although very anxious to see me, when I picked them up after school each day. I can still hear Christina's excited cries of "Mom! Mom!" when I arrived; she sounded like a baby bird calling out to me. It was a call that I can still hear, and it continues to haunt me because I now understand how difficult the separation must have been for her.

We wanted Christina to continue through EELP for another full year; however, we were told that since she was turning six (albeit not until the spring of the next year), she could not stay in the program without being formally classified as special needs. This spurred our first IEP meeting, and the result was not good. She was classified as Trainable Mentally Handicapped (TMH), and we were told she needed to be serviced by a TMH class offered at a different elementary school. Not only did they deny our request to keep her in EELP, but they were planning to bus her to a school thirty minutes away.

I was in shock when I left that meeting. I felt completely unprepared for the news they were delivering. I was pregnant with my fourth baby (the one I would soon miscarry) and was worried about Christina's health. She was constantly hyperventilating, extremely stressed, and getting weaker and sicker by the day. She became so fragile during that spring and summer that I truly feared for her life. Yet there I sat listening to three people tell me they had already passed judgment and decided my daughter was trainable mentally handicapped and needed to be bussed to a school miles from home.

I don't know if I even realized what the term Trainable Mentally Handicapped was or what it meant then. We were in the process of genetic testing at the time, but no one in the medical community had yet given us any conclusive diagnosis. I went into the IEP process wanting to get her an extra year in prekindergarten. To say I was caught off guard is an understatement.

Before that day, I had never seen an IEP before. The document itself was daunting: it was sixteen pages of handwritten notes basically telling me everything that was wrong with my child. (Today, IEPs are generally typed and completed electronically during the meeting.) All of Christina's delays and problems were laid out on paper, and seeing it like that was shocking. Of course, it was laden with education jargon and school code words that left me wondering what half of the convoluted report was even saying. How are "percentages of accuracy goals" measured? Who determines this, and how accurate are the findings? The worst part was seeing the label: trainable mentally handicapped.

They were labeling my baby. They were sending her too far from home to a school I was not familiar with. I didn't know how to react. I wanted so badly to keep my composure. I asked about a variance to keep her at our local school, but they said no; no waivers were available. I left the meeting very upset and feeling like I had failed Christina. I remember being dressed in my favorite blue maternity dress but wishing I could fit into a crisp, tailored black suit, thinking they would have treated me with more respect if I were in my professional attire. I even wished for that brief moment that I was a lawyer so I could have had just the right words to make them listen. (However, after dealing with enough school people, I now believe that being a lawyer wouldn't necessarily give you an edge, anyway.) More than anything, I hated feeling at a disadvantage during the meeting. I left feeling abused, beat up, and taken advantage of. Simply put, I was devastated.

Exceptional Student Education (ESE) is classified by intelligence quotient (IQ). Here is a simple chart that explains just a bit of the confusing education-speak. If only I had known this much before the IEP.

Trainable Mentally Handicapped (TMH): IQ range < 50
Educable Mentally Handicapped (EMH): IQ range 50–70
TMH teaches basic, functional skills, such as using the bathroom.
EMH teaches reading, math, and certain life skills.

After that first IEP meeting in June and after I had more time to play everything back in my mind and go over it all with Jeff, I called the person in charge of ESE to ask for reconsideration. When I started talking to her, all I heard were scripted, canned phrases. She carefully parsed her responses and used specific language like "We can have an 'expanded conversation.'" This woman was unreal and completely unyielding; she talked but didn't say anything original or informative. Nor did she seem genuinely concerned about helping us find a solution.

I hung up the phone and knew we were in trouble and needed help. I called my dad, a respected businessman with social connections who knows how to make things happen. He made a call to someone on the school board, and that's when we finally got some attention. Everyone who was anyone (or so it seemed) showed up at the next IEP meeting in August. There were a dozen school officials seated at the conference table, waiting for us. That's the only time I've ever reached out to get help in that way. With any other situation, I never call my dad to step in. Whether it's pride, a sense of fair play, or whatever, I just don't do it. In this case, because it was Christina and she was in such a precarious health condition, I had to put those feelings aside and get help wherever I could.

Prior to the second IEP meeting, Jeff and I agreed to visit some special education classrooms to see which one we felt would be right for Christina. Even though we wanted her to stay in the EELP program at our local school, the administration was still saying no. So we had to at least begin the process of moving toward the TMH classroom they said she needed. We scheduled visits with three classes at three distant schools. No TMH or EMH classes were available at our neighborhood school.

Around this same time, I called to request the help of a parent liaison. As fate would have it, a woman I had met eight months earlier at a neighbor's holiday cookie exchange party came to our aid. The funny part is I recall being so stressed the day of that cookie party that I almost didn't go. We were new in town, we were going through genetic testing, and I'm not fond of baking. I was running late that day, so Jeff ended up decorating all my cookies, just so I could go and get to know some of our new neighbors. Months later, when I called the parent liaison office and left my name, this woman recognized it from having met me at the party and intercepted my call. She has been a very good friend and helpful resource to me over the years, starting with accompanying us to visit the ESE classrooms.

Of the three classrooms, two were completely wrong for Christina. In one, the aide was clearly uninvolved and just there to physically help the teacher instead of being actively engaged with the children. The second class was designated as just TMH and had several much older and bigger, severely handicapped children in it. Jeff looked at me and said there was no way we could put her there; Christina was just too small and fragile for that environment. I remember looking around the class and thinking that if Christina belonged there, that would be one thing. But if she didn't, even if she didn't have the words to communicate her thoughts, she would realize on some level that something was wrong with her. Even the parent liaison agreed that the class was not a good match for Christina.

During the course of visiting classrooms, I was surprised to learn how many parents were willing to give the schools complete control over their child's care and development. My friend and liaison explained how some parents never attended IEP meetings; the liaisons attended in their place as the child's representative. It was an eye-opener to realize that some special education parents want no involvement with their kids. I love my kids and struggle for what is best for them all the time; I can't imagine washing my hands of them in that way. The thought makes me very sad for those children.

At the third school, we met the teacher who would end up teaching Maria for two years and Christina for one. She had a very aggressive personality and was a little gruff in how she dealt with the kids, but to this day, I've never seen a teacher work as hard as she did. She ran a class that serviced both TMH and EMH kids, and she was amazing with them. She taught her students to cook, had them doing yoga, and really encouraged them to try new things.

Jeff and I decided that if Christina absolutely had to go to an ESE classroom, we wanted it to be this one. However, we weren't quite ready to accept that the timing was right. We still wanted her to stay in EELP for another year. She was too young, weak, and sick. In fact, just the stress of visiting the ESE classrooms brought about another problem. In addition to hyperventilating, she began stuttering. As Jeff pointed out, we had already learned that stress behaviors don't necessarily disappear when the stressor is removed. Christina continued hyperventilating well after we stopped going to the speech therapy that triggered it. What if the stuttering became permanent? She already had enough problems with speech; we certainly didn't need to compound her difficulties with stuttering.

No. Christina was simply not ready for the added stress of being moved from the EELP classroom she already knew, and the additional stress of being separated from her sister, in a new school. It was just too much for one extremely stressed and sick little girl to endure. We pushed for the second IEP meeting with a purpose of requesting that she stay in the EELP program for another year.

Because of the phone call my dad had made, everyone was at the second IEP meeting, including the head of the department, the same woman who had been so evasive with me on the phone. I later found out she was there in case I said the magic words: "None of these options will meet the needs of my child. I want Christina in school, but the EELP program is the only one." Apparently, you have to demand, not ask, for what you want. If you ask, they won't budge. If you demand it, they can and will make exceptions. But you have to have that catchphrase; you have to know just what to say or nothing will happen. If I had said just the right words, she could then have responded with, "In this one instance, I will make an exception." She was the only one with the authority to make that decision, which was why she was at the meeting. Unfortunately, I did not know that going into the meeting, and we did not get the result we wanted. But neither did we allow ourselves to be railroaded into pushing Christina beyond her abilities.

Jeff and I went into that meeting with our talking points prepared. We had medical evaluations affirming Christina's physical, emotional, and mental ages were delayed by two years. Age was the main crux of the problem. She was turning five during the school year. If her birthday was three months later, none of this would have been an issue. She would have been allowed to stay in EELP without any question. But because she was turning five, the school's stance was that she needed to move into a regular ESE classroom. Our stance was that she was only five by chronology; developmentally, she was three.

Despite all our medical documentation and appeals for a waiver, the school representatives weren't interested in any of it. One of the men went so far as to make odd, veiled threats about Maria. "Well, we'll see if *she* makes it here," he said. Jeff took it same way I did. Only one person at that table acted like they remembered we were the parents. Everyone else had made their decision, and our concerns were irrelevant. I could see my husband, a man who is always controlled and logical, becoming very upset by the way we were being talked to and how our concerns were being dismissed. He didn't show it to them, but I could see it.

I, too, was extremely distressed by the way the meeting was going. All I saw was my sick little girl, who was so sick I feared for her very survival, being forced to be sent to an even more stressful environment that might take her away from us altogether. As if that weren't enough, we had already suffered severe emotional losses in the weeks leading up to this meeting. I was grieving the results of the genetic testing and the loss of my baby, and I was in the midst of making one of the most difficult spiritual decisions of my life: to make myself incapable of ever becoming pregnant again. Yet none of these things could come into play during the IEP meeting. Christina's well-being was the only thing that mattered right then.

At one point during the meeting, Jeff turned the tables. He said, "She's three years old mentally, emotionally, and physically. A three-year-old needs to be at home with her mother." He was visibly shaken but adamant that Christina was not going into any of the classes they wanted to put her in. His statement ruffled a few feathers; I'm sure some felt an underlying implication of judgment against them for putting their own kids in day care. Some educators don't want to hear that very young children may be better off at home. It's one of those philosophical divides that goes much deeper than one meeting or one child. They all reacted predictably by telling us why she needed to be in school. Everyone at the table said she would be better off at school, except Jeff. He told them Christina would be spending the year at home with her mother and little sister. That was it, and that was exactly what we did.

After the meeting, when we told Christina that she didn't have to go to school, that she could stay at home with Anna for a year, she was visibly relieved and excited. As we had thought, the stuttering was brought on by the stress, and as soon as she learned she would not have to go to any of those new classrooms, the stuttering stopped. For the next year, I homeschooled both Christina and Anna with a pre-K program. I took Christina to a new speech therapy class twice a week. She handled it fine and even hugged her teacher at each session. All in all, Christina had a really good year at home. Then when she went back to kindergarten the following year, she was ready. She started kindergarten still classified as TMH, but she was able to attend the same class as Maria (Maria was classified EMH), and they were both taught by the teacher we had met and admired from our classroom visitations, before that dreadful IEP meeting.

Giving Christina another year to develop made all the difference. When she went into the ESE class, she was ready. I know we did the right thing by standing our ground and keeping her at home for a year. In fact, Christina did so well in kindergarten that her teacher recommended reclassifying her to EMH. This triggered a new IEP, which fortunately was nowhere near as stressful as the first one; however, it also meant another home evaluation with a social worker, that turned out to be quite memorable.

Every time we've had an IEP, we've had a social worker come to the house to evaluate our girls. They ask us questions about our background, my pregnancy history, discipline philosophy, family routines, and so on. I'm not sure why it has been required for us, because we have friends who never have had a home evaluation. Yet we had one with every IEP. It's very awkward having someone come to the house, and it does feel like an invasion of privacy. After all, why do you have to have strangers in your home just because your child has special needs?

During the reclassification visit, our social worker was a nice man, but Christina was behaving very poorly. She was throwing tantrums, wouldn't listen when I told her no, and was just plain being intolerable. It was as if she decided to act out all of her worst behaviors at the same time. Of course, it was very embarrassing, especially because I knew that my reactions were being scrutinized as closely as her behavior. There's tremendous pressure as a parent to perform during these evaluations. I tried my best to carry on with the interview by showing him around and answering his questions.

At one point, he asked what Christina's best attribute was. She was pitching a fit by the glass door because she wanted to go outside. I didn't want to try to discipline her in front of him in case it didn't work. I felt like crying because of how badly she was behaving, but I answered, "Her personality." And then I started laughing hysterically because of the irony of her throwing a tantrum while I was commending her personality. He laughed, too, which helped me relax. I went on to explain how her personality is such that she gets you involved with her. She's able to draw people in with her. The teachers got so involved with her that she often got more attention in the classroom than other students.

To his credit, he was very patient with Christina throughout the evaluation. He showed her a sticker book that had a sticker in it she wanted. Her attitude switched completely. We talked more, and it became apparent that she was so agitated because of his presence in our home. While he had observed her previously at school, he had never had any formal contact with her. She connected that he was a stranger and saw him as a foe. She knew he was there about her but not why. But as soon as he gave her the sticker, she saw him as a friend. We both realized he should have done that at the very beginning.

In the end, he filed a positive report that confirmed the teacher's recommendation. The process took about eight months, but Christina was finally reclassified as an EMH student. Christina had continued making amazing progress and surprised her teachers year after year. She was an amazing little girl.

Maria

The firstborn babies always set the pace. They are the first to take us parents through various stages of life and child-raising experiences. Maria was my first, and with her, we had our first experiences with the school system. Wary with a growing sense of her delayed development, we held her out of prekindergarten to mature further, and I tried that year to homeschool her to help prepare her for kindergarten but without much success and with a lot of frustration. We enrolled her in September of 2002, in Virginia, for one month, before moving to Florida. She finished her first kindergarten year in Florida but showed little progress, so we agreed to have her repeat kindergarten the following year. I have to admit I went into the new year with some trepidation but also with high hopes. I really wanted Maria to succeed in her regular education class.

To help prepare her for her second go at kindergarten, I worked diligently through the summer of 2003, trying to teach her to write her name. I thought if we could just get her do to that one thing—write her name—she would be okay and would be able to stay in regular-education classes. But she just couldn't do it, and I felt so guilty for not being able to teach her that one skill. This, of course, was all happening concurrently with Christina's first IEP and the EELP debacle, my miscarriage, and the genetic testing. Needless to say, I was ready for something, anything, to work out right for the girls. I really wanted Maria's kindergarten class to work out. So on the first day of school, we dressed up, put on big, and happy smiles; and I took Maria to her new kindergarten class and open house.

She was so happy as we walked in the room. I remember holding her tiny hand while she said in her animated way, "Mommy, I don't need you." She was so excited about being a big girl and starting school, and she kept telling me how she didn't need me. I'm not sure I felt good about that, but I knew it was just part of her excitement about starting school.

Even though I was going through so much with Christina (we were scheduled to visit ESE classrooms for her all throughout that same week) and I had my six-week miscarriage D&C follow-up appointment with my OB-GYN that same afternoon, I tried to look past it all and play the happy mom of a kindergartener starting school. I wanted to get off on the right foot; I wanted to show the teacher that I was going to be an involved parent, one who could be counted on and whose daughter would be fine in her class. I talked to her about becoming the homeroom mom, and she responded with enthusiasm. I left the school that day feeling optimistic that maybe, just maybe, everything would be okay this time.

But it wasn't. My life continued unraveling over the following weeks. The school psychologist began evaluating Maria and expressed concerns; however, she didn't express the findings in a way that clicked. Perhaps I was too deep in denial because of everything going on with Christina's IEP that month. Whatever the reason, I still didn't see that Maria was heading for special education. It's interesting to look back now and see the clues that were unfolding, through the school's actions, before anyone actually told me anything. All I knew at that time was that I needed for her to write her name. I was becoming frantic on that point.

I wanted so badly for her to stay in her class that I took extra measures, including taking her to a well-known tutoring center. There, they assured me (without any form of diagnostic testing) that for a fee of five thousand dollars they would have her reading in no time. They presented themselves as miracle workers, not just teachers. As a desperate mother, I was willing to do nearly anything or pay any price to avoid the inevitable. In hindsight, I am very glad we decided against enrolling her. They would have taken our money but would not have been able to help her. She is sixteen now and just able to read at the first-grade level.

My initial realization that Maria was going to be moved to a special education classroom didn't come from the psychologist or from a report or assessment. It happened when I learned that another mother had been selected as homeroom mom. I knew right then that the teacher did not expect Maria to make it in her class. Why else would she pick someone else after she'd reacted so favorably when I had volunteered on the first day? I could read between the lines; I knew what was coming, and I was devastated.

While this may sound odd, my biggest fear at that moment was not what the future held for Maria but what was going to become of me? I was in such emotional turmoil; I was truly frightened that I might never be able to recover from the despair I was feeling. How much can one person go through without becoming jaded? I did not want to become a bitter person, yet I could feel myself slipping into that place.

October 10, I still remember the day, was when Maria's teacher finally summoned the courage to tell a mother that her child needed to be in special education classes. That must have been very difficult for her. She was a very kind woman and was so gentle and comforting in how she broke the news. As we talked, she told me she'd been up all night praying about us. I knew I was fortunate to have someone like her there for Maria at that time. Without trying to, she helped me remember that God works through other people. We are never alone. He brought this caring woman into our lives at a time when we needed the help she could give.

Another of the wonderful things she did for me was assure me that Maria had been treated well by her peers. She showed me some coloring Maria had done and explained how all the other kids had complimented her on it. "In all my years of teaching," she said, "this is one of the nicest classes I've ever had. You are fortunate. They've all been very nice to Maria." It's scary to think about the alternative, about how kids could've been mean or hurtful to her. And in a small way, it made me feel better about moving her to a class where she ultimately belonged.

After talking to the teacher, we had a meeting with the school administrators and went through all the paperwork for setting up Maria's IEP. This one wasn't as difficult as Christina's. We had already visited all the classrooms for Christina's first IEP and knew where we wanted Maria to go. I went back and met with the special education teacher shortly before Thanksgiving. I expressed my concern about Maria changing classes midyear. I wanted to start her at a time that would cause her the least distress. I was worried about how to tell Maria that she would be changing classes. I didn't want her to feel bad. How do you tell your child she is flunking kindergarten? The ESE teacher assured me she would be fine and suggested having her start on December 1, at the beginning of the "reindeer segment." The entire month of December was going to be devoted to holiday activities and would be a good time for her to make the transition.

After Thanksgiving, I said to Maria, "Guess what? You are going to go to a new school, and you are going to be doing all kinds of Christmas things for December." She was very excited and, in the days that followed, didn't miss the old school at all. The idea that there's a curriculum for special education and something called the reindeer segment seemed very positive and a bit humorous. It was refreshing to be able to look forward to something again.

Before Maria left her regular education kindergarten class, she was able to participate in their Thanksgiving pageant. Maria played an Indian. I sat in the audience with Christina and Anna, watching Maria in her play. Maria wasn't singing or doing anything. She was in her Indian costume. Her eyes were big, and she was just staring. I was a bit sad knowing that this was it for regular education. I remember I just wanted a picture of it, but I'd forgotten my camera. Another mom said she'd send me copies of her pictures, but she never did. She may have forgotten, but most likely it was too uncomfortable after learning that Maria had been moved to special education. The only picture I have of Maria in regular education is in the school yearbook.

After she changed classes, Maria experienced a great year with her new teacher. Then the following year, we were rezoned to a new school that was launching its first year of a new ESE program. But Maria was doing so well where she was, and Christina was just getting ready to start school after her year at home, I really didn't want to switch to a new school with an untested program. I protested, and this time, we were granted our request for a variance to keep Maria with the same teacher for a second year and to have Christina join her. It worked out wonderfully. They had a great year together. Maria helped Christina with little things, like putting on her jacket and getting her lunch. Christina loved going to school with her sister. And both of them made steady, if slow, advances in their functioning.

The following year, they were scheduled to move out of the classroom with the teacher we really liked and into a classroom with a teacher we really didn't care for. I had seen and heard enough about her in my two years of volunteering that I knew I did not want the girls going into her class. We opted instead to switch them back to the school we were zoned for, which proved to be the right decision. Both girls were able to continue in a classroom together with another wonderful teacher.

Through the years, we have been blessed with some great teachers, but the road wasn't always smooth. In the next segment, I will talk more about a year that went terribly wrong.

While administrators for regular education may balk at switching kids' schedules based on whether or not they like a teacher, special education parents are given more flexibility in finding the program and teacher that best meets the child's needs. We normally do not have to sit back and put up with an intolerable teacher. The teaching style and class dynamics vary by teacher, and what is right for one child isn't necessarily right for another. But the only way to really know what works for your child and what doesn't is to be intimately involved at the school. Get to know the teachers, observe how they interact with the students, talk to other parents, and don't be afraid to make discerning decisions based on any of the factors you see first-hand. The schools will work with you—usually.

Curse of the Minimo

Given Christina's history of speech problems, we weren't surprised that communication was a struggle for her in kindergarten. To help, the teacher gave her a specially designed book with pictures representing basic school-day needs, along with pictures of the main people in Christina's life. She could then point to those pictures to convey information to the teacher and aides. That spring, when the teacher put together her assessment, she made two recommendations. The first was to have Christina reclassified from Trainable Mentally Handicapped to Educable Mentally Handicapped. The teacher gave us a glowing report about Christina's progress during the year; her excitement was very evident. We've noticed this happens a lot with Christina. At first glance, she looks like she has great disabilities, but when you start working with her, you soon discover that she has an exceptional memory and is a pretty sharp little kid.

The second recommendation she made was for the school to provide Christina with an experimental communication assistance device called "Minimo." The Minimo would be Christina's constant companion at school. Essentially, the device was designed to help children like Christina, whose speech challenges are severe enough to hinder basic communication, by electronically articulating words for the user. For instance, if Christina needed to use the bathroom, instead of struggling to formulate words, she could raise her hand, and then when the teacher acknowledged her, she could press a button on the device. A computerized voice would then say, "May I go to the restroom?"

Even though Christina had made good progress that year, communication was still very difficult for her. The device seemed like it would be helpful given Christina's challenges up to that time, so we signed papers authorizing Christina to use the Minimo during the following year. This was in the spring, at the end of the school year. Over the summer, Christina made a quantum leap with her speech. So Jeff and I talked it over and reevaluated our position on allowing the school to introduce the Minimo. We concluded that she was making good progress, and we didn't want to interrupt that or cause her to backslide because of a reliance on technology. More so, we did not want her to become dependent on such a device.

In our view, every time she used an assistance device, she would lose an opportunity for further speech development. Practice is one of the most important components of traditional speech therapy. We also saw that by the beginning of the school year, Christina was having running conversations with her sisters at home. This told us that she was physically and cognitively able to speak; therefore, implementing an assistance device would allow her the option of not speaking in full sentences, a choice she was likely to make. Nor did we want her denied an opportunity to speak in class because of it. Ultimately, we wanted her to learn how to speak and overcome the developmental issue of poor tongue coordination rather than learn how to push a button.

What had seemed like a potentially helpful tool four months earlier now clearly was a step in the wrong direction. So when the school year started in August, we told them we had changed our minds and no longer wished for her to use assisted communication technology in the classroom. Little did we know that the school's speech therapist would ignore our wishes and implement the device, anyway. Several months passed before we learned that the Minimo was being used. We didn't find out until close to the holidays, and when we did, we also realized what was behind so many other behavioral problems we'd suddenly started having with the girls at home.

Whenever a new piece of technology is introduced into the classroom, the teachers need to make sure all the children in the class are comfortable with it. Because of this, they were letting all the children practice on the Minimo to see how it worked. They were also programming all of their names into the Minimo for Christina's use. This, of course, attracted a lot of additional attention toward Christina, which had negative behavioral consequences for both Christina and Maria. Christina became anxious from being at the center of the attention, while Maria, being in the same class, felt left out by the added attention being shown to her sister. Neither was able to express those feelings, so they manifested them through behavior.

For weeks, we couldn't figure out why Maria was acting out so often. Then when Christina had multiple "accidents" in school and in her religious education class at church over the course of just a few weeks, we knew something was wrong. She hadn't had an accident in over a year prior to this. I remember the stress of both girls' sudden change in behavior was so great that it triggered a horrible, debilitating migraine for me that lasted for days.

When we learned that the Minimo was being used at school, we immediately understood what was causing so much havoc in our home. We called it "the curse of the Minimo," and we wanted it stopped. It took six weeks after contacting the school to get the device removed from our lives. We never understood why the speech teacher was so adamant about using it; even after contacting the school, she continued insisting that Christina needed it. Our only guess was that she wanted to have it on her resume since it was a relatively new piece of technology. Luckily, we had the support of Christina's main classroom teacher, who agreed that Christina could manage fine without the Minimo. Only then was the device removed from the classroom. We were all relieved when the curse was finally lifted.

The Mystery of the Matrix

Money. When we talk about school programs, it seems to always come down to money. Which schools will get much needed funding to run good programs? Or to hire qualified teachers and support teams? To purchase equipment and materials to enhance learning? These are questions that plague every school administrator for both regular and special education classes. We all know that standardized test scores are directly tied to funding for regular education programs. But what determines funding for our special needs kids? The answer is the *matrix*.

I first learned about the matrix when I began looking into private school options. While visiting one of the prospective schools, I was asked if I knew the girls' "matrix numbers." I discovered that a student's matrix number determines the amount of funding a public school will receive from the government, or the level of funding available to private schools, through the McKay Scholarship. This scholarship was created here in Florida to give parents an option to choose private or charter schools for their children and have the money follow the child.

So I asked the girls' teacher about the matrix, and she readily gave me their numbers. A short time later, we decided to leave the girls where they were and stopped looking further into private school options. Two years went by, and both girls were progressing well and were enjoying their classrooms and teachers. The following year, however, when Christina's hyperventilation problem escalated and she began having seizures, we once again decided to look for alternatives. We knew the stressful setting was contributing to her increasing health problems, and we thought a change of schools would help. I requested their matrix numbers again, but when I received them, I noticed they had changed. This made me curious. Why the change? Why did Christina's number go down while Maria's went up, even though this appeared to be the opposite of their actual needs. Christina now needed much more assistance, yet her lowered score dictated less support. And there was no way Maria's number should have been higher than Christina's; as time marched on, and Maria showed no progress, her score should have risen but not to exceed Christina's—who clearly needed more support at that time.

Seeing such an inexplicable change in numbers prompted me to go back to the school in search of an explanation. What *exactly* is the matrix, and how is it calculated? This was when things got a little odd. No one wanted to tell me. Every time I asked a question, whether it was to the teacher, a classroom aide, a parent liaison who'd always been so forthcoming and helpful in other situations, or the head of the ESE department at their school, they all skirted the issue and avoided answering my question. Their reluctance was clear, but the reason for it was not. It felt like "the matrix" was a big, top secret conspiracy that only those on the inside of the system could know about. Yet it was in *my* child's file, and it was directly connected to my child's education.

Whenever I pressed the issue, I received an answer along the lines of "Why do you want to know?" I tried to explain that if it was in my child's file, I wanted to understand it. I have that right, as a parent, to be fully involved and informed about anything pertaining to my child. Still, they refused to give me any solid information. Even when I confronted the person in charge about the secrecy, telling her that I knew through a relative that other school districts are very open about the matrix, she balked at releasing anything that explained how the matrix score is calculated. Sometimes, I received half answers from the people I asked, which gave me a sense that I understood it. At least until I tried explaining it to Jeffrey, that is. With his logical mind, he asked me so many specific questions that I realized I still had no idea how the matrix was calculated.

Reluctantly, they finally gave me copies of the completed matrices. A start toward understanding. Then an administrator at one of the private schools we had visited gave me a copy of the matrix handbook and explained how the matrix is completed. Basically, there are twenty-one defined areas of eligibility. Each is related to a different special needs area, ranging from autistic to visually impaired. Each of these areas, or domains, is then broken down into five levels of service the child may require. There is an assessment team (in our case six different names were shown) whose members rate the child based upon their perception of the child's needs.

The final number is used to calculate the amount of money that will be allotted for their specific educational needs each year. For public schools, the funds are transferred from the state or federal government; for private or charter schools in Florida, this determines the qualifying amount to be provided through the MacKay Scholarship.

With Christina's newly lowered score, her allotment decreased by $3,398. This was a significant decrease that was based on subjective evaluations without any parental involvement. When I finally received the file, I understood why they didn't want me to see it. It was very, very subjective.

The secrecy surrounding the matrix was maddening, but more distressing was learning what goes on behind the scenes. After an IEP meeting, parents think that's all there is. They leave, but the administrators stay and have another meeting. During this time, they determine the matrix number. I found the idea of them having a secondary meeting about us without our presence very unnerving. I still don't understand why there is so much secrecy. My only guess is that due to the subjectivity, school administrators don't want to be questioned about the accuracy of their assessment. I suppose making it unattainable to parents is one way to avoid demands for reevaluation, but that is hardly the right answer. Parents have a right to know this information, and we do need it. Having it withheld only exacerbates the stress and confusion of trying to select the correct educational setting for our children. Note: Our school district has since given educational seminars for parents about the matrix.

Parents' Role in Education

One of the most important aspects of excelling in the special education system is remembering that parents have a role. Decisions should not be made unilaterally. There is a partnership between the schools and parents that has an objective of providing the best education possible. However, because of the sheer number of students that schools serve, parents must be the child's primary advocate for achieving that goal. While we may not have a complete say in everything, there are many areas of our child's education that we can control.

First and foremost, parents of special needs children have to make sure their child is in a positive classroom environment. Every child has different needs, and therefore, not every classroom is the same. Since teachers have the most influence over that environment, your child's teacher will also have the most impact on his or her school experience. Over the years, we learned to look for the following criteria when evaluating a potential classroom:

- Teachers and aides who are actively engaged with the students. Good teachers are constantly working on helping the child grasp whatever concept they are teaching; they truly want the child to improve and meet the learning objective. We had one teacher who had the girls come in early so she could bring them up to speed on a skill they were struggling with. Some teachers, however, show little concern.
- Classroom aides who are as aggressively involved as the teachers. It is easy to see which aides enjoy their work and which ones treat it as "just a job."
- Teachers and aides who are able-bodied. This is not meant to sound judgmental, but special needs children often require quick, physical intervention. In the next chapter, I will recount how having a teacher who was obese and not physically able to intervene with Christina's hyperventilation contributed to a situation that rapidly escalated beyond the classroom.
- Do they have a curriculum? Some teachers or schools use regular programs; some make up their own. Others seem to just wander from day to day.
- The classroom environment needs to be orderly and calm. Too much chaos means the teacher may not be sufficiently skilled in classroom management to handle a special needs class. Continual disruptions can create a hyper-stressful environment for some special needs children, leading to a manifestation of new problems or health issues.
- Teachers need to be organized and demanding. One of our best teachers was also the toughest. It surprised people to learn we had chosen her for both Maria's and Christina's first year in ESE, but her tough edge made her the perfect choice. She was always in control of her class and had the

students engaged in a variety of activities that helped them make great progress that year.

- How teachers interact with parents is important too. Do they answer questions and communicate what is going on in the classroom and with the child? Do they demonstrate respect for parents?

- Do the teachers plan parties and classroom activities that include parents? Smart teachers will use holidays as an opportunity for parents to come in and see what's going on in class and meet other parents. The social aspect of special education classes is much more important and takes a higher priority than in regular education. This also gives the children a chance to shine, which can easily be overlooked.

Beyond evaluating teachers and classrooms, getting to know and maintaining contact with other parents is an important aspect of being a special education parent. The reason for this goes beyond building a social circle of parents facing similar issues; parents who have more contact with each other make the teacher's job a little easier. When parents know each other and each other's children, all parties have a better understanding of the interpersonal dynamics in the classroom. When problems come up, they are easier to resolve because all parents involved know the behavioral quirks of their child, as well as those of the other children.

For example, one year, Maria was in class with a daughter of an acquaintance of mine. These two girls did not get along during the first week of school to the extent that the school nurse wrote a "prescription" to keep one away from the other. Because I knew the mother and the girl—and I know Maria's idiosyncrasies—I was able to dismiss most of what I was hearing without getting too upset by it. If something more drastic was going on, then it may have been best to separate them, but the other mother and I recognized that this was just a personality clash our girls needed to work through.

In another situation, Christina kept complaining about a little boy hitting her, squeezing her hand, and pulling her hair really hard. One day when I picked her up, she complained about her head hurting. The teacher explained that this boy had pulled her hair so hard he ended up being sent home for the day. I was wondering what was going on with this child, and then I met him and his mother and understood. Unlike Christina, who is very sensitive and doesn't like loud noises, this was a boy who needed excessive stimulation to feel anything. That's why he holds hands too tightly and likes things loud and rough. Our children each had very different personalities, and the boy's behavior was not a result of meanness or lack of discipline. In fact, the mother was so sweet; she sent me a note apologizing for her son's behavior. It was clear she felt very badly. I told her it was fine. Once you realize what's going on, you remember that each child has a unique set of problems.

In addition to classroom social events, birthday parties are wonderful opportunities to gather with other parents. Not only can everyone get to know each other (parents and children included), but parties are a great chance to discuss school issues and compare notes on teachers or classrooms. Be wary of gossip and rumors, but any chance to gather credible information and stay abreast of what is going on in the school helps parents make better choices about their child's education.

Being involved at school and spending time as a parent volunteer in the classroom helps give a clearer picture of what happens inside the school on a daily basis. It also helps the parent see how the children interact with each other and provides an opportunity to build a familiar relationship with the teacher. Having a good parent-teacher relationship has many benefits. Not only will teachers be more communicative throughout the year, but the parent will be better able to respond appropriately to unexpected situations.

For instance, when Maria was in sixth grade, there was an incident of a male student inappropriately touching a couple of the girls in the class while they sat on the floor in small groups. His hands never went under the clothing, but it was still distressing. When the administration learned about it, the boy was sent to another school. Yet the parents of one of the girls involved also chose to move their daughter to a new school. I had a good relationship with the teachers and could see how upset they were to learn this had happened in their classroom. Even though Maria was not involved, I felt confident that the level of concern shown by the teachers and administration meant that steps were being taken to limit the likelihood of it ever happening again. I could also tell it bothered the teachers that they never had a chance to clear the air with the girl's mother. Since the mother was never involved at the school, it's understandable that her immediate reaction was to simply remove her daughter.

When these situations happen, it will come down to your relationship with the teacher and what you think of the teacher. I had conferences with the teachers about the touching incident. They both were visibly upset. If you know the teachers, you can see their point of view. I could put myself in their shoes and imagine how badly I would feel if that mom didn't give me a chance to talk to her. I had to ask myself if I believed they were capable teachers, and I did.

During the puberty years, situations like inappropriate touching are not uncommon in special education classrooms. The challenge is figuring out if the behavior is stemming from an intellectual issue or is a normal part of adjusting to puberty. In the latter case, the behavior is something that can be fairly easily corrected. By moving the boy, is that child being served well by the education system? Is he being taught the behavior is wrong, or is it just transferring the behavior to a new environment where it might happen again? Granted, if my child was being touched, I'd be emotional too. But as you start thinking it through, you can begin to see other perspectives. Does the boy even know it's wrong? One of the hardest parts about dealing with situations at school involving our children is removing emotion. This is even harder when you don't have the full perspective.

Sometimes, regardless of how efficient and professional the school staff is, accidents can happen. Kids can get hurt. No one wants this, but realistically, no one can completely prevent the unexpected; all anyone can do is minimize risk. The schools have protocols to create the safest environment for our children that they can. We, as parents, can only teach safe habits to our children and then hope they remember those when not under our direct supervision. Then if something does happen, we also have an obligation to handle the situation in a manner that is both rational and assertive.

Recently, Maria was involved in an accident in the parking lot. She has always had a problem remembering to look for cars before crossing the street or parking lot. She will turn her head and go through the motions, but she isn't really looking to see if a car is coming. On this particular afternoon, a mother happened to enter the carpool lane from the wrong direction and hit Maria. Although she was travelling very slowly, Maria was knocked down. Thankfully, she was not hurt, just scared and a bit sore. A visit with her doctor later confirmed that she had not sustained any injuries.

I arrived at the school a few minutes after the accident. Everyone was there attending to Maria: school staff members, the driver of the car, and even another parent who was an orthopedic doctor and had seen the accident and immediately assessed Maria's condition. Maria was fine, so I was able to breathe a bit easier. The other mother was distressed, and although the afternoon is a bit of a blur now, I do remember hugging her and assuring her that everything was okay; Maria was okay. Afterward, I wondered if that was the right thing to do. Was I serving my daughter's best interest by comforting this woman? I didn't know she had been driving the wrong way, but I did know that Maria doesn't look both ways.

In the days following the incident, I slowly started learning more details. I found out that the barricade was not up preventing cars from entering the carpool lane from the wrong side. I also learned that there was a video of the accident and that the administration had reviewed it several times without telling me of its existence. I don't know if a formal accident report was ever filed, but technically, I believe this is a standard procedure. I didn't request one, but I should have.

After I found out about the parking lot video, Jeff insisted that I go to the school and watch it. He believed that I needed to present myself as a mother who was not going to be dismissed when harm befell her child. What, he asked, would happen if one of our girls was touched, accosted, or hurt by another student later when they are in high school and not under continuous supervision? What would the administration's reaction be? Would they notify us appropriately or assume that we were not that interested? Additionally, since I did not see the accident firsthand, viewing the tape might provide other clues that would have been helpful for understanding both the specific incident and how our daughter behaves and reacts to an unexpected situation.

You want the school to know without a doubt that you are the type of parent who is going to march in and demand to see any video footage of the offense. That is part of establishing balance and boundaries with the school—a mutual respect of each other's role in the child's life. The schools need to know the parents are involved. If getting hit by a car doesn't invoke a parental reaction, what will it take to get upset enough to demand accountability? Yes, we want to maintain a good relationship with the school, but as parents, we also need to think of the consequences of remaining silent.

I never planned to sue the school, but I could tell that was the question on all of their minds. It was very uncomfortable for a while and put a strain on our otherwise good relationship. I felt I needed to address the elephant in the room and met with the principal to assure her we had no intention of filing a lawsuit. It really bothered me that the existence of the video had been withheld. By the time I asked to see it, I was told that too much time had passed and the surveillance cameras had looped and overwritten the accident footage. But I had to look at the bigger picture. I had two children at the school and expected to be a part of this school for many years. I didn't want to let one incident ruin my relationship with the teachers and administrators.

When it comes to surviving and excelling in the special education system, keys to success include balance, building good relationships, and standing strong when you need action. Part of this includes understanding the hierarchy of communication. If something is happening within the classroom, whether it is a social issue between the students, concerns over the curriculum, or questions about the type and length of homework assignments being given, it's very important to communicate directly with the teacher first. If the teacher cannot resolve the matter to your satisfaction, then you can take it to the next level. Similarly, keep the lines of communication open with any of the specialists who have regular contact with your children during the school day. Using notebooks to jot notes back and forth can be a very effective way to ensure teachers, specialists, aides, and parents are each abreast of pertinent developments, either large or small at school or at home, that might affect the child's progress or behavior.

The school and district administrators are typically very responsive to parental requests, but they should only be utilized as a last resort. Administrators should know you and that you are involved in your child's education. But like the boy who cried wolf, going to the principal or vice principal should only be done sparingly to preserve the effectiveness. Everyone in the school wants to do what is best for your child; sometimes defining what is best is the hardest part. If you've built mutually respectful relationships with everyone, including the support personnel, addressing and resolving concerns and differences of opinion is much easier.

Maintaining good relationships is about more than dealing with problems. Often, it's all about dealing with difficult people. I've had my share of bad moments and encounters at the school. A teacher once told me that Maria and Christina would never learn to read and would end up in a care home (and this came from one of our favorite teachers!). Then one of Maria's middle school teachers, in response to our concern that the homework was conceptually too hard and was causing her to have self-esteem issues, replied that "Maria's not a little girl. She needs to grow up and take responsibility." (Yes, that hit a nerve!) Such comments can be very painful or insulting at the time, but I've never let someone else decide my child's fate or bully us into compromising my daughters' well-being. I've never given up fighting for my girls to receive the best education and opportunities Jeff and I can provide. I've never stopped giving Maria and Christina a chance to prove those people wrong, and Maria and Christina have learned to read. Even the best teachers can be wrong sometimes.

Fortunately, the special education community is filled with many good-hearted people. There have been countless times when teachers, aides, bus drivers, and, of course, other parents have helped me through very difficult times. Fate, I believe, brings us together at just the right moment. Most people enter a career of working with special needs children because they have genuinely caring personalities. In many cases, special education teachers and paraprofessionals have been touched by special needs on a personal level; perhaps their own children have developmental challenges. While I'm not saying that you need to become best friends with every person at the school, being involved and getting to know all the people in your child's life simply makes good sense. Stay open to the miracles that can come through them. More importantly, never lose sight of what is really at stake—the health and happiness of your child.

Helpless

Invasions of Personal Privacy
When Overzealous Professionals Cross the Line

Child abuse and neglect can affect any child, but children with disabilities are at much greater risk of maltreatment than children without disabilities. According to the various research that has been done, children with disabilities may be physically and sexually abused from two to ten times as often as children without disabilities (see http://www.childwelfare.gov and publications from the Child Welfare Information Gateway, Children's Bureau/ACYF, 1250 Maryland Avenue, SW, Eighth Floor Washington DC, 20024; 800.394.3366).

This sad and disturbing statistic shows not only how vulnerable and helpless special needs children can be; it also demonstrates why it is so incredibly important for parents to be especially vigilant with their special needs children to protect them from falling victim to these abuses. Sadly, this also means that families of children with disabilities are particularly prone to becoming targets of investigation, even when they've done nothing wrong. Threats, accusations, allegations—one wrong word to the authorities and a family can soon find itself embedded in a tangled web of legal battles to keep from being torn apart.

Jeff and I have twice experienced authorities overstepping their boundaries and putting us on the defensive to protect our family: once by an overzealous school psychologist and once because of a false allegation filed with social services. Neither incident was warranted, nor do we believe either would have happened if we didn't have special needs children. Our ignorance of our rights beforehand, coupled with a too trusting naiveté, made these situations even worse.

We were fortunate that both situations were resolved without serious implications, but other families have not always been so fortunate. Children may be taken from their homes, the legal system can egregiously intrude on parental rights, or threats of such measures may be used as leverage to intimidate parents. Of course, no one, including us, wants an abuse to be perpetrated or continued without consequence to the abuser. The safety of children, especially special needs children who lack the capacity to seek help, is clearly the priority. However, the system has become so powerful that innocent parents can feel trapped and helpless once the door of an investigation is opened. And once "the system" enters, it is nearly impossible to extricate without lengthy, expensive legal recourse.

Just Breathe

Christina hyperventilates—a lot. She started hyperventilating when she was five. We believe this was triggered by the stress of starting school before she was emotionally ready. Even though we pulled her out to give her more time to mature, she has never stopped hyperventilating. We've taken her to a multitude of doctors and specialists: a pulmonologist, a cardiologist, an endocrinologist, a neurologist, and a psychiatrist. She's been tested, evaluated, and reevaluated for years, but so far, no doctor has been able to find a systemic cause or an effective cure.

For Christina, hyperventilating is an anxiety-induced habit, a behavior that she uses to deal with stress similar to how a nervous person might bite his or her fingernails. Unlike chewing fingernails, however, hyperventilation can be dangerous. Over the years, I've done my own research on hyperventilation syndrome, which is described as overbreathing associated with anxiety. This is a cyclical condition that begins with an emotional trigger causing a person to become anxious and overbreathe. Typically, the cycle begins with rapid shallow breaths that quickly escalate in intensity. Accompanying symptoms include muscle stiffness, a sensation of pins and needles on the arms and around the mouth, and abdominal bloating. As the person experiences more physical discomfort and increased difficulty in breathing, his or her anxiety level increases and exacerbates the cycle. The critical issue with overbreathing is that levels of both carbon dioxide and oxygen are reduced, causing a chemical imbalance in the bloodstream. The resulting oxygen deprivation can lead to muscle spasms, dizziness, and fainting.

Christina's hyperventilation can quickly escalate into full-body spasms. When she loses physical control of her body, she can fall and further injure herself. We know of at least one incident when she fell out of her chair at school and struck her head. Her attacks happen frequently, sometimes as often as ten times in an hour, so it's imperative that we are always aware of her surroundings. Sometime after Christina first started hyperventilating, she also began having seizures. While the doctors have not yet been able to definitively link the seizures to the hyperventilation, we suspect there is a correlation.

Because of the seriousness of the condition, Jeff and I have a protocol we've developed and had approved by Christina's psychiatrist on how to intervene at the onset of an episode. With responsive help from an adult, Christina can usually regain control of her breathing. Someday, she should be able to catch it herself, but she isn't developmentally mature enough yet to stop hyperventilating without adult intervention. We want her to learn to control her attacks, or I should say regain control when attacks happen, but we also know that Christina will not learn to do this until she is ready. In the meantime, prompt and consistent intervention is the only effective way to help her.

The protocol we created comes from years of trial and error, discovering what worked and what didn't. Essentially, it was Christina who taught us how to help. By progressing through a series of distraction techniques, we can usually help her to stop overbreathing fairly quickly. Sometimes, all it takes is having her count out loud to ten, which interrupts the rapid breathing cycle and gives her something besides breathing to focus on. Sometimes, we take away a toy or stop her current activity. If these steps fail, we progress to physically inhibiting her ability to breathe too deeply. Crunching is a good example. When she was little, we could hold her, so she rolled up into a ball on our lap. That slowed her breathing. Of course, as she's gotten bigger, we've had to find new ways to achieve similar results. Now we wrap our arms around her and gently help her bend forward to disrupt the rapid breathing cycle. Eventually, the goal is to train her to slow her breathing on her own before the attack progresses beyond the point of self-correction.

It Starts Innocently Enough

Jeff and I have always placed our daughters' care and safety as our top priority. We are extremely forthcoming with their medical providers and educators. For years, I've worked closely with their teachers, often spending hours helping in the classroom to ensure that every need is addressed. I know the teachers, aides, parents, and administrators; and they know me, so I was shocked when a seemingly simple observation by Christina's teacher turned into a yearlong battle that culminated with the school psychologist threatening to report us to social services.

In retrospect, I believe the situation really began at the start of the 2006–2007 school year. This was when Christina and Maria—the girls were in the same class at the time—had a new teacher enter their lives. Their teacher the previous year possessed a wonderfully calm and soothing demeanor. The girls liked her and were happy in her class. She and her paraprofessional were able to handle Christina's hyperventilation episodes swiftly and without incident. Unfortunately, she accepted a job elsewhere during the summer, and her replacement did not have the same nurturing personality or ability to respond to Christina's hyperventilating.

The classroom dynamic changed drastically that year as well. The previous teacher used classical music to help calm the students; this soothing music was now gone and replaced by frequent, disruptive commotion. Because the class was changed from "special education" to "academic support," there was no longer a full-time aide in the classroom, and the curriculum was much more difficult. The young, good-natured teacher from the prior year was replaced by an older, sterner teacher whose physical limitations required frequent use of a motorized scooter for her to ride on to get around the classroom.

Maria had her worst year ever, and Christina's anxiety escalated. Other parents also noticed subtle differences; and although none of us could put our finger on any specific fault of the teacher—she spoke to all of us in an exceedingly sweet voice—many of us felt a negativity that wasn't there the year before. One parent removed her child from the class immediately. Jeff and I were concerned enough that we began looking for private school options, even though it would've meant a lengthy commute every day.

Because Christina suffers from acute anxiety, small disruptions are often problematic. One of her triggers is the disruption of someone entering or leaving a room. This, along with the new structure of the class (or rather lack thereof), was a recipe for disaster. Instead of being in a closed room with the same group of students all day, there were now groups of children requiring "academic support" continually rotating in and out of the classroom. Christina was now in an extremely stressful environment, and as with any cause-and-effect relationship, her hyperventilating problems became more and more acute.

I remember approaching the principal and asking if there was anything I could do to help him get an aide in the classroom. He was nearing retirement and brushed me off, apparently not realizing how badly an aide was needed in that room. And did I sense resentment on some level that I was questioning how he was allocating his aides?

Christina began hyperventilating with increasing frequency under the care of a teacher ill-equipped to handle the situation, and her attacks progressed past the point of rapid breathing to full-body spasms. The teacher, who I don't believe intended any harm, reported Christina's hyperventilation to the school psychologist and asked her to come into the classroom and observe. That was all it took—one comment from a teacher to a school psychologist—to set off an unbelievable string of events.

I often wonder how differently the situation might have evolved if the teacher had contacted me first. I believe parents should be the first line of communication when a situation with a child arises. At the very least, I would have been given an opportunity to better explain our intervention protocol with the teacher. I probably should have done that, anyway. That was my mistake; I realize that now. But that does not excuse the chain reaction that started in the fall of 2006.

When the school psychologist first called, she told me Christina was having a problem with frequent hyperventilation. She wanted to work directly with Christina to try and help her, and she requested permission to view Christina's medical records. At the time, I did not think much of her call because I was well aware of Christina's health problems and had been dealing with them for years. I explained Christina's condition and medical history in detail, believing that would be enough to assuage the psychologist's concerns, but I declined signing the medical release consent she requested. I saw no need to allow her to view Christina's private medical records. That choice is my right as a parent. At that point, the entire situation should have become a nonissue. She had done her job by reaching out to us. She was able to confirm that Christina was already under the care of a professional medical team. As parents, we were doing everything we could, and that should have been apparent to the psychologist. Theoretically, confirming that parents are aware of a problem and offering assistance if they choose to accept it is the extent of the school's role in a situation like this. When I declined any further assistance, her involvement with my child should have stopped. But it didn't.

I thought the issue would be closed once I explained the full scope of Christina's condition and ongoing medical care. However, there was something very unsettling about the school psychologist's call that caused me to have lingering concerns. I must have had some kind of maternal intuition that the situation was going to get worse before it got better. I remember writing in my journal about a sudden eye twitch that started later that day. I had noted it was likely caused by this unexpected call. The twitch lasted for weeks.

Of course, I can't prove they were related, but the coincidence was remarkable.

That nagging concern also prompted me to go out of my way to meet this person. We had spoken on the phone but never actually met. I wanted to introduce myself so we could get a better sense of each other. I wanted her to know that I was a concerned parent. I'm not irresponsible or neglectful. As I mentioned before, I am very involved at the school and have an excellent reputation there. I had hoped that by associating a face with the voice on the phone, we could establish a better understanding of one another. While I always intend to be professional, courteous, and helpful, I am not easily manipulated; nor am I going to waver in my choices—not then and not now.

Crossing the Line

The school psychologist continued monitoring Christina in the classroom without my knowledge. She called again and said she felt strongly that Christina needed respiratory therapy and even offered to help me find a therapist. I doubted her premise, but I listened to her suggestions and agreed to look for a respiratory therapist and let her do the same. I queried Christina's pediatrician, neurologist, and endocrinologist; and I called a pulmonologist. None of them were supportive of her recommendation. Even so, I searched extensively for such a therapist, partly to placate her and partly to leave no stone unturned.

Ironically, there are no respiratory therapists in Florida who do the kind of breathing retraining she was suggesting. Respiratory therapists generally work with patients who've suffered a traumatic injury, similar to how a physical therapist helps people learn how to strengthen injured limbs to become mobile again. Christina did not need to learn "how" to breathe correctly—her breathing was fine when she was calm or sleeping. She just needed to learn to control her breathing during periods of anxiety. Every expert I consulted with sympathized with our problem but regrettably admitted that they did not treat her type of hyperventilation.

For a time, we didn't receive any additional calls from the psychologist. Then in the spring of that school year, I learned that we were not out of the woods yet. Christina was still in a very stressful class environment, with a teacher unable or unwilling to follow our suggested protocol. As her hyperventilating worsened in frequency and intensity, her teacher continued turning to the school psychologist for help. The worst attack happened one day on the playground. Christina began hyperventilating, and no one stepped in. By the time an adult finally intervened, she was already convulsing with full-body spasms. This attack prompted the new principal to call me and request a meeting. Luckily, I received great advice once years ago to always have Jeff come with me to school meetings. It definitely changes the dynamics to have a man in the room; it is much more empowering to have your spouse with you than to be sitting alone across the table from the supposed authorities.

Jeff and I walked into a meeting that I now consider to have been nothing less than an ambush. We walked in expecting to discuss Christina's IEP with the principal and were confronted with seven members of the administration, including the psychologist, all proffering their recommendations for treating Christina's hyperventilation. They all admitted to having no experience in treating hyperventilation, yet they continued with relentless prying questions about her care, treatment, and the qualifications of our doctors. They made suggestions for alternate doctors and recommendations for different therapies. They accepted no responsibility for failing to intervene properly, or for endangering our daughter's health and safety with their lack of responsiveness, while subtly implying that our parental care was inadequate. In the end, they had no solutions; nor did they offer to provide Christina the classroom aide she so desperately needed. I regret to say that by the end of the meeting, we were emotionally exhausted and mentally beaten. They coerced us into consenting to a treatment plan to be developed by the school psychologist that would have no input from us.

We had previously resisted this because the intervention methods she was advocating directly contradicted those we had successfully implemented and had been approved by Christina's psychiatrist. The school psychologist's plan was to first offer Christina assurance that she would be okay and then verbally instruct her on how to hold her stomach and move her diaphragm. We knew such instructions would mean nothing to Christina in the midst of an overbreathing episode; it would be a completely ineffective strategy that would waste time and prolong the attack. Also, knowing from experience how important consistency is for Christina, to have the school psychologist completely out of step with the methods advocated by our expert medical team was particularly worrisome. Up to that point, we had chosen to trust our team instead of listening to her. But now we would have to accept a technique that conflicted with our own and constantly worry about the hyperventilation escalating out of control.

A month later, during the last days of the school year, without our knowledge, the school psychologist filed a formal evaluation report. I only learned of it by chance—when I bumped into her at a grocery store later in the summer. She asked how Christina was doing. I started to tell her that Christina was actually quite sick. Her anxiety had escalated even more over the summer, and she had experienced her first full seizure. We'd spent three long days and nights at the hospital and were very worried about her. The doctors had put her through more tests, including a sleep study test to see if she was breathing properly at night. Those test results determined that her breathing problems were not physiological, because she breathed normally while sleeping. This was good news, but it also meant that they still couldn't figure out what was causing either the hyperventilation or, more critically, the onset of seizures. Christina was getting sicker and sicker, weaker and weaker, and no one could seem to do anything to help her. She was already a very petite girl; watching her become so fragile with each passing day was devastating. It was an unbelievably difficult, frightening, and trying summer—one I hope we never have to go through again.

While I didn't tell the school psychologist all of this, I told her enough for her to know that Christina was very fragile and getting worse. She didn't respond; she didn't even seem to be listening. I found this behavior odd considering the battle she had spearheaded under the guise of being concerned about Christina's welfare. Wouldn't someone who was that concerned show a dash of interest about a sick little girl, even off the clock?

"Have you picked up your copy of my report?" was all she said.

"What report?" I asked.

"My evaluation of Christina. Your copy is at the school." That's when I found out she had filed a formal report that was now to be part of Christina's permanent school record and, of course, would be on file within the higher echelons of the school district. Later, when I actually read it, I was surprised and concerned with the precision with which she wrote her side of the story. She came across as being very professional and competent. I can understand how someone not familiar with the full story could read it and think that she was the expert and we, the parents, were standing in the way of allowing her to help our child. The report also admitted that, just as we had expected, the school psychologist, with her treatment plan, had been completely unsuccessful in her attempts to "rehabilitate" Christina's overbreathing problem. However, we found little consolation in being right.

The contents of the report were disconcerting but didn't become truly frightening until the new school year began. Maria had struggled a lot during the previous year and was reassigned to a different class for the new year. Christina, unfortunately, was not. She went back into the same stressful environment, now compounded with her proclivity for seizures. Jeff and I were overwhelmed with worry about Christina's weakened condition. So when the school psychologist called me once again just a couple of weeks into the school year reasserting her demand for me to find a respiratory therapist, I was even more adamant about not putting more stress into Christina's life.

Frankly, I was exasperated by her relentlessness; and given the fragility of Christina's health following a summer of seizures, tests, and hospital stays, I was in a near panic. I told her we knew for a fact that her overbreathing was not physiological and that our medical team had already determined through the sleep study that she could breathe normally. Anxiety was the cause, and adding a new therapy would only exacerbate her anxiety level, potentially causing more trauma and more damage. At this point, my only concern was to save my daughter's life. Jeff and I fully believed that any additional stress on Christina, in the condition she was in, could have been fatal.

I painstakingly explained to the psychologist, once again, the level of care Christina was receiving from our medical team. I told her we were doing everything possible and that additional therapy was not a solution. It was becoming quite clear that she was on a mission to have her way, and nothing, not even my parental rights, was going to stop her. Keep in mind we had already given her permission to work directly with Christina the year before. The only reason she was back on the "respiratory therapist" crusade was she was not making any progress with Christina, with *her* intervention techniques. This was no surprise to us; we had told her repeatedly her methods weren't applicable for Christina's unique condition. But the psychologist had made her stand, gotten the permission she demanded, and then failed. This, apparently, was not setting well with her, so she decided to up the ante and insisted we pursue respiratory therapy.

She tried to coerce me by promising to get Christina a classroom aide, if I would agree to seek respiratory treatment. This was tantamount to bribery. An aide was the one thing that truly would have helped Christina more than anything else. I had repeatedly requested an aide for over a year to no avail. Now I had this psychologist dangling an aide as a carrot in front of me if I would only agree to do the impossible. And let's face it, even if there was a respiratory therapist within reasonable distance, it was not the correct therapy and would most likely cause further harm, not good. That logic was lost on her, as was the fact that Christina was physically and emotionally extraordinarily fragile at that time. Jeff and I were fighting for Christina's life, and it seemed the psychologist was fighting to save face.

Not only was she trying to bribe us with a desperately needed aide, but she decided once again that she must review Christina's medical records to prove her point that respiratory therapy would be beneficial. Again, I said no. Why should she be given access to every detail of Christina's medical history when she was not a medical doctor qualified to provide credible care? But this time, she was not taking no for an answer. She called me on Monday morning, September 24, 2007, and demanded that I sign the medical release forms, or else she would report me to the Department of Children and Families (DCF).

Complete shock set in first.

Terror rushed in waves next.

I don't know what you would do, but I panicked. I was intimidated by her threat to take such extreme action and the consequences that could come from it. The last thing any parent wants is for child welfare to open a case against them. To make matters more frightening, there were several newspaper articles published around that time about failings within Florida's social services and stories of caseworkers abusing their power and wrongfully taking children out of their homes. The ramifications were profoundly unthinkable. Coerced and unprepared for having my rights violated in such a manner, I signed the release forms immediately.

But it wasn't a case of just "sign here" and the situation would go away. She had clearly overstepped her boundaries. What else was this woman going to do? How far was she going to take this? This was a real problem with no end in sight.

When one person decides they know more about your child than you do and they decide to use their position in a school or medical agency against you, you are immediately put into a defensive position. The Department of Children and Families (DCF) seems to have a mentality of "take the child first; ask questions later." Threatening parents with DCF is wrong in the fullest sense of the word. Any investigation would be intrusive and difficult for the family to endure. But for a family with special needs children, it would be extremely traumatic. With Christina's weakened state, we feared the trauma of being forcibly removed from our home would very likely have triggered seizures of sufficient magnitude to kill her.

I didn't know where to turn that day, but I went into full overdrive trying to figure it out. I spent hours looking up and trying to read legal code. I wanted to find the statute that explains parental rights and defines the boundaries for external agencies. I was sure our rights had been violated. After hours of research, I realized I needed professional legal help.

I called attorneys. I contacted activist groups. By nightfall, when the girls were tucked in bed, oblivious to the threat hanging over our family, I still didn't relent. Exhausted but desperate, I sent an e-mail to my friend, the head of parent resources, asking for any advice she could offer, any course of action I could take to protect my family. She responded the next day, saying she would help me but only over the phone. In cases like this, no one wants an e-mail or written record of what they say, even if they are just trying to help.

Jeff and I launched into a day-and-night campaign to find a solution. We had no idea where this was heading, but we knew we had been bullied, and we weren't going to roll over and let her ramrod our family or further endanger Christina. I was compiling notes, logging dates, and cataloging conversations from the previous year in preparation for a court battle. At one point, I recall contacting the principal for help. I was astonished to learn she was aware of the psychologist's inappropriate threat but hadn't taken action to rectify anything. Thankfully, within a few days, we found a wonderful attorney who provided us with detailed advice on how to proceed.

Once we had the support of legal counsel, I notified the numerous doctors and specialists that the forms authorizing release of Christina's medical records had been signed under duress. I sent them copies of the formal report the school psychologist had written the previous spring, hoping to give them an idea of her intentions. I was furious to learn that one of our doctors had not only talked to her but had entertained her ideas. In my opinion, this just fueled her fire. I was shocked because that same doctor had previously told me that he did not agree with the psychologist's position. Another doctor later told me that the psychologist was very obstinate in her views during their discussion. "Unwilling to consider other opinions" is how he described her. When the school psychologist was asked by Christina's doctor if she knew of anyone who worked with children who hyperventilate, she conceded that she didn't. When reminded that there weren't any respiratory therapists who could provide a magical cure within hundreds of miles, she responded that "If I needed to fly to

Alaska to get help, I should be willing to do that." At yet another doctor's office, the staff reported that she was verbally abusive toward the office manager and she began yelling and acting very unprofessionally when told the records could not be released to her due to privacy laws.

With help from our attorney, we were finally able to end her unyielding crusade. He confirmed that our parental rights had indeed been violated. He explained that by threatening to take my child from me, she had deprived me of my legal right to refuse consent. Just because my children are in special education does not mean that I have to forego my federally protected parental rights. The school psychologist, regardless of whatever altruistic intentions she had claimed, had overstepped her boundaries and had no authority to impose her opinions for Christina's medical care onto our family.

In the end, a well-written letter sent to the principal and to a number of school district officials brought the ordeal to a close. Following our attorney's advice, Jeff sat down and typed a formal letter requesting all contact between the school psychologist and Christina cease immediately and releasing the school from responsibility. Releasing the school officials from their responsibility to provide treatment was essential. Legally, they do have an obligation to treat the children in attendance. By putting in writing that we did not want that service, from their perspective, they were covered against future liability issues. If only we had known that a year earlier.

We met once more with the school principal, and she was amenable and open to working with us. The best thing for Christina was to move her to a lower-functioning class and alleviate much of the pressure and stress she had been experiencing. She was moved to a class of eight students in a contained setting, with a teacher and two aides who could intervene with the appropriate techniques whenever Christina began hyperventilating. This, combined with our written request to cease all contact between the psychologist and our daughter, brought a peaceful end to a long, insidious, and emotionally traumatizing ordeal.

Other than this episode (and the "curse of the Minimo"), we have been very pleased with the schools our girls have attended. We stand in awe of the majority of teachers and administrators who show exceptional levels of concern and dedication in educating and supporting the students. And I have not ceased being active on various committees or in their classrooms and continue to do my best to support in any way I can.

Visible Symptoms of Hyperventilation Syndrome

- Sighs or yawns frequently
- Breathless after exertion or when stressed
- Has trouble breathing while talking or eating
- Frequently tired or unable to concentrate
- Child appears dizzy

Proceed with Caution

- If you open the door, they will come in.
- Be wary of who you allow to have access to your family.
- Even professionals who seem competent and cordial are capable of overstepping boundaries.
- One person with power and obstinate opinions can create a parental nightmare.

An Ounce of Prevention

- Take early precautions to protect your family.
- Research parental rights and laws within your state.
- Find an attorney who specializes in family law and understands the unique challenges of disabilities. Keep his or her number readily accessible. When problems arise, you may need immediate counsel.
- Keep records of dates, written correspondence, and notes of verbal conversations.
- Visit websites of the advocacy groups listed under Resources for more information on how to protect the rights of your child and family.

Letter to Principal

October 1, 2007
Mrs. Xxxx Xxx Xxxxxx
Principal, Xxxxx Elementary School
XXXX Elementary Drive
Xxxxxxx, FL 33549

Dear Mrs. Xxxxxx:

The purpose of this letter is to provide information concerning the medical treatment of our daughter Christina Ann Ames.

Christina is presently under the care of the following doctors:

Name	Specialty	Phone Number
Dr. T	Pediatrics	813-000-0000
Dr. D	Endocrinology	813-000-0000
Dr. G	Neurology	813-000-0000
Dr. R	Pulmonology	813-000-0000
Dr. B	Psychiatry	813-000-0000
Dr. C	Cardiology	813-000-0000

Christina is receiving careful care and monitoring of her physical, neurological, and psychological condition.

We are in regular consultation with each of her doctors and affirm that all medical advice from these licensed caregivers has been and is being followed without exception.

We believe the care prescribed by Christina's doctors is appropriate, that her doctors possess the proper level of expertise, and that they are closely monitoring her status and will advise us of any additional treatments or tests that should be considered.

We are also in receipt of advice and directives from Mrs. V, Xxxxx Elementary School Psychologist. Her advice and directives are in conflict with the medical care prescribed by Christina's licensed doctors, listed above. Despite Mrs. V's professed good intentions, we are most concerned that her involvement is interfering with Christina's present treatment protocols. Mrs. V's insistence on further tests, which have not been recommended by her doctors, may at best be merely fruitless fishing expeditions, but at worst, may very well exacerbate Christina's anxiety disorder and further threaten her health.

We have given our permission to Mrs. V. to contact any of Christina's doctors to verify that we are following their prescribed treatments. However, aside from that, we must insist that she cease any further involvement in Christina's treatment. Since Christina is under the care of a licensed psychiatrist, there is no need for any further treatment by Mrs. V.

We freely and with full knowledge relinquish our right for Christina to be seen by the school psychologist and place our full reliance on the treatment she is receiving from her licensed psychiatrist and other doctors. We release Xxxxx Elementary School from any responsibility for psychological treatment of Christina Ames.

Sincerely,

Signature_____   Signature_____
Jeffrey M. Ames   Date   Julie Ann Ames   Date
Christina's Father   Christina's Mother

Christina Doctor's Appointments for 2007

Date	Doctor	Specialty	Reason
2/5	Dr. G	Neurologist	EEG
3/5	Dr. T	Pediatrician	Annual well checkup
3/9	Dr. B	Psychiatrist	Anxiety
3/23	Dr. B	Psychiatrist	Anxiety
3/23	Imaging	Bone age study	Check growth
4/20	Dr. B	Psychiatrist	Anxiety
5/25	Dr. B	Psychiatrist	Anxiety
7/9	Dr. G	Neurologist	Seizure
			Sleep study to check seizure activity
7/10	Dr. G	Neurologist	Seizure
	Dr. S	Pediatric critical care	Pediatric procedures under sedation
	Dr. R	Pulmonologist	Breathing
	Dr. C	Cardiologist	Heart (EKG and Echocardiogram)
	Dr. T	Pediatrician	Primary care
7/11	Dr. G	Neurologist	Seizure
	Dr. T	Pediatrician	Primary care
7/25	Dr. R	Pulmonologist	Sleep lab to check breathing
7/30	Dr. B	Psychiatrist	Anxiety
8/20	Dr. G	Blood test	Ordered by Dr. G
8/23	Dr. G	Neurologist	Six-week follow-up
9/5	Dr. G	Blood test	Ordered by Dr. G
9/10	Dr. T	Pediatrician	Sick appointment
9/13	Dr. B	Psychiatrist	Anxiety

9/15	KR PA-C	Urgent Care	Three staples
9/17	Dr. M	St. Joseph's emergency doctor	CAT scan
9/25	Dr. A	Urgent care	Remove staples
9/27	Dr. D	Endocrinologist	Premature puberty/ thyroid
9/27	Dr. D	Blood test	Ordered by Dr. D

Hyperventilation Behavior Modification Program

Following are five intervention measures that have proven effective in controlling Christina's habit of hyperventilating. They are listed as increasing levels of control. These measures work at home and in the classroom when they are consistently applied.

1.   Count to Ten

Tell Christina to count to ten. Counting out loud to ten makes it very difficult to hyperventilate. It also helps distract her, by having her focus on her counting. If she is still hyperventilating after counting to ten, have her count to ten again. Keep repeating this until she returns to normal breathing.

2.   The Takeaway

If she starts to hyperventilate during an activity such as eating, reading, writing, and playing with a toy, "take it away!" Explain that when she stops huffing, she will get the item back. If she continues to hyperventilate, have her "count to ten." Examples:

Eating—take away her food or utensil.
Reading—take away her book.
Writing—take away her pencil.
Playing—take away the toy.

3.   Isolation

This is when she is isolated or taken away from an activity. She is seated at another table or put in the corner for time out. She will also focus her attention on a timer when it is used. The timer insures she has enough time to completely settle before she is allowed to resume her activity. Otherwise, she will stubbornly claim to have stopped huffing when in fact she has not.

4.   The Crunch

When she is having a very difficult time with hyperventilating, "the crunch" normally works. This can be performed while she is seated or while standing. "The crunch" is when an adult gently and firmly wraps their arms around hers from behind, helping her to slightly bend forward. This crunching action makes it difficult for her to breathe deeply enough to hyperventilate. Also having her "count to ten" will help her reach normal breathing more quickly. Note, if she is seated, you may need to pull her chair out a few inches.

5.   The Mask

When nothing is working, have her wear a painter's mask. This works because it interrupts her breathing patterns, and she doesn't like the mask. This helps motivate her to correct her breathing. At times, it is effective to set a timer for three to ten minutes. The goal is to return to normal breathing in the shortest amount of time.

Note: The comment "It's going to be okay" only applies if she is not feeling well. Christina's tendency to hyperventilate can be triggered by boredom, transition, difficulty of the task, etc. Christina hyperventilates the way some people bite their nails. One can ponder, do people really enjoy biting their nails? Why don't they stop? When do they bite their nails? Regardless of the answers, it is a harmful voluntary behavior. Christina has a behavior that she can decide to stop. But she needs to be told to stop by someone in authority. Not stopping the hyperventilation can be a health hazard. Hyperventilation causes a person to get dizzy because the carbon dioxide levels start to drop in the body. This can then lead to stumbling, falling, and getting hurt.

Investigated

An Unexpected Visit
Dealing with Child Protective Services

Our home state of Florida ranks third in the country for sexual offenders. This is not a statistic we are pleased about, but it is a reality. Just like all responsible parents, we take regular precautions to protect our children from victimization. Living in a state with a nearly sixty thousand registered offenders and knowing that special needs children are at an even greater risk for abuse, we must be even more proactive about our children's safety. Nothing can be taken for granted. No risk can be overlooked. Making sure our daughters do not become another statistic is never far from our minds. We are not paranoid, just prudently cautious. Our protective instincts are internalized not from fear but from reality.

We viewed the dangers of our children becoming victims of molestation in the same way many parents do—yes, it exists but not in our home. Because of the level of care Maria and Christina have required, abuse was, in fact, a near impossibility. I say this for two reasons. First, the girls have always needed our constant supervision. Second, both Maria and Christina have a heightened sense of what is "their space," have sensitivity issues when it comes to touching things, and are very uninhibited when voicing objections to other people's misbehavior. Once, while visiting our very good friends next door, Maria unabashedly noted very loudly to the mother, "You haven't made your bed yet!" They simply would not allow someone to touch them without causing a scene. Child molesters rely on secrecy; our girls are not wired for that.

While I have enjoyed some peace of mind, believing that our children have a decreased risk of being molested, I have not been spared the horrors of false allegations, interrogation by a social services investigator, and the seemingly unlimited power of the "Child Protective Services." In August 2010, I abruptly learned how vulnerable families with special needs children are to becoming victims in someone else's sick game. Much to my astonishment, at the end of one peaceful summer day, an unexpected visitor would prove just how exposed we, as a special needs family, are to allegations of molestation and abuse.

Because I had no prior experience dealing with Child Protective Services (CPS) and because I never thought I would be in such a situation, I was completely unaware of my parental rights or how to react to protect those rights. I didn't know how to defend my family's privacy when an official with a badge showed up at my home and demanded to be let inside to check the safety of my children. I didn't know that it was possible to comply without exposing my family to invasive questioning and the risk of escalating an already frightening situation.

Now I know that being armed with this knowledge before it's needed is just as important as teaching my kids not to talk to strangers. All parents need to educate themselves ahead of time on how to react and how to retain their parental rights if the unexpected happens. Once the situation begins to unfold, it is too late. There is no time to think or look up answers online when the CPS investigator is standing at your threshold, telling you that she can take your children if you don't let her inside—you need to know what to say, what not to say, and what to do before you open the door.

Collateral Damage

It was a Friday evening in mid-August. We had returned home from a nice dinner with friends. The girls were bathed and tucked in their beds. The house was clean and calm. It was 8:30 p.m., and Jeff and I were just about to relax and watch a movie when the doorbell rang.

Jeff answered the door, and I could hear a woman's voice saying, "My name is Dana*, and I'm an investigator with Child Protective Services." In a moment, I was standing beside Jeff, shocked and confused about the situation that was unfolding. "We've received a report that one of your children has been the victim of child abuse. I'll need to speak with both you and your children as soon as the police officer arrives." A police officer? This, presumably, was for either her safety or to assist with removing our children from our home if she determined they were in danger. Both implications were very distressing.

At that moment, we were too stunned to consider the full ramifications of what was happening. We knew we had nothing to hide, so all we could think to do was to be as compliant as possible and answer her questions. At no point were we informed of our rights as parents. We didn't know the limits of her authority to enter our home and interview our children. At first, Dana would not tell us the nature of the claim, who it was made by, or who was accused of the alleged abuse. She did explain, however, that when a complaint is filed, CPS has to investigate within twenty-four hours to ensure the safety of the child.

We later learned that we did the right thing by letting her see our children that night. When CPS responds to a claim regarding abuse, they have extensive rights to enter a home to check the welfare of the child. Once they ascertain the child is not in danger, however, CPS's rights of access to the child become much more limited. Dana didn't mention that. Even worse, she told us we were not allowed to be present while she interviewed the girls, even after she had determined they were quite healthy and safe in our home.

While waiting for the officer's arrival, Dana asked to speak privately with Jeff. By this time, both Anna and Christina were awake and buzzing with excitement. Maria was sleeping soundly. Jeff showed Dana to our bedroom, where they could talk without the girls overhearing. I took Anna and Christina into the kitchen for some milk.

A few moments later, a police officer arrived. Dana told Jeff he could not disclose any of their conversation to me and then stepped outside onto the porch to confer with the police officer. Naturally, I was becoming alarmed; Jeff assured me that *we* were not under investigation. Someone had filed a report that one of our daughters— once we learned the dates, we deduced that they were inferring it was Maria—had been molested when she was six years old (which would have been eight years prior) by another family member. (We were not told until later in the evening which relative was being accused of the molestation.) Initially, we were not too distressed, because we knew there was no possible way such an incident could have taken place. With the exception of my mother, our daughters have never been left alone with anyone else in the family.

To add to the absurdity of the allegation, the abuse supposedly caused the child to "become retarded." This alone should have raised flags about the validity of the claim. Retardation is not caused by psychological trauma. Our children have special needs caused by a genetic abnormality they were born with. Their challenges are innate, not induced by some form of abuse. Jeff and I both explained this to Dana that evening. We even signed release forms for her to confirm it with the girls' doctor. We thought that being forthcoming and providing succinct medical information that invalidated the claim would expedite a swift resolution. We were wrong.

While Dana conferred with the police officer outside, I sent the girls back to bed; it was late, and they needed to calm down from the excitement. Having a CPS investigator and a uniformed armed police officer in our home after nightfall was as unsettling to them as it was to us. When Dana and police officer reentered, we explained the impossibility of the accusation. Dana, however, insisted she needed to question the children. She and the police officer went to Anna's room first. They told us we were not allowed to be in the room during the interview. I stood in the hall, on the other side of my daughter's closed bedroom door, anxiously trying with no luck to pick words out of the muffled voices. Jeff went and sat with Christina on her bed; he refused to allow them to speak with her privately because she could easily be agitated to an overly anxious state, which we knew from experience could easily escalate to hyperventilation and seizures.

We should have been allowed to stay with Anna too. Our lawyer later informed us that our rights had been violated when the investigator insisted on a private interview with Anna. To this day, I don't know exactly what was said to Anna, but I know Anna was very frightened by having a stranger in her room asking her questions while an armed policeman stood at the door. She told me later how she could not stop shaking. I tried to downplay the situation when I talked to Anna afterward and laughed as she showed me how her legs were trembling. Anna did not appreciate my weak attempt at humor and said, "You'd be scared too if there was a stranger and policeman with a gun in your room." She was right. I was scared too.

During Christina's interview, Jeff and I stayed in the room. Dana asked about good touch and bad touch and if anyone had ever touched her in a private place. She answered with outstretched arms, shrugged shoulders, and a broad grin, which I knew meant she did not understand. When Dana asked Christina if she knew anyone named Daniel, I spoke up and said, "Yes, he's in her class." I was then reprimanded for answering for her, but I knew that is what Christina would have answered if she were speaking. She wasn't, however. With both Jeff and myself at her side, Christina remained calm, and we avoided the usual hyperventilation and associated risk of seizures.

This was also when I began to figure out the "Daniel" that the investigator had asked Christina about was not a classmate but instead my cousin, who is a very upstanding man with a wife and small children of his own. The pieces of the puzzle were coming together slowly, but they still didn't fit. Our family and Daniel's family only see each other once a year at Easter. These are very large family gatherings, centered around an Easter egg hunt for the children. I love to go to catch up with relatives, but Jeff dreads it, because he is on constant alert for Christina's hyperventilation and subsequent seizures from all of the excitement. Our three girls stay together at such events, and Jeff never takes his eyes off Christina, so no one would ever have had an opportunity to be alone with our children, let alone perpetrate any inappropriate acts with them. In addition, the year the alleged abuse happened—seven years earlier—Daniel and his wife did not even attend the Easter gathering. Something wasn't adding up.

Our attorney later described the case as "the blind man with no hands being accused of playing the piano." That summed it up completely. There was never an opportunity for my cousin to commit the crime; nor would he, even if he had had an opportunity. When it was my turn to be interviewed that night, I explained all of this to Dana. I thought that by telling her as much as possible, I was helping her prove the charges to be unfounded, if not impossible, which would allow her to quickly close the investigation.

Thinking back on it now, I see where she manipulated me into providing extra information. She had a pleasant tone and phrased statements to make us believe she was on our side and was going to help us. She was very crafty in her questioning and kept me feeling falsely secure enough to continue divulging what I thought was helpful information. I think back on it now and compare it to the crime shows on television. I had never noticed how much the detectives mislead suspects during questioning. I was always rooting for them to catch the bad guy and thought it was just clever script writing. When it happened to me in real life, however, I realized how much indignation there is in being the one to answer questions honestly, only to later find out that the openness was not reciprocated. I felt like my willingness to help was being taken advantage of and that I had been used.

Luckily, nothing I said that night was later used negatively against us or Daniel; however, whenever a person is being questioned by an investigator—even if they aren't the suspect—an attorney should be present to keep the discussion focused and limited and to make sure that nothing is misconstrued or taken out of context. All it takes is for an investigator to hear the information wrong or to hear it the way he or she wants to hear it, and unimaginable consequences can follow.

Throughout all of the events that night, Maria remained asleep. (At least one of us got some rest.) Dana wanted to talk to her, and although I tried to wake her, Maria was too exhausted from a full day of activities. Dana finally relented and agreed to interview Maria another time; however, she did snap photographs of each of our girls in their beds before leaving. She also took a picture of the contents of our refrigerator, which is apparently a standard procedure too, but odd since Jeff and I were not under investigation.

Two hours after that first ring on our doorbell, Dana and the officer finally left. It was 10:30 p.m. We were emotionally and physically exhausted but way too upset to sleep. As we regained our wits and began to contemplate what had really happened, we began to realize that the entire allegation was likely fabricated by an estranged family member as an act of retribution directed at my cousin. This family member has a criminal history and a record of mental illness. A few days later, we learned that a second, similar claim had been filed on that same night, accusing another family member of abuse. This only served to strengthen our suspicions and prove the fallacy of the claim. This person's actions were a direct attempt to cause harm toward certain family members; our daughters were simply collateral damage.

The Aftermath

By morning, I was terribly shaken from the realization that a social worker and a police officer had been in my home without forewarning and, at night, questioning each of us and taking pictures of my girls in their beds. I felt sick. And I was so angry because it was all based on false allegations by someone most likely suffering from severe mental illness. Why was the claimant not investigated prior to disrupting the lives of innocent people? To make matters more distressing, we knew that Daniel and his family would soon be going through the same thing—only worse because his children were going to be questioned about their own father.

Monday morning, we found an attorney who we knew was experienced in handling disability cases, and we felt we could trust. After hearing our story, he told us we had done the right thing by allowing CPS into our home. They have to be able to verify the children are safe. If we had refused, they could have forcibly removed the children that night. I shudder to think what this would have done to Maria and Christina—they most likely would've needed to be sedated in order to control their skyrocketing anxiety.

Allowing CPS to inspect the children's safety was critical to avoiding a disastrous situation. After that, though, we should have asked the investigator to leave and schedule the interviews for a more appropriate time. Dana's demand for private interviews was a complete violation of our parental rights. In fact, we had several options available, that we weren't aware of, until we had consulted with our attorney. We could have insisted an attorney be present during the interviews, we could have videotaped the interviews, or we could have asked to have them conducted at a child advocacy center—all of which would have been under our supervision. Parental supervision in such situations, particularly when special needs children are involved, is even more important because these children can easily be led during questioning. According to our psychiatrist, not only do children with lower IQs have difficulty comprehending the line of questioning, but they don't have the same concept of time to discern between something that happened a week ago and something that happened years earlier.

In the days that followed, we consulted with Maria's psychiatrist, who advised against allowing Maria to be interviewed. We were worried about further aggravating Maria's anxiety level, especially when we knew the allegations were unfounded and had been filed with malicious intent. So when Dana called to schedule Maria's interview, we said no. The next day, her supervisor called Jeff, demanding access to Maria. Jeff again refused and gave him our psychiatrist's contact information to call instead. By this time, we had consulted with our attorney and were better prepared to handle CPS's requests and strong-arm tactics.

Several weeks later, we heard from Dana once again. This time she was requesting a follow-up interview with Christina and Anna. For reasons she wouldn't tell us, she said she needed to take more pictures of them. We had no intention of granting her further access to our children. Then she astounded us by stating, "We've already talked to Maria at school." It was as if she was trying to tell us resistance *was* pointless. We were outraged. We were told nothing about this, nor had we given her our permission to speak with Maria. We called the school immediately to find out the details. Yes, we were told, an investigator and a police officer had indeed come to the school to see Maria. The investigator told the principal that she had just been to our home the previous night. (That was a lie—some time had already passed; was the lie devised to create a sense of urgency to conduct the interview that day, before we, the parents, became aware?) Fortunately, the school counselor insisted on staying with Maria during the questioning. She assured us that the interview was uneventful and that Maria had not been aggravated by the questioning. Maria answered the investigator's questions, affirming that she knew the difference between good touch and bad touch and that no one had ever touched her in the bad way.

We were very upset that the investigator had gone behind our backs to gain access to Maria, but we were relieved that neither Maria nor Christina displayed any signs of distress after the questioning. Anna, on the other hand, was deeply upset by the incident. It was very traumatic for her, just nine years old, to be asked sensitive questions by a stranger with an armed police officer standing nearby. Dana planted ideas in Anna's mind about "bad touch" that she never would have considered before. As a result, Anna suddenly decided she no longer wanted to go to gymnastics, because she felt uncomfortable with the coach touching her.

"Anna," I said, trying to reassure her, "there is nothing inappropriate about how the coach touches you. She has to touch you in order to help you." But Anna didn't waver. She only became more upset because she thought I wasn't taking her seriously. I had to promise to watch even more carefully from the viewing deck before Anna would agree to go back to her gymnastics class.

Prior to Dana's intrusion into our lives, Anna loved gymnastics. I know without a doubt that this new resistance was caused by something said in their private conversation. I asked Anna to tell me about her conversation with Dana. In a single heartbreaking reply, Anna looked me square in the eye and said, "It's none of your business." I was utterly shocked to hear my young daughter say that to me. At that moment, I felt like Dana had taken much more than a bit of our privacy and some pictures; I felt like she had destroyed a piece of my daughter's trust in me. She had driven a wedge into a mother-daughter relationship that had not existed before.

As much as my heart sank, I knew that Anna was confused and scared inside. I sat with Anna for a long time that evening, talking and telling her stories about events in my youth that had upset me. I told her that whenever something had happened that bothered me when I was a girl, I would tell my mother and she was always able to help me. I needed Anna to understand how important it was to not keep secrets from me and that I would always be there to help her and protect her. Always. Hearing this made an impact on her. I could visually see the tension leaving her body; I sighed with relief knowing that my innocent, trusting little girl wasn't completely lost to me.

Reflecting back, I think one of the most troubling aspects of this entire situation is how long it stretched out and how manipulative Dana's tactics were. For instance, when I spoke to her just days after her visit, I was still trying to help her. I told her who I thought made the allegations and why. I also reiterated that I had no worries whatsoever about the safety of my children around my cousin Daniel. I asked her if I should tell Daniel what was going on. She said no; she wanted to see his reaction for herself. Since she was conveying a tone of believing me and implied a shared purpose of wanting to prove the allegations were false, I thought that she was expecting to see Daniel's surprise, thereby proving his innocence. I now believe she had ulterior motives and quite possibly wanted to see a reaction that proved his guilt. Fortunately, another relative alerted Daniel to the situation, so he was prepared to protect himself when she knocked on his door.

Daniel's Story

I received a call out of the blue from a distant relative on a Monday morning. He told me a crazy story about how CPS had been to Julie's house over the weekend and about these absurd alle-

gations made about me. At first I thought he was joking. When I realized he wasn't, I became rightfully concerned and confused. I called Jeff to get the full story. Then I called my business attorney for immediate advice. And then I waited. I knew the investigator would be showing up soon, but I didn't know when.

Dana came to my home two days later just as my wife was putting dinner on the table. I remember that she was wearing a blue polo shirt with the sheriff's emblem on it. She said she was an officer of the court, but at no point did she present a search warrant to enter my home. Just as she did with Jeff and Julie, she said a police officer was en route and that she would need to ask me questions when he arrived. I was glad I had already spoken with an attorney. Following his advice, I told Dana that I wanted my attorney present before answering any questions. "In that case," she responded, "there's no need for the deputy." She canceled the call for the officer but then said she still needed to come inside to check the welfare of my children.

I should have called my attorney again right then. She made it seem like I didn't have any choice about letting her come into my home, and yet she had just cancelled the dispatch for a deputy, which didn't make sense. Even though I thought I was prepared for her, she still managed to manipulate and control the situation by playing off my fear. I was terrified that one wrong move would lead to devastating consequences.

When you are being accused of such horrendous deeds and you know that even though you are innocent, the person standing at your door has the power to take your children and completely destroy everything about your life, you don't think clearly. Everything happens so fast. There's no time to think. Try as you might to remain level-headed and practical, the fact is that the threat is real. The situation is real. One misstep can unravel everything and turn your life into a nightmare. They know what they are doing; you don't.

An honest law-abiding citizen doesn't know how to react when faced with being accused of a felonious crime. A traffic ticket is unnerving enough. This was so far out of the realm of anything I ever thought I would experience; my only instinct was to protect *myself and my family. I knew to say I wanted an attorney present, but that wasn't enough. Before I could sort out what was happening or what my alternatives were, I found myself agreeing to let her come into my home and check on my kids.*

In my mind, since I had told her I wanted an attorney present during questioning, this included the entire family. I didn't think she would question my kids without my permission, especially without a deputy present. However, that is precisely what she did once she was inside. Dana went into the playroom where the children were playing and shut the door. She told us that we needed to wait in another room. Not only was she skirting my insistence for an attorney's presence, but she was now asserting authority over me and my wife in our own home, telling us that we could not be with our children to protect or comfort them in the presence of a stranger. We felt totally helpless. Later, I learned that I could have complied with her request to verify their safety without letting her inside the house. I should have brought them to the door so she could see they were fine. She would not have been able to isolate them and talk to them unsupervised.

By the time Dana finished talking to the kids, my wife was in hysterics about the impact this was having on them. When Dana came out of the playroom, I rushed in to check on them. In her panic, my wife agreed to go into another room and talk to Dana. I didn't know until it was too late to stop her. Even though I had been very clear about wanting an attorney present, Dana still managed to speak with my wife and kids alone. She finally left, saying she'd call to set up an interview with me. "So we can put this behind us," were her words.

Initially, I tried to be responsive and agreeable, hoping that I would help her finalize the investigation and refute the allegations quickly. I wanted to meet her halfway. We scheduled an appointment for my interview shortly after she came to my house. However, just as my wife and I were getting in the car to meet her and my attorney at the sheriff's office, Dana cancelled without giving a reason. At that point, I became nervous enough about the inconsistencies in her behavior combined with the seriousness of the allegations that I decided to hire a criminal attorney. He made it very clear that under no circumstances was I to speak to anyone from CPS. He took over all communications on my behalf. In the meantime, Dana still attempted to call me directly even though my attorney had already contacted her and her superiors. When she realized that I was not going to talk to her, she began contacting other family members, asking them if they ever felt unsafe leaving their children with me.

The absolute inability to control the situation was maddening. Even though the case has been closed and the charges determined "unfounded," I am still very upset about how devastating this could have been. This could have ruined my reputation, my career, my family, and my life—all on the basis of a false anonymous report. CPS won't tell us who filed the charges, and my attorney has advised against pursuing the matter any further. There is no telling what a person is capable of, and none of us want to spend the rest of our lives looking over our shoulders in fear of retaliation. Apparently, anyone spiteful or hateful enough can maliciously and purposefully set out to destroy an innocent person. Meanwhile, the innocent are left without recourse or justice for the turmoil thrust upon them and their families.

While I was going through this, I remember that in addition to a profound fear of the unknown outcome, I was incredibly frustrated by the complete lack of resources available. I couldn't find any information on how to protect myself and my family. When I learned Julie was writing this book, I was glad for a chance to share what I had learned in order to help other families facing similar difficulties.

- *If a CPS investigator shows up at your home, immediately close the door and call an attorney.*
- *Unless they have a search warrant, do not let them inside your home.*
- *Keep them at the front door until an attorney can provide guidance.*

- *If they insist upon checking the children, it is okay to bring the children outside of the house if needed.*
- *Most importantly, you have rights! Don't allow yourself to be intimidated or bullied into foregoing them.*

I'm glad to finally have this episode behind me. For a long time, my wife was very upset and felt like our home and privacy had been violated. My children, luckily, have never brought it up again and seem to have forgotten about the lady in the blue shirt. For that, I am grateful.

*****

It was six weeks after that initial traumatic night when Dana finally gained access to Maria at school. This was despite our insistence, with her doctor's support, that she not be interviewed. There was no reason for Dana's insistence on seeing any of our daughters again, yet she was still adamant that another meeting with our other two daughters was needed. We didn't know to what lengths she would go in order to gain access to Christina and Anna. Would she intercept them at school? Barge into our home again? Accost us on the street or at gymnastics? Would we even be present to guard against Christina's hyperventilation and seizures or Anna's further traumatization? We had no idea where she would stop.

Jeff was in continual contact with our attorney during those weeks. Eventually, the attorney had to contact CPS directly, demanding that they abort their attempts to reach our children. Without due cause or a court order, any further contact with our girls would be illegal and a violation of our rights. This was finally the end of our ordeal with Dana. However, we still had one more unexpected visit in late October. Two detectives with the sheriff's department showed up unannounced on a Thursday morning to follow up on the initial report. I remember thinking how odd it was to be surrounded by all the festive Halloween decorations while standing on my porch yet again explaining Daniel's innocence, the suspected reasons for the allegations, and my daughters' medical conditions. It was also a stark reminder of just how long this had drawn out. What started as a quick follow-up to an anonymous tip in August still was not resolved at the end of October.

The case was supposed to be closed within sixty days, but we never heard another word from CPS. We never received a copy of Dana's report, nor were we told the outcome of her investigation. Finally, over a year later, I requested a copy of the sheriff's report containing the findings of the various deputies who accompanied Dana during her interviews, along with the final report from the officer who conducted the follow-up visit in October. While a great many details were blacked out for privacy, the one that brought me the most comfort was the single word in bold at the top of each page: *unfounded*.

A Word on Safety

The story I've just shared is one that addresses false accusations and how malicious adults may use other people's children as pawns in weird, twisted games. I've talked a lot about how to protect your family from CPS, but I also think it is important to note that CPS does have a valuable job to do. I can only imagine the horrors CPS investigators see when they find true cases of abuse, molestation, and neglect. I'm sure it is an emotionally tiring and thankless profession. If my children had been victimized, I would have been grateful for the dogged persistence of the investigator. Because they weren't abused, we instead became victims of a bureaucratic machine. The unfortunate reality is that this is not uncommon, especially with special needs families.

Special needs children are much more likely to be victims of abuse, which in turn means they are also easier to be used in claims of abuse. Since special needs kids often have difficulty communicating accurately, they either aren't able to tell when they've been abused, or they can't dispel an inaccurate report. This makes them particularly vulnerable to becoming a different kind of victim—a victim in wars of spite between adults.

When I say that I was confident my girls have a decreased risk for being molested, I was not trying to sound like an unrealistic mother wanting to ignore facts. I am far from that. I am always alert to the ways of predators and try to stay cognizant of our surroundings at all times. I made my statement based on my knowledge of my daughters' unique personalities. Maria and Christina are both acutely anxious and protective of their physical space. They wouldn't need to know in their minds that what a predator was doing was wrong; their nervous systems would take over and cause them to react physically. A pedophile would not be able to get close enough without setting off their internal alarms and the chain reaction of symptoms that overtakes them when they become agitated. By contrast, Anna is a normal little girl who could be manipulated and victimized if we let our guard down.

In his brilliant book *Protecting the Gift*, Gavin de Becker explains how predators find victims. According to de Becker, there are two types of predators: power-predators and persuasion-predators. The first is the kind most of us fear in dark alleyways—the kind that use force and violence to abduct victims. The second is equally terrifying to parents. They employ a variety of techniques to build trust in children and parents, biding their time, and creating an opportunity to either abduct or molest a child. This is the one that frightens me most and keeps me alert. This is also the type that I suspect recently tried to victimize Anna.

We were at a very large crowded sporting activity designed for special needs children. Hundreds of kids participate, including Maria and Christina. They have a great time and look forward to the season each year. Because we are there each Saturday, all three girls have developed a level of familiarity with the surroundings and certain faces they see every week. Some of the participants they know from school, church, and other places we frequent regularly. During one recent season, the girls developed a routine of running up and excitedly talking to a lady they knew well. Maria and Christina would become overexcited, telling her about whatever had happened that week; Anna would show off her latest gymnastics tricks, and Jeff and I would be busy trying to regroup all three and get Maria and

Christina on to the field with their team. We never paid any attention to the husband, who was always quietly there, in the background. Not until the last game of the season, that is.

On that last day, as the chaos of the moment carried on, I caught an unnerving sight out of the corner of my eye. It happened so fast it was a blur. This man, whom we barely knew by name, was somewhere off to my right. Maria was stumbling and bumbling, a behavior that stems from her obsessive-compulsive disorder (OCD). Christina was hyperventilating. Jeff was watching the action on the field. The man had crossed behind me to where Anna was, on my left. Anna recounted to us later that he had told her, "I want to show you something." Within a flash, he had his arm around Anna's shoulder and was guiding her toward his car in the parking lot. Alarms sounded in my head as I pieced together everything that was happening so fast, less than ten feet from us. Before I could react, Anna had slipped away from him and was running back to me, terrified.

I can't say with 100 percent certainty that this man had bad intentions, but I do know the situation was just odd enough to raise a red flag—and the hair on the back of my neck. The parking lot was a long way away and fairly deserted at that time. Was this man really planning to walk with his arm around my daughter all the way past hundreds of people as if he were her father? Or did he just have very, very poor judgment? I'm thankful I did not have to find out the answer.

De Becker talks about trusting our instincts and knowing the key indicators persuasion predators rely on: access, cover, and escape (ACE). In this situation, if the man did have devious intentions, he had all three working in his favor. According to de Becker, if a pedophile has these three elements, a child can be victimized in a matter of moments. Not all victims are taken for long periods of time.

It is also important to note that besides behavior, there is no clear-cut physical profile or warning signal to recognize predators. As an example, de Becker repudiates the myth that pedophiles are predominantly homosexual. Statistics show that nearly all are heterosexual, married men who wouldn't normally be considered suspect by those who know them. Even more frightening is the fact that most abusers have perpetrated over thirty acts of abuse before they are ever caught. This is why all parents must remain on constant vigil for warning signs. We cannot let our guard down, even in places that *seem* safe. In fact, any event that brings a lot of kids together in one place requires extra caution. Organized activities and athletics should have security personnel on hand watching out for just this type of behavior. Our sports organization for special needs children employs undercover personnel to monitor suspicious activity amidst the chaos of hundreds of energetic children. They watch for people who look like they don't belong there or don't have children participating, and they routinely check the bathrooms to ensure children are not being violated in this common trap. I strongly recommend becoming an advocate for establishing this kind of undercover security in your child's recreational activities.

When it comes to protecting our children from abuse, parental instinct is the most powerful tool we have. As parents of special needs children, we need to hone those instincts even more. Trust is a luxury we cannot always afford when it comes to defending children unable to defend themselves. While I don't believe we should live in perpetual fear, I am saying that we must always be aware. We need to educate ourselves to the dangers surrounding our children, exercise extreme caution in granting others access to them, and be ever alert to our own intuitions. Even if our special needs children never mentally or emotionally understand sexuality or intimacy, we still need to arm them with a vocabulary so they have the ability to verbalize an abuse or to deny one, depending on the circumstances. While it might not always be easy to think about the ugliness in life, it is important we periodically challenge ourselves to face those truths so we are better equipped to protect our children and keep predators at bay.

Medical Treatments

"Dr. Livingstone, I Presume?"
Lost...and Found...in the Medical Jungle

Let's face it; the medical world is confusing and stressful enough for laypersons under the best of circumstances. Between the hard-to-get appointments, crowded waiting rooms, endless forms and questions, insurance forms, copayments, deductibles, and unfamiliar terminology, there's no wonder as new parents we are often anxious about finding the right doctors for our precious babies. After all, we are putting all our trust in these experts and their advice. Now take all of the normal medical experiences, concerns, and confusion and amplify it for special needs. Instead of one doctor, we have nine, not including occupational therapists and dentists. For our girls, the list has grown from the usual visits with a pediatrician, to include ongoing treatment with the cardiologist, allergist, neurologist, psychiatrist, gastro-enterologist, endocrinologist, and ophthalmologist. Along the way, we've also seen a geneticist and an ophthalmic surgeon.

We've run the gamut from truly exceptional, wonderful professionals to complete quacks. We've seen great offices with helpful and intuitive nurses and staff, and we have seen those that are sorely lacking in organization and qualified personnel. We have left bad doctors, and we've been asked to leave a dentist (Yes, we were fired! He was not able to handle Christina's anxiety-related challenges). Over the years, we have learned more about the ins and outs of the medical world than we had ever wanted or expected. We've followed advice and made medical decisions we now wish we hadn't, but we can also look back and see where our prudence paid off. The one truth we've learned through it all, however, is that the need for constant medical care will never go away. As such, well-qualified physicians and specialists are indispensable to the special needs family.

Welcome to the Medical World

Finding a good doctor is daunting. Referrals are great, but the patient-practitioner relationship is so personal that not every practice is right for every family. It's important to do research, investigate a doctor's qualifications, certifications, and education beforehand, and most importantly, ask questions. A lot of people forget that they are hiring the doctor to work for them. The degrees and knowledge doctors have may be impressive, but that does not mean that we need to blindly trust them or be intimidated by them. As a parent (or patient), you have every right to ask questions. Physicians typically charge more for new patient visits because these visits are more comprehensive and take longer; in essence, they are charging extra and allowing time for questions. Use it. Arrive at your appointment prepared to ask about their professional experience, philosophical approaches to treatment, after-hours availability, and how they stay abreast of medical research and trends. This is your time to learn about the doctor and the practice and to ascertain if the fit is right for your child.

Background Check

There are a couple ways to do a little research and find out about your doctor's professional record and credibility.

- Check with the American Board of Medical Specialties (www.abms.org) for board certification.
- Court records are public and searchable for lawsuits.
- Each state has a medical regulatory board. Check the website for disciplinary action and license status.
- www.docinfo.org and www.docboard.org both have searchable databases for past sanctions anywhere in the country.

A good doctor will not be offended by your questions, nor will he or she take it personally if you decide to interview other doctors or seek second opinions. Steer clear of doctors who are too busy, brusque, or condescending. You will have too many questions along the way, and you'll want to know that your doctor will take the time to make sure you are informed before making major medical decisions. Also be wary of doctors that disappear for extended periods. We had one doctor who was often gone for weeks, citing altruistic mission trips. These trips, we later learned, were really to rehab, and the doctor eventually committed suicide. This example certainly isn't the norm, but the point is that you should always stay vigilant in assessing your doctor. Even after you find a practice you are happy with, keep your eyes open. If you start seeing warning signs or begin to feel less than confident during or after a visit, it may be time to move on. Follow your intuition. If something doesn't feel right, trust your parental instincts—they are stronger than you think.

When assessing a new doctor, pay attention to the vibe you get from the personality of the physician, the support staff, nurses, and the environment; but don't get caught up in trivialities like decor and magazines in the waiting room. Focus on the critical aspects. Sometimes, the physicians in a group may be wonderful, but the practice itself may be in disarray. If the staff is surly or incompetent, that's an indication that there is a lack of proper management and organization, which often equates to poor job satisfaction and poor quality of care. You don't want to entrust your child's care to a practice where the staff do the bare minimum because they dislike their work environment.

The support staff can make or break a practice. When Christina was in the hospital, she was treated by a specialist who was very competent and good with her. Afterward, however, when I needed to get a copy of the report from his office, I had a horrible time. I had to call so many times that years later I can still remember the assistant's name. When I mentioned the difficulty I was having to a different specialist who was waiting to see the report, he immediately knew the office in question. It turned out that this office had a reputation in the medical community for being difficult. I couldn't help but wonder why such a good physician would continue employing an assistant like that.

In other instances, the office personnel and nurses have gone above and beyond to be helpful and caring. One example that comes to mind happened shortly after Christina was born. She was such a fragile newborn that when Maria came down with the flu, I was very concerned about Christina becoming ill. It was a rough time of trying to take care of Maria while not being able to get too close to her. I didn't want to transfer the germs to Christina. To make matters worse, Jeff had to go out of town, so I was home alone juggling the needs of a newborn and a sick toddler with bad diarrhea that leaked out of her diaper and through her pajamas wherever she was sitting. The messes alone were exhausting.

By the time we went to the pediatrician for one of Christina's well-baby visits, I was extremely stressed. One of the nurses picked up on my emotional distress and went out of her way to spend some time talking with me. She was very supportive and encouraging. Later I realized that she was probably trying to assess whether I was just a stressed mom or if I was suffering postpartum depression. I was fine; I just felt bad that I couldn't hold and cuddle Maria more, especially as she was also adjusting to having a new sister. In retrospect, I appreciated how sharp the nurse was to check. It demonstrated a deeper level of concern for both my well-being and the safety of my children.

Developing a good rapport with your physician is a two-way street. Yes, we may be assessing them and their staff when we first go in, but too many people forget that they are also making first impressions with the doctor. This, in my opinion, is a mistake. Doctors may try to be objective and treat all patients the same, but I don't believe it is that simple to avoid the innate human tendency of forming opinions (and on some level, passing judgment). I want doctors to form a positive opinion about how I present myself and my girls. I believe this creates a more mutually respectful relationship, and with that, they will take me and my concerns more seriously.

When you stop to think about it, most business transactions take place in the upper-middle class. A doctor appointment should be treated like a business transaction, which includes dressing to put a professional image forward. This doesn't necessarily mean that you have to wear expensive clothes, but cleanliness and the care you take with your appearance matter. And whether we like it or not, we are often judged based upon our appearance. Going to the doctor is not a time to allow the kids to play and show up with dirty clothes, hair, and nails. The way we present ourselves is a representation of the orderliness (or lack thereof) with which we choose to live our lives. This is not a reflection of economic status as much as it is of self-respect. If we want others, including doctors, to treat us with respect, it starts by putting forward an image that says we respect ourselves. I'm concerned that too many parents, especially moms bedraggled by the challenges of raising young children, do themselves a disservice in this regard.

Ever since the girls were little, I've tried to make doctor visits a fun and special event. They like getting dressed up for their appointments. The ritual makes going to the doctor exciting; and with all of the appointments we have—some of which have involved unpleasant procedures—having built this level of excitement into the experience has been really helpful over the years. I can't imagine how hard it would be if they hated going and fought me with every visit. To keep it fun, I've also used a couple of tricks like letting them pick a prize for good behavior (I keep several inexpensive goodies on hand to use as rewards). Sometimes, the promise of an ice cream or a trip to play in the tunnels at their favorite fast food chain is enough to keep them on their best behavior. I keep special coloring books and crayons packed for the doctor's office. Since these are only used at appointments, the girls don't get bored with them.

Having a good, quiet form of entertainment is invaluable in crowded waiting rooms or when trying to converse with the doctor without interruptions from an impatient child. The goal, of course, is to be able to make it through the appointment without incident and to be able to ask the questions and take in all the information the doctor is saying. I want to leave the office with a good understanding of what our next course of action, if any, will be. I also know that I'll need to be able to relay everything that happened to Jeff since he is rarely able to attend appointments.

I've found that reading online medical sites is very helpful before going to see specialists, particularly when we are dealing with specific health issues. I don't read them looking to self-diagnose or to look for new problems but rather to have a better baseline understanding of certain conditions and treatments before seeing doctors. That way, when the doctor mentions something, I have a better foundation of knowledge to start the discussion, and I can better formulate my questions while I'm in the exam room.

Taking notes is helpful for remembering everything the doctor suggests or explains. Little details are easy to forget after any doctor visit, but when emotions and stress levels are heightened because of a medical crisis, it's almost inevitable that you won't remember everything or will have new questions later. This is when having a doctor who is patient and accessible is a blessing beyond measure. None of us ever expects a crisis, but when one does occur, having done early research to screen doctors will pay off in spades when we are at our most vulnerable with an extremely ill child. That's when it's most important to know we can trust the medical professionals we've chosen.

Keep in mind that when making medical decisions for your child, you should never feel embarrassed or too intimidated to ask for more information. If the doctor doesn't answer your questions in a way that makes sense, ask again. If the answer doesn't resonate as reasonable (we once had a doctor suggest that Christina's seizures may be connected to lunar cycles) or if the doctor's recommendation seems too lax, too aggressive, or too radical, never be worried about seeking another opinion. Even if you like your doctor personally, you aren't obligated to them. First and foremost, your responsibility is to get the best possible care for your child, regardless if that means leaving one doctor for another whose treatment plan makes more sense to you. In the end, it's your child's health on the line. Follow your instincts.

Ins and Outs of Occupational and Speech Therapy

Our introduction to occupational therapy was at a large prestigious academic institution, and it was not promising. We took Maria for an evaluation shortly after Christina was born. A full team of therapists sat with her while Jeff and I observed from behind a mirror. We watched as the occupational therapist directed Maria to insert pickup sticks in a hole. Jeff turned to me and said, "We're going to evaluate her based on how many sticks she puts in a hole the right way?" How is that a reliable indicator, especially with a child that young?

The rest of the experience did not bode well, either. The report was riddled with errors, and we felt an inordinate amount of pressure to pursue treatment. It was as if they were strong-arming us to take their recommendations, almost as if Big Brother would come after us if we didn't. Yet they weren't able to provide us with any conclusive evidence that she needed therapy. Being engineers, we are both very analytical and like to see the data, but they couldn't provide that for us. We had brought our little girl to them for help, but we left with a deeper doubt of the soft sciences.

In the years since, we have sought the help of occupational and speech[6] therapists for both Maria and Christina. We've seen a mix of results, which has left us simultaneously grateful for the help we've received from talented therapists and skeptical of new therapies and techniques that were long on fanfare and short on data. In many instances, we have been confronted with the failings of medical experts who claimed to have had the answers. But as far as we know, most of the successes our children have realized have simply been through trial and error and persistence. Lots of persistence. When the experts recommended walking therapy, Maria learned to walk by herself within the same time frame as prescribed by the therapist. When another therapist recommended feather treatments for their tactile defensiveness, Jeff's approach was more effective. "The way we get over tactile defensiveness," he said, "is we force them to bathe, to get in the tub, and to shampoo." After a few difficult baths and an onslaught of Mr. Bubble, they got past their bathing issues.

We know there isn't a proven process that will work with every child. Some kids benefit from some treatments, while different therapeutic approaches work better with others. The problem is that

---

[6]   Specially trained speech therapists work in the area of feeding therapy.

some experts claim that if you don't reach them and fix the problem before the age of three, the child will be stuck with the problem forever. Parents are frightened into believing they will forever lose the opportunity to correct the problem. Our opinion may not be popular with some therapists, but we think this is counterintuitive. If a child is behind and suffers from anxiety issues, how does piling on more training and more pressure accomplish anything? I look at our kids and know that when they were that small, they were just trying to get their bodies to work. Instead of pushing them, we gave them a calm, peaceful, stress-free, loving household. Instead of going to therapy multiple times per week, we gave them the time and the love they needed until they were more ready—physically, mentally, and emotionally—to work on their challenges.

There's no data to say for sure that early intervention works. In fact, there is no data to prove it either way. That's the challenge. There is no way for a child to walk both paths and then compare results. Clouding the issue is always the question of financial incentive. Are we, as parents, avoiding additional therapies due to cost? Or are the specialists recommending therapies for more business and profit? These practitioners are no doubt emotionally involved in their practice and philosophy. Most are sincere in their desire to help, but perhaps they lose a little balance in their perspective on seeing the part versus the whole, and they fail to fully see the overall effect on the family. For parents, especially moms, the pressure to "do what's right for the child" is emotionally draining. Having someone put a time clock on the child's future abilities is an emotional manipulation, especially when there is no evidence to substantiate these claims.

I know other families whose children enjoy going to therapy sessions, but with our girls' anxiety issues, therapy is an added stressor. We need to be selective in our treatment choices. As such, I don't like the girls being guinea pigs in new treatments. Whenever a therapist says, "I just learned…" or tells me about a seminar they just attended, that's a red flag. I am not interested in being part of their experiment while they try out some new approach. Hearing this immediately makes me skeptical and can start our therapy sessions on poor footing.

Not long ago, Maria needed to return to feeding therapy. From day one, something was missing for both Maria and Christina—they seemed to lack either the physical coordination or the electrical wiring to perform the simple process of chewing and swallowing. After years of searching, we finally found a speech therapist trained in treating eating disorders, who was willing and able to work with them. After six months of therapy, she had made good initial progress with both of them and recommended we take over, working with them at home. She gave me a program to follow, and I began working diligently. Christina continued to improve, but Maria did not. So eighteen months later, I admitted defeat and decided to return her to feeding therapy. We were waitlisted for several months, then finally got our first appointment with a new therapist. We had had good results with Maria's first feeding therapist who used a lot of games to motivate Maria, so we were disappointed that she was not going to be available to help us this time. I went to our first session hopeful that the new therapist would be just as good. When she mentioned a recent seminar, I cringed and left the appointment unsure if I wanted to go back. Since we had to wait so long to get in, I decided to go three more times before making a decision; any more than that might be a waste of time and money. She didn't use any of the methods that had been effective in the past and focused primarily on our mealtime environment at home. This philosophy may sound great in theory, but we were living with the issue on a daily basis. We felt like we were way past an environment issue. We needed Maria to learn to chew and swallow in order to eat something other than liquids and soft foods.

The feeding program the therapist presented consisted of twelve weeks of intensive mealtime rituals with three therapy sessions per week. Needless to say, the bulk of the work would fall on me. We were told that if we didn't do everything and follow the program to a T, Maria wouldn't see any results. I looked at the program and felt defeated. Mornings were hard enough. How was I going to follow all of these extra detailed steps every day for twelve weeks? It was unrealistic and set me up for failure before even starting.

I had had enough. It was a rough morning; I'd had trouble with both girls that day. Christina was feeling sick and missing school again, and by the time we got to our session, I was already on edge. At one point during the session, the therapist insinuated that I wasn't doing enough with Maria at home. I felt my face flush hot, and in a rare moment of losing my cool, I snapped, "I have had it! It's everything I can do to just get here! Look at them!" Maria, fifteen years old, was sitting at a little child's table, unable to chew; and Christina, thirteen, was lying on floor whining, for the thousandth time, about not feeling well. I felt bad about losing my temper, but the obstacles were overwhelming. A few minutes later, when I calmed down, the therapist and I were able to have a rational discussion about the future of the twelve-week program.

As it turned out, she knew that it was unrealistic to expect a parent to do everything every day. It simply doesn't happen. In trying to avoid setting up false expectations for results, she overcompensated by stressing the importance of having to "do it all" in order to see any results. I understand why she did this, but she was inadvertently creating a situation where I felt like I had the weight of the world on me. Once we talked and changed the perspective about expectations for both following the program and the anticipated results, we were able to look at the program as an opportunity, but not a guarantee, for improvement and then determine the best way to move forward with helping her. I am pleased to say that we did end up making substantial progress—Maria is now able to take a bite of cheeseburger without choking on it—but it was very touch-and-go at the start. Communication proved essential for creating realistic expectations on both sides.

Much of success with therapists comes down to the relational capital between the therapist and parents, even more so than with physicians or surgeons. If therapists don't relate well with the parents or if the parents don't have confidence in the therapist's approach, it isn't worth the time or effort to move forward with that therapist. Since therapists have various styles, finding one you trust may take some time. Be wary of therapists overstepping boundaries and making you feel inferior. Some therapists don't want to accept that their approach hasn't worked. Instead of owning the failure and trying something new, they'll shift the responsibility to the parent, making it seem as if the parents' inability to follow through is what caused the approach to fail. This is unacceptable. No parent who is desperately trying to help his or her child needs to be made to feel this type of blame.

The simple fact is that not every child responds the same way to the therapy or the therapist. Unlike traditional medicine, occupational therapy is highly personality driven. We see different characteristics as positive or negative, and both children and parents are motivated by personality traits they can connect with. A child is not likely to make progress with a therapist he or she doesn't like. Similarly, if the parents don't care for the therapist, they won't be as willing to accept or follow through on the suggested therapy techniques.

Sometimes, however, "clicking" with a therapist can be a detriment. If we like them, we are more prone to look past their flaws and, perhaps, incompetence. I experienced this with one of Christina's speech therapists at her school. Initially, I was impressed because the therapist communicated so well with me. Communication is a trait I appreciate, and her frequent notes home gave me a false sense of confidence in her abilities. It wasn't until Jeff and I went to meet with her, and she revealed her only goal for the entire year was to teach Christina two sounds, that we realized Christina wasn't going to make any substantial progress. The therapist gave us a very impressive sounding spiel, but Jeff saw through it immediately. When we left, he told me that he couldn't believe I had been so impressed with her. I was a bit surprised myself. Two sounds? In a year? In hindsight, I know the only reason I missed seeing the signs was the notes she sent always made it seem like they were working on a lot of material. If she had been a private therapist, we would have started looking for someone else. Since she was a school therapist, we didn't have much say other than to press her to develop a more aggressive plan for the school year.

We have seen a stark contrast between the quality of treatment children receive in public school and that provided by private practices. Private therapists know they have to produce results; therefore, they are more proactive in their efforts. Unfortunately, private therapy is very expensive, so having some form of help through the schools can certainly be beneficial (as long as the therapist is not doing anything to stress the child and cause a backslide or trigger new problems—such as we experienced when Christina began hyperventilating during her early speech therapy sessions and then later with the "Minimo" ordeal). Sadly, we even experienced some school therapists who appeared to care very little about helping some of the children and acted like nothing more than glorified babysitters. Here again, the only way parents will know what is really going on in school-sponsored therapy sessions is to remain involved and constantly ask questions.

Graduation Day?

Therapists sometimes like to celebrate completing a program with a "graduation." We don't necessarily agree with this. In our opinion, there is no finish line when it comes to improving in these areas. We don't want the girls, especially Maria, who is prone to stubbornly refusing to participate in her therapy, to think they are done. Yes, we let them know how proud we are of their accomplishments, but we don't want to imply they can stop trying.

No More Pills, Please!

Deciding whether or not to put a child on behavioral medication is never easy. There are so many potential negative effects and consequences. And if undesirable side effects do occur, the doctors may simply prescribe more drugs. It's a vicious cycle that only stops if all medications are removed, if that is ever possible. Unfortunately, sometimes the effects are not reversible, yet no one—not parents or medical experts—can definitively say if a child's new problematic behavior or condition is a direct result of the medication or if it would have developed regardless. For us, we will always be left to wonder if the antianxiety medication, Lexapro, was the cause of Christina's seizures.

We were first prescribed an antianxiety medication in 2007 for Maria's OCD and anxiety. It was the generic version of Zoloft. The medication seemed to work in the beginning. Eventually Maria's anxiety condition worsened culminating with Maria picking her lips until they bled. We were at our wits end. Her psychiatrist then switched her to Lexapro, and she responded well. However, by the summer of 2010, Maria's other behaviors had become unbearable. The all too frequent periods of incessant crying, wailing, spitting, and stumbling about (known as "stimming") were too much. This was around the same time that she started puberty, so hormones may have been a contributing factor, but the medication was our primary concern. She was so out of control during those months that Jeff quietly put a picture of her as an adorable three-year-old on our fridge to remind me of better days. The doctor wanted to keep increasing her dosage, saying that more medication would help, but we felt that this was making things worse rather than better. We weaned her off the antianxiety medication completely. She has been off it since and has nearly returned to her normal sweet, albeit sometimes stubborn, disposition.

Because Maria responded well to Lexapro in the beginning, we went ahead and put Christina on it around the same time. Her anxiety has always been an issue, and we hoped that medication would help calm her enough to curb her huffing and hyperventilating. Although she seemed to respond well, only two months lapsed between starting the medication and her first seizure that put her in the hospital for three days. Years later, I read that seizures were a known side effect of Lexapro. At the time, however, no one connected the medication as the potential cause. Christina continued taking the medication for two more very long distressing years. She was so sick all the time, vomiting and having frequent seizures, that we'd finally had enough. We wanted her off everything so her body could have a chance to recover. However, we did not dare stop her seizure medication, Trileptal, since her seizures were so severe. But we did successfully get her off the antianxiety medication.

I now know Lexapro is a possible link to seizures. What I will never know, though, is if our decision to allow her to take behavioral medication was the cause of a life-threatening condition that has forever changed our lives. Her neurologist tells me she might have started having seizures, anyway. This lessens but does not alleviate the guilt of wondering if we could have prevented the seizures. We've also been told that serotonin levels may be a factor, but Christina would have to undergo a spinal tap to have her serotonin tested. Since serotonin fluctuates and the test results are not always accurate, we aren't willing to put her through such an invasive procedure. Even if we could pinpoint the cause, the doctors know of nothing that can be done to eliminate her seizures. All we can do is manage them.

Today, Maria only takes medication for her thyroid. Christina continues taking Trileptal for seizures. We have to take her in for blood tests every three months to manage her dosage and make sure she isn't experiencing any organ damage. At one point, Christina's doctor also prescribed Resperdol, an antipsychotic that is used to treat bipolar disorder and anxiety. However, I couldn't bring myself to give it to her after learning that it can cause severe tics. We did not need to add any more problems in trying to treat the ones we already had. This is the same reason I've been resistant to consider our neurologist's suggestion that Prozac may help reduce hyperventilation. He gave me a medical journal article to read that reported Prozac significantly helped Rett syndrome patients, sometimes with results in just a couple of weeks. While I would love to stop the hyperventilating, I am not ready to experiment with another medication. The risk, at least with Christina, is already too great.

I feel fortunate that she is only on one medication right now. I know other children who are on multiple medications, and their parents are filled with anxiety about wanting to wean them off so many pills. It's hard to find the right balance. In my view, Christina is doing well. She is happy. We are managing her seizures for now, and we are helping her learn how to self-calm and stop hyperventilating. Why add another drug into the mix? Why risk it? We will continue with as few drugs as we can for as long as we can.

Side effects are not the only concern with these prescriptions. Cost is also a major factor. Even with good insurance, many of these drugs are insanely expensive. Christina's Diastat, which we have to have on hand at all times in case she has a severe seizure, comes in two dose packages and costs around five hundred dollars. (Diastat is a suppository used only in emergencies that immediately slows the nervous system to help arrest a seizure.) But it could save her life, so we can never risk not having at least two doses readily available (I can administer one or two doses safely; any more has to be given by a paramedic or at the hospital). Once, we had a liquid medication that I calculated cost five dollars per teaspoon. I don't need to describe my frustration when my resistant daughter spilled her dose on the counter instead of swallowing it. Five dollars wasted. It's hard not to look past that.

I do buy generics whenever they are available. Our neurologist believes brand-name drugs are more effective, but we haven't noticed a difference, at least not with the ones our girls have taken. The cost savings can be amazing; when one of our brand-name drugs was finally available in a generic, our bill went from three hundred dollars to thirty dollars a month. With that kind of price difference, we decided to continue with the generic as long as it remained effective. The main difference between the name brands and generics are the inactive ingredients and binders. These can cause different side effects, so we are watchful for new symptoms.

I typically use drive-thru pharmacies for the convenience of not having to get the kids in and out of the car. The cashier has to collect before releasing the product, and most are sensitive to the financial pinch prescriptions can create. Usually, when they break the news of how much my bill is (often in the hundreds for us), they are very kind and go out of their way to make sure it isn't too much of a shock. I pretty much know what to expect now, but I still appreciate the effort. Once, however, there was once a cashier who seemed to take pleasure in announcing the total. She had an odd smirk and acted like it was a game to see what kind of reaction she could evoke. I thought it was incredibly rude and inappropriate, especially since prescription costs are a true hardship for so many people. Maybe management found her behavior to be unprofessional, too, because I never saw her there again.

A lot of people may take their pharmacies for granted. Medications are expensive. We have to go out of our way to pick up prescriptions. And we may never really appreciate the value of a good pharmacist until something out of the ordinary happens. The summer Christina started having seizures, she was so ill that we were going through a dose of Diastat every other day. The hospital had sent her home with a course of antibiotics, but these gave her such bad diarrhea that her body could not absorb the medication intended for preventing seizures. In her weakened condition, she was seizing constantly, which is why I was using so much Diastat.

When I went to refill her Diastat, the pharmacist told me he couldn't give me any more. I panicked. Diastat was the only thing keeping her out of the hospital. I had no idea what would happen if I couldn't get the refill. The pharmacist was also concerned; he did some research and discovered the problem. Apparently, the way the prescription had been worded made it appear that Christina could only receive a limited quantity within a three-week window. This technicality resulted in the insurance denying the refill and the computer flagging the prescription as nonrefillable. At that point, I didn't care if the insurance paid or not. Christina desperately needed this medicine. We couldn't wait three weeks. Every day was a battle for her life.

Fortunately, the pharmacist kept pushing to get the glitch resolved. When he called to tell me the refill was ready, I was more relieved and grateful than words could express. I went straight over to pick up Christina's life-saving Diastat and felt myself tearing up as I thanked him. I will never forget how much it meant to have a pharmacist who was genuinely concerned about my child's health when we most needed his help.

Ambulances and Urgent Care

Christina's seizures have provided us with several opportunities to become familiar with medical emergencies. When she had her first seizure, we called 911. Having the paramedics come into your home is a surreal experience. They often have large physical statures, are dressed in dark colors, and are very fast in their movements. One minute you are on the ground holding your frail, unresponsive child, and the next, a swarm of EMTs are working on her and firing a barrage of questions at you. They need to know exactly what has happened in the moments, hours, or even days that led up to the crisis so they can treat her safely and effectively.

After the first episode, I learned to always keep a pen and paper handy. As soon as Christina begins having seizure activity, I start writing everything down. Sometimes, she will have a series of mild seizures over the course of several days, so it's imperative that I have everything—times, medications, durations—documented in the event that I end up having to call the paramedics.

When calling an ambulance, there are a couple of things to keep in mind. Not all ambulance services use the same drugs. With a situation like Christina's seizures, she can only have so much Diastat. I can administer up to two doses at home; any more might send her into respiratory failure. The paramedics can give her more because they have the equipment on hand to monitor her respiration, but they need to know how much she's already had, especially if they are using a drug from the same pharmaceutical family. One ambulance service that responds to our home uses a drug from a different family that doesn't act as a sedative for the entire body like the Diastat does. And since it is a different class of drug, it may also induce other effects as well.

If you have a child with a chronic condition that often requires emergency service, it's a good idea to know which pharmaceuticals the different responding ambulance companies use. A quick phone call is all it takes to learn this valuable information. Then you can consult with your physician to make an informed decision on which drugs will be safest in the event of an emergency. When you call 911, they will generally dispatch city or county ambulances, but you can request a private ambulance company if you've done your research ahead of time.

When investigating ambulance companies, you also want to know how far they go and which hospitals are in their service area.

Not all hospitals are the same, and the closest hospital might not be the right choice. The EMTs will likely ask which hospital you prefer, so you need to know which ones your doctors and specialists have privileges at and which hospitals are within your insurance network. If you aren't prepared to answer the question, they will automatically take your child to the closest hospital. If that hospital is not equipped to handle the situation, they will then have to transfer your child to one that is. This means a second ambulance is dispatched for the transfer. Most insurance companies will only pay for one ride in a twenty-four-hour period, so the second trip will end up being an out-of-pocket expense. We experienced this with Christina's first seizure. Considering that each ride can cost around five hundred dollars, you don't want to pay for any unnecessary trips. We now know we have to go further to a hospital with neurology, for Christina's seizures. Here again, doing a little legwork before an emergency can save both time and money during a crisis.

Whenever you take an ambulance to the hospital, you are ensured immediate admittance. Whereas if you drive to the emergency room on your own, you may end up waiting quite a while to be seen, depending on the situation. We've found that with respiratory issues and seizures, Christina is always seen immediately—whether we go by ambulance, drive to the emergency room, or when we've gone to urgent care facilities. If she begins hyperventilating, even when I've taken her in for stitches or a skin rash, the emergency staff treat it as respiratory distress. They never want to take a chance with breathing issues in case something else is going on that can become a life-or-death situation.

I don't typically take her to a hospital unless she is having seizure activity or symptoms that are preludes to seizures. If I do decide to take her to an emergency room, I always go to the hospital where her neurologist works just in case her symptoms are related to her seizures. You never know what symptoms will be a part of the puzzle. For instance, once she was zoning out at school for two to three minutes intervals. During one episode, she fell and cut her head severely enough to require stitches. In this case, I took her to the hospital instead of urgent care. I knew they would want to test her for abnormal brain activity. Over the years, we have seen a correlation between sinus infections and an increase in seizure activity. So when she is severely congested, we have learned to treat it as a component of her seizures rather than just a typical cold or flu.

For non-emergencies, I always start with her pediatrician or after-hours advice line. If the situation warrants it, we'll go to an urgent care facility. We've had mixed results with urgent care, but it is a decent intermediate solution for nonlife-threatening conditions. The best part about urgent care is that they can usually get things done faster, like blood tests and X-rays. Conversely, although they usually have a doctor on premise, you aren't always assured of being seen by the doctor. With Christina's complex medical history, I always want to make sure the most experienced person available sees her. Once, however, when I explained my concerns and how she was prone to seizures, the urgent care facility refused to see her at all. They said I needed to take her directly to the emergency room instead.

Seeking treatment with a child like Christina is always a judgment call. Based on her history, we need to make quick decisions to decide which level of action to take. For any child with chronic medical issues, those decisions are never far from your mind. Every day, parents dealing with these issues are accustomed to evaluating each cough, sniff, or change in behavior. It becomes second nature. But we also can't let it stop us from having a normal life. We need to continue having regular adult activities with and without the child. Parents of special needs children need to have those breaks and to find balance to maintain their own physical and emotional health. The key is to be prepared. Have a complete list of emergency contacts—physicians, pharmacists, hospitals, urgent care, neighbors, relatives, schools—posted near the phone so that anyone, even a sibling, can get help immediately.

Being a Proactive—Not Overreactive—Parent

I think most moms will agree that it's easy to get caught up in worrying about our children's health. If a doctor expresses a concern, we are likely to take it seriously. We can also misconstrue a casual comment into a full-blown diagnosis. I caught myself doing this not too long ago. I took Christina for a routine pediatric checkup; and when I asked about Christina's posture—she seemed to be leading with one shoulder—the doctor said she might have a slight case of scoliosis. At fourteen, this is around the age when scoliosis, a twisting or curvature of the spine, typically begins to present. The doctor wasn't concerned enough to have X-rays, but I couldn't stop thinking about it. After the appointment, I talked to a friend who is a physician and had been treated for scoliosis as a teen. She told me that the severity determines the treatment, and if it's bad enough, the patient may require surgery to correct the spinal deformation.

Later, when I told Jeff about the prospect of Christina having to have surgery, he helped bring it back into perspective for me. "You are assuming she has scoliosis," he said. "What if she just has bad posture? You already have her on a gurney on the way to surgery." I was able to laugh at how easily I had overreacted and agreed that maybe we weren't facing yet another medical crisis with Christina. Instead of pushing for X-rays and expensive treatments, I spent some time manipulating her shoulders to help her stand up straight, which seems to have helped. It's easy to look beyond the simple explanations, especially for parents of special needs children; we are conditioned to dealing with so many situations that are quite serious.

Medical care is too expensive to pursue every possible treatment or recommended therapy. As parents, we have to be able to discern what is a necessity and what isn't. Clearly, Jeff and I aren't going to take any chances with something like Christina's seizures, but when it comes to pursuing any type of therapy, we are more selective. A lot of programs sound promising, but when you look deeper, you see that they want exorbitant fees for something you can accomplish on your own or that may or may not produce results. We opted against one such program, for Maria. It was called binocular vision therapy and would supposedly cure her inability to solve math problems—for a mere cost of just over ten thousand dollars. We could have easily been swept up in the emotions of wanting to solve Maria's school problems and committed to the program before realizing it had no track record of success. It's always best to take a step back and make these decisions from an analytical, not emotional, mind-set.

When evaluating a new behavior or medical development at home, I usually try to stay levelheaded while determining the severity of the symptoms. Maria has a tendency to become very upset when she doesn't feel well, so I have to be able to see through her behavior and decide when she needs rest or when she needs to be seen. The challenge is that if she's being overly dramatic and I cater to her attention-getting behavior, it only encourages her. I have to be very careful to use nonleading questions with Maria, or else her answers will be useless. Usually, I try to placate her and put her at ease and then see how it goes. If she continues carrying on, I may recruit Anna; she has a sibling sense and can usually tell if her sisters are serious or not. With Christina, I have to assess her health on a day-by-day basis, but she's better than Maria about letting me know what's truly going on.

Sometimes, it is tempting to reach out to my neighbor and good friend who is a doctor when an unusual development comes up. I appreciate that she is there for quick advice, but I never want her to think that I'm counting solely on her. I always make sure I've contacted my usual doctors before asking her for guidance. I never want her to think that if anything goes wrong in this household that she's liable or that I would direct blame toward her. When families have friends or relatives who are in the medical profession, it's important to respect the professional boundaries and not put those individuals in a position of liability.

Dealing with a child's medical challenges is often stressful and overwhelming. There are many decisions that need to be made along the way, and it's important for both parents to be involved in the process. It isn't always feasible for both parents to attend appointments, but whenever something more serious develops or if the parent who can't usually attend begins having doubts or unanswered questions, the best course of action is to schedule the next appointment where both parents can be present. This may take some juggling and forward planning, but ultimately, the efforts are needed to make sure neither parent is excluded from making informed medical decisions.

As hard as I try to relay to Jeff what the doctors have told me, he inevitably will have more questions than I can answer. He thinks of things that I might not think to ask, and vice versa. It takes both of us to decide what is reasonable and what will work with our family and our beliefs. We both need to have confidence in the doctors treating our children. I also believe it's important that both parents meet with the doctor in person at least once. If the physician's competence ever comes into question, you don't want to open the door for marital discord if one parent blames the other for choosing the wrong doctor. Raising special needs children presents enough challenging situations for a marriage; don't allow potential strains to be created that can be avoided by early communication and mutual involvement. Clearly, both parents want what is best for the child, and the child is counting on parents to make the best decisions possible. This can only happen when both parents work together as a team when making medical decisions and ask the right questions of the medical experts treating their child.

Stay Organized

Keeping your child's medical records, test and lab results, and pharmaceutical records, and keeping your notes organized in an easily accessible location are important in the event that your child faces a health emergency. You also want this information to be handy if you want to seek a second opinion or if something should ever happen to you and another family member needs to step in.

I've found the best way to do this is to keep everything in one large binder (per child) with dividers for each doctor (by specialty) and one for labs and tests. Add records chronologically to the correct section, along with your own notes of what the doctor was looking for or treating; and then you will always have a portable, comprehensive health history at your fingertips.

Tampa City Center: Believe it or not that's me on the tallest
building in Florida at the time, at the topping off party.

Julie working at a Tampa Steel drafting table.

Marrying the man of my dreams!

July 1996—My Brother and I with our father at Maria's Baptism.
My niece is six months old and Maria is three months old.

October 2001—Maria and Christina realized that Anna could play with them. Suddenly, she became interesting to them.

March 2003 Maria and Christina started school in Florida. Maria was in Kindergarten and Christina was placed in the Early Exceptional Learning Program to provide her with additional support. She wasn't mature enough to attend school until she was 6 ½ years old. Christina started hyperventilating due to the stress she experienced. This behavior is still with her today.

This was taken on April 5, 2003 when the girls were 7, 5, and 28 months. Three days later, I would learn about the girls' genetic situation.

August 2, 2003 The girls visiting Dad and Granddaddy at work.

August 7, 2003 Maria was allowed to repeat Kindergarten. Christina was going through the Individual Education Plan process. Thankfully, she ended up at home with Anna. Christina's stuttering immediately stopped at the realization that she would be staying home.

December 2003 Maria started in a special education class at a different school. We explained to Maria that she would be doing all kinds of Christmas things at her new school. She never missed her old school.

Christmas 2003 Our girls were 7, 5, and 3 years old. Our fourth baby was due that December. The baby was dead when I went to my 16 week appointment. The Dr. could not get a heartbeat. I was scheduled for a D&C. I was very depressed. My dreams for our family were gone. How could I survive? What would the future hold for our girls?

This is my favorite photo of the girls. It was taken April 2004. I used to look at it with great anguish wishing what I had been told was not true. Our 4th child would have been 4 months old in this picture. There were many tears. (8, 6, 3yrs 4 months)

Christmas 2004: During the 2004/2005 school year their teacher told me our girls would never read and they would one day live in a home. I decided to prove her wrong. Their teacher gave me a gift. I realized I could live with the worst case scenario, but I refused to accept it. To this day she is one of the best teachers they have ever had. (8, 6, 4 years old)

1st week of school in 2005. The girls working on a project after school. Anna started Pre-K4. It was my first time alone at home in years. (9, 7, 4 years old)

April 16, 2007 (11, 9, 6 years old) Christina would
have her first seizures that following July.

Our Disney trip in January 2009 was a dream come true! With
Maria's and Christina's difficulty in handling the stress of new
situations, we dared not risk a Disney trip before then. This
is a picture of our 2nd Disney Trip in November 2011.

The Girls First Communion May 2009 (13, 11, and 8 years old):
Anna had her first communion with a hundred other children.
Maria and Christina had their first communion and confirmation
in a small chapel by themselves. It was a beautiful ceremony.

Christmas 2011 with Grammy Clark. She has been a Godsend,
helping with the girls. Note: Maria is holding our 9 month old
black Peek-a-poo, Lady. The girls are 15, 13, and 11 years old.

February 2012 Stone Mountain, Georgia—This was our first trip with the girls out of state since moving to Florida in 2002. Stone Mountain was the closest place we could find that had snow. (15, 13, 11 years old)

Christina graduated from Middle School in June 2013. I also completed this book in June 2013. (17, 15, and 12 years old)

June 2019 Anna's High School Graduation.
The girls are 23, 21, and 18 years old.

Part 3

Daily Challenges

Seizures

Lights and Sirens

I will never forget the day any parent's worst fear—the sudden death of a child—nearly became our reality. It was a warm summer morning in the second week of July 2007. Maria and Anna were playing, as usual, while Jeff read the paper and I prepared to start our weekday morning routine. I thought it was odd that Christina wasn't up playing yet. She is normally an early riser. Yet it was already 6:15, and she wasn't up. I went to her room to check on her; when I opened the door, I saw her facedown on the floor, convulsing uncontrollably.

I screamed to Jeff for help as I rushed to where Christina was lying. She was blazing hot and soaked in sweat. We turned her over; her eyes were wide open yet vacant. She wasn't there. Jeff, fearing a high fever, swooped her up, her tiny body still jerking violently from left to right, and rushed her to the bathroom to immerse her in cool water. I grabbed the phone and called 911. What was happening to her? We'd never experienced anything like this before. The operator ran through a list of questions and, realizing we had a severe seizure situation on our hands, told me we needed to get her out of the water immediately.

The next few moments seemed to last a lifetime. Jeff had her wrapped in a towel, cradling her in his arms. Her body would not stop shaking; her eyes were still empty. We heard sirens in the distance. Jeff passed her to me and ran outside to flag down the ambulance. I sat on the floor, holding her in my lap and listening as the sounds of help approached. It's funny how the mind deflects trauma by focusing on details that don't really matter. I can vividly remember hoping the paramedics would not have to cut off her favorite blue *Dora the Explorer* nightgown; it had been a gift from her great-grandmother, and Christina insisted on wearing it every night. Blue was her favorite princess color, and Dora was her favorite character. I knew she would be upset if it were ruined. I would later hide that same nightgown from her because the sight of her wearing it was too painful a memory for me.

Before the paramedics arrived, it did not occur to me just how close we might be to losing her. My mind had gone into crisis mode, and I was not thinking about that yet but would later, after she was in the hospital hooked up to monitors and undergoing neurological tests for brain damage. Jeff knew, though. He knew while he was holding her convulsing body for those eternal-feeling moments waiting for the ambulance. He later confided that he thought she was going to die in his arms before help arrived. Thoughts like, "Where will we hold the funeral?" raced through his mind as he held her, helpless, straining to hear the first sounds of sirens.

The paramedics came in, fast and efficient, taking her from me and putting her on a stretcher while asking questions about her health history. I now barely remember answering. On the way to the hospital, I rode in the front seat with the driver. Jeff followed in the car with Anna and Maria. The familiar sights along the way looked new and different to me, as if I were traveling those roads for the first time. In a sense, I was. My life had changed—my daughter was in crisis. Our world had been turned upside down; nothing would be the same again.

When we arrived at the hospital, the paramedics rolled her into the emergency room. Christina was still unresponsive. I went with her as they took her in for an MRI. I remember a rough-handed nurse allowing Christina's head to hit the side of the gurney as they moved her. I was so upset. So much time had passed since I first found her on her bedroom floor, and she had yet to regain consciousness. While the hospital staff tended to Christina's limp form, Jeff and I tried to figure out our next step. At home, Maria and Anna had blended into the background, staying out of the way but taking in all the commotion. I scarcely remember noticing them. But at the hospital, they seemed to be constantly underfoot and demanding of our attention; they didn't understand what was happening to their sister or why we were so worried. The excitement had worn off. I needed to get them back home where they would be safe and allow us to take in everything the doctors were saying without being interrupted. Everything had happened so fast that morning; I hadn't had a chance to shower or even get dressed. Jeff and I decided that I should take Maria and Anna home, clean up, and pack for Christina's hospital stay while waiting for my mother to arrive at our home to take care of Maria and Anna.

I rushed home with the girls and found my mother waiting there for us. It was only then while I was sitting down with my mother, explaining the events of the morning in more detail, that I began to realize the full impact of what was happening. I'd always been somewhat aware that we might lose Christina at a young age. We'd had other scares with doctors testing her for degenerative disorders, such as Rett syndrome, that are known for early mortality. The thought had been there before, but it had never been real. The seizure made it instantly and undeniably real—Christina had almost died, could still die, that day.

That's when I broke down. The emotions hit me so hard; I couldn't stop the tears. Crying, I told my mother about the concerns for Maria's and Christina's life expectancies that had been weighing silently on me for years. No one in the medical community fully understands what the chromosomal translocation means for their futures. I've always worried that they might have some kind of genetic unraveling when they reach a certain age. No one can tell me if they will live well into adulthood or if we are already on borrowed time. The seizure brought those fears to the surface. What if this was the beginning of Christina's unraveling?

But it wasn't just fear of facing their loss that was causing me so much pain. Yes, losing any of my children would be unbearable. With Maria and Christina, there is more to it than that. I also fear not being able to protect them. I remember confessing to my mother during that traumatic morning that my only goal was to outlive them by one day. Just one day. All I wanted was to know that I would be there for them each precious day of their lives to help, guide, and watch out for them. Those thoughts were not easy to voice, and they were even harder for my mother to hear. She was still coping with learning about their genetic anomaly (we had only recently told the family), and any discussion about the loss of one of her grandchildren was more painful than she could bear, especially during the midst of a medical crisis. Luckily, caring for Maria and Anna was going to keep her attention diverted for the next three days while I stayed with Christina in the hospital.

Talking with my mother allowed me to release some of those pent-up worries. Regaining my composure, I continued gathering up clothes and items I thought we might need at the hospital. Before I could finish, Jeff called to ask why I wasn't back yet. Christina had had another seizure, and the doctors wanted to transfer her to a different hospital that had a neurology team better equipped to treat her. Jeff wanted me to be in the ambulance with her when they moved her, but he was concerned I wasn't going to get there in time. Instead of delaying her move, I agreed to meet them at the new hospital. I felt bad about not being there to ride with her, but I did not want to further jeopardize her condition by having them wait for me. As it was, by the time I reached the new hospital, Christina was already admitted and settled into her room.

Four hours after the crisis began, Christina finally woke up. Jeff and I were with her. She didn't understand or remember what had happened, but she seemed to be aware that something was wrong with her. This became even more evident when my father came by to visit later in the afternoon. During that visit, I witnessed a tender moment between them that I'll never forget. It was as if Christina knew he was there for her. Even though they hadn't had a lot of direct interaction before her seizure, she fell in love with her granddaddy that day. I could see it in the way she responded to him then and every time since. In fact, the next time he came to our house after she was feeling better, Christina was so overjoyed to see him that she jumped into his lap and threw her arms around him. Her eyes sparkled excitedly as she laughed and talked to him. If anything good came from such a frightening day, it was that she and my father were able to create a wonderful bond.

For the next three days, a neurologist, a cardiologist, and a pulmonologist treated Christina. They ran tests, recorded her movements on film, and monitored her brain activity with electrodes adhered to her scalp. That first night, she had so many wires going everywhere that several nurses were needed to help disconnect her whenever she needed to use the restroom. Since I stayed with her overnight, they tasked me with pressing a button to record every involuntary muscle twitch. The first night was the longest. I was glad the neurologist had told me to expect her feet and hands to cramp periodically; otherwise, I would have been terrified when she cried out for help during her midnight trip to the bathroom. Her feet were curled up so much that she couldn't stand up. She was frozen and scared. It was frightening to see, but having been forewarned, I didn't panic. I carried her back to her bed and tried to comfort her until the cramping subsided.

The next day, the doctors removed the electrodes, which made her a little more comfortable. However, she made it clear that she did not want to stay in the hospital. "Go home," she said again and again, becoming increasingly adamant as the days passed. Maria was known to be our strong-willed child; stubbornness was a behavior we weren't accustomed to seeing in Christina. We knew there was no way to explain to her why she had to stay, so instead we tried to divert her attention by watching cartoons or playing card games. I remember looking at her at one point and noticing how her normally fine, straight hair was now wild and curly, mirroring her strong new attitude.

Throughout Christina's hospitalization, she continued having seizures and involuntary muscle contractions in her hands and feet. She also ran a high fever, which the doctors suspected might have been contributing to her seizure activity. After more tests, they put her on antibiotics for a sinus infection. Finally, on the fourth day, the doctors agreed to send her home. For the three days of her stay, I had been with her the entire time while Jeff juggled hospital visits, work, and helping my mother with the girls at home. Everyone was anxious for Christina's recovery and release from the hospital.

Jeff came to pick us up the morning of her release; and armed with medications to combat a sinus infection and stop her nausea to prevent bouts of vomiting that could trigger seizures, antiseizure medication she would take from that point forward, and emergency doses of Diastat in case she went into another grand mal seizure, we took our wild-haired, feisty daughter home. Considering everything she had been through, she was feeling great that morning and was still displaying an uncharacteristically strong-willed attitude. Maria was at school, but Grammy and Anna were there to greet Christina with excited hugs and smiles. We were all happy she was home.

I knew the girls had missed each other, and our hearts over-flowed with joy as we watched Maria and Christina's reunion later that afternoon. As soon as Maria got off the bus from her morning at summer school, Christina bolted across the yard to her. "Ma-reee-aaahh!" she cried again and again. She flung herself onto her older sister, wrapping her arms and legs around her in an embrace as if they'd been apart for years. Maria was so happy to see Christina; she carried her all the way back into the house. All three girls were inseparable for the rest of the day, playing together in Anna's room while Jeff labored to switch beds, giving Christina a standard twin that would be safer for her than the loft-style bed she had been using.

My mother was a great help to us throughout this crisis. Without her help at home, I wouldn't have been able to stay with Christina. She even stayed all day, on the day of our return from the hospital, helping out with so many little details. Finally, we set-tled the girls and prepared for our first quiet evening in many days. Mother prepared to leave so that we could get back to our routine. Before she left, however, she said something that has always stuck with me. In observing the way the girls had all interacted that after-noon, she commented on how it was as if Christina—the one who always seemed quieter than the other two—was actually the silent leader of the group. I don't know that I would have ever noticed that, but I think there continues to be truth in that observation. She is such a special little girl with a unique gift for drawing people to her, including her sisters. In her own quiet way, Christina finds a way to touch everyone's heart.

The Weeks that Followed

As relieved as we were to be home, hoping that the worst was over, we were not prepared for what the next few weeks would bring. Christina was a long way from being out of the woods. Every day brought a new challenge and close calls and return trips to the emergency room. While she was at the hospital, they put her on antibiotics to treat a sinus infection. Because of the infection, she battled an unrelenting fever. The antibiotics also caused her to have severe diarrhea. Both the fever and the diarrhea further weakened her and left her prone to a series of seizures in the days and weeks that followed.

Jeff was able to stay home for a long weekend right after Christina came home. She was so happy Daddy was there with her. I was too. By Monday, however, he had to go back to work, and I was on my own to juggle our very sick daughter along with Maria and Anna. Between the diarrhea, constant vomiting, and being on alert for a seizure every moment of the day and night, I became increasingly sleep deprived and stressed. Nor did it help that the messes were so frequent and extreme; I had to put a plastic shower curtain down under the blanket Christina was lying on while she rested in the living room, and I kept her trash can for vomiting always within reach.

It seemed like an endless cycle: Christina was hyperventilating constantly, which led to the vomiting, which in turn led to seizures. This was the same period of time that we went through so much Diastat that the pharmacist needed to come to my rescue by figuring out how to refill the blocked prescription. We were fighting for Christina's life every day. Even a week into regular dosages of her antiseizure medication, she wasn't improving. During one of her many follow-up visits with the doctors, I asked why the Trileptal wasn't working yet. Why hadn't the seizures slowed down? The best he could determine was that the extreme diarrhea caused by the antibiotics and the vomiting caused by the stress and hyperventilation were not only keeping her weakened and dehydrated, but they were making it impossible for her body to absorb the Trileptal.

By this point, I had already called the pediatrician's office twice because of her diarrhea. Neither time did they suggest a solution or offer to put her on a lower strength antibiotic. Needless to say, I was exasperated with my inability to provide my daughter with any relief. She hadn't eaten or even been able to keep fluids down for over eighteen hours by that point. Her hands were cramping more than ever. I vividly remember one moment during the height of the ordeal. When I checked on her following a horrible bout of vomiting, she opened her eyes, told me in her weakened voice that she loved me, and then faded back to sleep. She was so weak, so exhausted, I just couldn't let her go through her torture another day.

Frantic to provide her with some relief, I called the pediatrician and said I wanted her off the antibiotics immediately. A sinus infection could be dealt with later, if needed. At that moment, her body needed a break from the onslaught of seizures. I also contacted the pharmacist who'd been so helpful with refilling her Diastat and asked for advice on getting the diarrhea under control immediately. He recommended a safe dosage of Imodium and assured me I was following the right course of action by taking her off such a strong antibiotic at that time. I'll never forget Christina's reaction when I told her she didn't need to take the antibiotics and that we had something to stop the diarrhea. "No more diarrheeeaaa!" She breathed excitedly.

Getting the diarrhea under control was a turning point, but as she began to feel better, she also had a tendency to become overexcited. This, of course, led to hyperventilating and more vomiting. The cycle was relentless for me. I ended up canceling several appointments and activities for Maria and Anna, something I rarely do, because the stress of Christina's health was just too much. Routine errands became nearly impossible. The simple task of getting to the store for a gallon of milk was monumental. Finally, three weeks after the crisis began, the stress of the entire ordeal—the seizures, the hospital stay, the tests, the weeks of no sleep, huge messes, and constant worry—finally took their toll. I lost it. And not in a controlled way—I lost it in front of the girls and threw my keys into the car in anger (and yes, I felt very guilty about it afterward).

The incident had been building up all day. Christina had been throwing up so much from being overexcited—she wasn't even trying to slow herself down. But it wasn't the vomiting that upset me as much as it was the fact that she wasn't trying to calm herself down that made me angry. Just a couple of days earlier, I had spent hours cleaning the interior of the car because of so many accidents over the preceding days. The day I lost my temper, we'd gone to the store, and she vomited for what seemed to be the entire ride home. I always have bags in the car in case she vomits, but that day, we'd run out. With no bags, there was nothing I could do except get her home. Christina, along with the entire backseat, the floors, and the backs of the front seats, was covered in vomit. The combination of events was just too much.

When we got home, following my momentary outburst of anger, I took Christina to the side of the house and cleaned her up.[7] Anna was grossed out by the mess but got a towel for me to dry Christina. Maria helped by going inside to retrieve fresh clothes for her. I was touched that both girls wanted to help. Although, after we got Christina settled watching TV, Anna told me that she didn't want to be a mom because she didn't want to clean up messes like Christina's. That bothered me. Not because I didn't think Anna would never become a mother; I understood it was a momentary reaction. It bothered me because ever since the special needs diagnosis entered my life, I had never wanted to feel like I was a victim because of it. I especially did not want Anna to see me as a victim. I didn't want her to have a negative view of motherhood because of what she saw at home. A woman's biology is designed for motherhood; I can't imagine how damaging a negative connotation of motherhood would be on a young girl's self-esteem. I was honest with Anna. I told her that I didn't enjoy cleaning up messes, but

---

[7] It was a very warm summer day in Florida. The water from the hose is the same temperature as that in the house.

I'd gotten used to it. I assured her it wasn't as bad as it seemed and that, in the end, the whole mess would be cleaned up in less than a half hour. Still, I can't begin to describe how relieved I was when Jeff brought dinner home that night so I wouldn't have to cook after the long and arduous day.

For three weeks, our lives were turned upside down. The worry, the fear, the stress took their toll. I could only hope that normalcy would return soon. I didn't know when, or if, it ever would. Finally, nearly a month after that unexpected, terrifying morning, Christina was well enough for the family to return to church. I have to admit the Sundays we didn't go were a welcome break. Sometimes, I think life would be easier on us without going, but Jeff and I have always known that going to church keeps us spiritually connected. Sunday mass is something our family enjoys and looks forward to every week. Going back to church was a momentous day for us. It meant Christina was still with us and was getting better. We didn't make it through the entire service, but we made it there. That was the important part. Simply being able to attend, even if just for twenty minutes, gave us reason to rejoice, knowing our family was still intact and that life was slowly, if uncertainly, returning to a new normal.

Always on Alert

Rest is crucial. If Christina becomes overly tired or stressed, she will start hyperventilating. And hyperventilation has been a consistent precursor to her seizures, often because it leads to vomiting, which leads to dehydration, and exacerbates the physical stress on her body. When her seizures have been at their worst, relentlessly coming one after another for days or weeks, giving her a prescribed adult-strength antinausea suppository has been our main line of defense. There have been many times when I felt certain the antinausea medication kept her out of the hospital.

When we did end up in the emergency room, I could not help but wonder if I had done enough early enough. Was it my fault for not following up with a Diastat soon enough when the vomiting didn't stop? The antinausea medication is very potent, so I never want to give her more than she needs, and Diastat is a last course measure because it shuts her entire body down. But I have to live with the guilt of not knowing if an extra dose of antinausea medication or the Diastat might have allowed her body enough of a break to stave off a seizure. These are questions I always have to live with. These are consequences I have to consider when making those judgment calls on any given day.

When Christina starts hyperventilating, it's imperative we get her to slow her breathing back to normal. Ideally, we catch her at the huffing stage. We've tried teaching her techniques to self-regulate her breathing when she begins huffing. We never get angry with her for hyperventilating; however, we have had to be very stern with her when she doesn't try to control it on her own. The consequences are too severe. We know we can't always be there to intervene for her; it's a skill we need for her to learn.

Her huffing is a daily occurrence. It isn't easy to differentiate between a normal episode and one that might escalate into an emergency situation. We can't always drop everything the second she starts huffing. If I have food cooking on the stove or I am in the shower, even if I just want to finish putting on my makeup in the morning or finish writing one last sentence before losing my train of thought, I always have that nagging fear of not knowing how much time I have until I must drop everything and intervene. Will two minutes be too long? Or thirty seconds? This is why we continually work with her to be able to stop huffing and hyperventilating on her own. We are acutely aware of the sequence that could follow on any given day: vomiting, suppositories, 911, hospitalization.

Christina knows when she isn't feeling well and will keep a trash can in hand in case she needs to vomit. Externally, I notice that her eyes seem to go vacant. Sometimes, she will stare straight at me, but I can tell she really isn't looking at me. When she slips into a deeper seizure, she will drift left. I remember one day walking through the living room where the girls were sitting on the floor watching cartoons. Anna was looking straight ahead at the TV, but Christina had her head turned at a ninety-degree angle, staring over her shoulder. With a slight seizure, her hands will clamp up. When I see that happening, I ask her to wiggle her fingers so I can assess the severity.

I find myself constantly checking her when she looks off into the distance, asking her questions to see if she is responsive or is in the midst of a seizure. With her, no seizure is the same. Many are violent but not all. Some are very subtle and would be easy to miss. One of my biggest fears is that she will have a seizure and die during the night when no one is there to help her. Many times, I've gone in at night to make sure she is still breathing. For years, I slept with a baby monitor so I could hear her throughout the night. Over the years, I've become more in tune to her sounds and can hear if she is in distress even without the monitor; however, I will still use it if she is sick. Because her seizures are often precluded by vomiting, Christina will wake up and call out to me when she feels nauseous. She always sleeps with a trash can within reach. Even though she is now pretty good about recognizing when a seizure is coming on, she doesn't always remember after seizure activity passes.

I recall one night when she started vomiting and having slight seizures around 2:00 a.m. I was there, monitoring her until she went back to sleep. I curled up next to her in her bed so I would be right there with her if anything else happened. When she woke up at her normal five thirty, she was startled to find me in her bed. "Why you in my bed?" she asked. I had to explain that she'd had another seizure; she didn't remember. Thankfully, she woke up feeling fine, and we went on with our day as usual.

I never know when I might need to react. There have been times when I've needed to pull off to the side of the road repeatedly during a short drive to help Christina stop hyperventilating. Once we had just gone through a drive-thru on our way home from school and I saw her seizing in the backseat. There was no warning other than Christina complaining that her legs had been "freezing" during the day. Freezing was a new term she started using to describe a symptom that has only recently developed. Unlike her other seizures, Christina is aware when she "freezes." She explained it to me as not being able to talk or move her legs.

She wasn't freezing in the backseat as we came out of the drive-thru that day, however. Her body was violently jerking left. I stopped the car, jumped out into the pouring rain, and ran around to where she was in the back. By the time I got there, she had stopped jerking, but I decided to give her Diastat, anyway. That seizure came on so suddenly; I was sure another would follow before I could get her to safety.

With Christina's seizures, there is always a fear that you don't know what will happen. It's always possible that she can suffer permanent brain damage. Once we feared she'd had a stroke because she was only able to smile with one side of her mouth. The doctor told us this was a common after-effect called Todd's Paralysis that can last for up to twelve hours following a focal seizure. It's her brain's way of letting itself recover. To this day, however, if she goes vacant or disconnects, we'll have her smile to see if both sides of her face are still working properly. So far, to the best the doctors can tell, she has not sustained any permanent damage from a seizure. She's been fortunate, we know. But we are never complacent. There is always the very real concern that one of these times she may not survive, that we'll get to the hospital too late and will have lost her.

Living with Seizures

Seizures may have become a part of our life, but that doesn't mean we have to let them dictate how we live. Yes, keeping Christina safe is always in the forefront of our thoughts. But we decided early on that we did not want autism or seizures to keep us from offering our girls a spiritually fulfilled and happy childhood. However, despite our best efforts to create a sense of normalcy, the unpredictability of seizures has required that we integrate new precautions into our routine.

One of our main concerns is making sure that Christina does not overexert herself, especially when she isn't feeling well. We need to monitor her all the time for seizure warning signs. If she isn't feeling well, I know that I need to make sure she gets the rest her body needs. Unfortunately, this means she misses a lot of school. While her teachers understand why she needs to stay home, we still have to be careful balancing her health issues with her school attendance. If she misses too many days in a year, the school can lose her funding allotment. So even when she is experiencing extended periods of frequent seizure activity, I can't keep her home as often as I would prefer. Every morning is a judgment call.

If Christina is feeling under the weather but doesn't show signs of being imminently at risk of a seizure, I usually will try to get her to school in the morning. I let the teachers know what's going on so they can take extra precautions to keep her calm, such as having her sit out of PE class. At the first sign of a seizure, the nurse contacts me to come pick her up; I never chance being away from my phone or too far from the school to respond at any given time. I am prepared to verbally walk the school nurse through administering the Diastat if I need to. Fortunately, we have not encountered that scenario so far; Christina has only experienced mild seizures at school that have been successfully managed.

We've become very conscious of scheduling activities and making sure Christina can take breaks when she needs them. When we go to church or social events, if Christina needs to rest, she rests. I don't try to force her to participate when she's not feeling well. For the most part, we can usually find ways to allow her to rest when she needs it. Sometimes, though, situations do come up that are beyond our control, and those can be frustrating. For example, one year her special education class was having a holiday show that was scheduled too late in the day. I tried to get the school to move it up, but they wouldn't. I was upset because I felt like it was pushing Christina to her limit. Since she was a participant, we didn't want her to miss out. Our instincts turned out to be correct, however. We were there way too late. I could see her beginning to hyperventilate on stage. Then just in time, the show came to an end. We gathered the kids quickly, headed out the door, and got them home and in bed without any further incidents.

Jeff and I were annoyed about the school's lack of judgment with scheduling the program so late in the evening. But we were looking at it from the perspective of parents who know that she gets very stressed around the holidays. In the years since her first seizure, she's ended up back in the hospital twice in January and once in February. Between all of the holiday festivities at home, in school, at church, and just in general, there is so much excitement, and that leads to an accumulation of anxiety. We know she has a history of increased seizure activity during and after the holidays, which was why it was aggravating that the school wouldn't consider our concerns; I'm confident Christina was not the only special needs child who would've benefited from an earlier program time.

One of the hardest parts about managing Christina's seizures is finding a fair balance for Anna and Maria. If it were just Jeff and me, perhaps things would be different in managing Christina's care. But it isn't. We have two other children who need to be allowed to have their own experiences. Christina also needs those experiences—birthday parties, activities, vacations; but for Maria and Anna, we can't let Christina's health keep them from participating in life.

Many years ago, when we first started seeing a psychiatrist, I was told to be very careful about maintaining balance in the household in regard to Anna. The psychiatrist said that regular education kids often develop resentment toward their special education siblings if the parents allow the special needs child to dominate the family dynamics. I've expanded that idea to include Christina's seizures. Yes, we have to be cautious, and her sisters are very conscious of her health, but it wouldn't be fair to either of them for me to constantly ask them to skip social functions because their sister isn't feeling well. Unless Christina is in seizure territory, we try to continue with our normal routine. It may not be the ideal situation, and I would prefer to keep her home on many occasions, but if all she needs is rest, she can rest anywhere. Why should her sisters sacrifice any more than they already have?

As an example, when Maria was in seventh grade, her class had a field trip to a day camp that offered a range of outdoor activities from rock climbing to paddle boats. Families were invited, and since Anna was homeschooling at the time, she was looking forward to it as much as Maria was. On the morning of the field trip, Christina wasn't feeling well. I knew she couldn't go to school, but I didn't want to disappoint Maria or Anna. It was one of those days that I would've preferred to stay home, but we made concessions. I packed a blanket in case Christina felt like resting on the grass outside, but I was also prepared to stay in the van with her if that was what was best for her. When I had volunteered to drive for that field trip, I had expected to be there more for Maria and Anna, enjoying the day with them, but staying with Christina in the van was a small sacrifice to make so the other two didn't have to miss out on a fun day.

Other times, the pressure is more subtle. When I promised Anna I would take her to lunch and to play on tubes after one of Maria's soccer games, I didn't expect Christina to be ill that morning. I knew going to lunch was a minor thing, but I caught Anna's disappointment when I suggested we skip lunch that day. I realized it was unfair to keep Anna and Maria from doing something they enjoy and had been looking forward to doing. We did go to lunch, and I had Christina lay down quietly at the table while the other two played. As the afternoon progressed, we knew she was having moments of slight seizures and was in dangerous territory. When I told the girls we needed to leave, Anna was having too much fun playing and didn't want to stop. This was where I had to draw the line and say, "We came because I had told you we would, but your sister is not feeling well, and now it is time to go." Anna understood; she was disappointed, but she understood. This is the fine line we walk daily. I don't want Christina to have a seizure, because I took her into some situation, but I need to make sure all of the girls' needs are being met.

The balancing act never ends. One year we decided to take them to Disney World. We live in Florida, but none of our children had yet experienced the childhood magic of a trip to the happiest place on earth. Jeff and I wanted for them to have this special childhood experience. As parents, we wanted it for ourselves too. We wanted to see our girls light up with excitement while meeting their favorite Disney princesses. We wanted to make those special Disney memories with our girls, but we also knew the risk. In order to minimize the excitement, we decided not to tell them until after we knew Christina had made it through the Christmas holidays. We didn't want to build it up and then have to take the trip away. Because we live within driving distance, we were able to plan the trip as a long weekend instead of a full week or multiweek trip, which helped.

Disney is wonderful for helping parents with special needs children. They offer passes for guests with special needs that allow them to go to the front of the line. We didn't feel like we needed to utilize that option with Maria, even though she technically would qualify, but I was concerned about Christina. If she became too excited, exhausted, or overly anxious, the trip would be over for all of us. We decided to get the pass for Christina, knowing that with her weakened stamina, she could go into seizure territory, and then the trip would be over for Maria and Anna. We didn't want that to be their memory of their first trip to Disney World. To our delight, the trip went really well, and we lost ourselves in the fantasy world for a few memorable days. But the bubble burst a few days after returning home, when Christina experienced another seizure. It was a minor one, though, and we refused to let it dim the afterglow of our wonderful trip.

We went through a stage when we thought Maria might be having seizures too. She was demonstrating odd behavior with her mouth and was shushing more frequently. Her psychiatrist recommended we have her evaluated by the Mayo Clinic in Jacksonville. Before taking such drastic measures, we took her to Christina's neurologist. He had Maria undergo a twenty-four-hour, overnight test to check her brain for seizure activity. The timing and expense forced us to choose between an upcoming family vacation and the neurological test. The choice was easy; we needed to know what was going on with Maria.

Fortunately, the tests came back negative and proved that Maria was not experiencing seizure activity. Of course, we were very relieved at the results; however, there was also some frustration with going through all of that—the expense and stress of the test— only to end up back where we were: not having any answers and not knowing what was causing her new behaviors. We did not want the tests to prove something was wrong, but we wanted an answer. With answers, we can at least begin moving forward with solutions.

Without answers, we are left guessing, wondering, and worrying. All any parent really wants is the ability to help their child.

A Day at the Water Park

On a nice early summer day a few years after we'd adjusted to Christina's seizures, I decided to take the girls to the water park while Jeff was at work. Waterslides are a fun treat that they enjoy, and since the end-of-the-school-year fieldtrip to the water park had been rained out, I knew the girls would be excited for me to take them. They all seemed to be doing well, and Christina's seizure activity had been relatively minimal in the weeks leading up to that day. But when it comes to seizures, there are no adequate predictors. I've learned to take precautions. In addition to packing all the usual accoutrements needed for spending a day in the sun and water, I also made sure I had Christina's seizure medication packed in our cooler. Carrying her medical kit with us wherever we go has become the norm.

All three girls are fairly independent and able to carry their rafts or tubes up the waterslide stairs, get on them at the top, and then emerge safely from the pool at the bottom of the ride. Now that they are older, we are also able to use the buddy system so everyone can go on their favorite rides. Anna is very good about staying with and protecting her older sisters. The park is designed so that there is a main staircase that splits off near the top into smaller stairs leading to different rides. The same grouping of slides then empties into one large pool. We can go most of the way up together and then meet again at the bottom. As long as Maria and Christina are with either me or Anna, I'm confident they are safe and will get the help they need if something out of the ordinary happens.

On this day, Anna and Christina decided to take a couple of turns on one ride while Maria and I chose another. Maria and I were carrying our rafts up the stairs when Maria tripped and fell, cutting the inside of her wrist. I found the nearest lifeguard and told her we needed first aid. The park has first aid stations, but as I explained to the life guard, Anna and Christina were already on another ride, and

I couldn't leave until they got back. The life guard called for someone to come to us. The responder who treated Maria was very nice; he cleaned her wound and wrapped her arm in a waterproof bandage that had purple hearts on it. Maria was quite pleased with how it looked—like she was wearing a cute bracelet instead of a big ugly bandage. By the time he finished, she was ready to go on the rides again.

In the meantime, Christina and Anna came down the ride and found us. I told them they could go again while I finished completing the accident report. Afterward, Maria and I went to ride again, and although I had to carry her raft for a while, she did all right and finally was able to manage on her own after a couple of rides. We continued going in pairs to different rides and enjoying our morning.

At one point, Maria and I had chosen a ride with a longer wait, so I was still at the top when I saw Christina and Anna land in the pool below. I was watching and waiting to wave to them, but neither looked up. As I watched, I saw them put down their rafts and stand together for a couple of minutes before walking over toward the lifeguard. Christina stopped and went back to her raft. She bent over and looked like she was stuck in that position. I could see Anna pulling at her arm, but Christina wasn't going anywhere. At that instant, I realized that Christina was disoriented and having a seizure.

I was about sixth in line; the group at the top seemed to be taking forever with getting ready to go down the slide. I felt trapped up there. I knew my daughter needed help, yet I was stuck on that staircase, too far out of earshot for me to even call out to Anna. I knew the slide was the fastest way down. Going down the stairs, struggling to go against the flow of the crowd with everyone carrying bulky rafts up the stairs would have taken too long. I didn't have any options, and I couldn't wait any longer. I told the group ahead of me that my daughter was below having a seizure and asked if they'd mind if I went ahead of them. I figured Maria would be fine waiting to take her turn and would be behind me soon. No one objected. They cleared a spot for me at the entrance of the tube; I put my raft in and just went.

Going down that slide was surreal; it was as if I was part of a cartoon. This was something that was usually fun, but all I could think about was how soon I would hit the bottom. *Please, just let me get there in time!* The ride whooshed and twisted at an adrenaline-pumping pace, but I didn't notice it. Instead, I felt helplessly stuck inside that tube. The entire way down I was running a play-by-play in my mind of what I was going to do when the rushing water finally shot me out into the pool.

Jump off the raft. Get to Christina. Get help.

When I got there, the first aid people were there tending to her. Anna had retrieved our cooler with Christina's medicine in it. Christina seemed to be okay and had snapped out of it by the time I reached her. Relief washed over me. I ran the scenario back through my mind, being stuck up there and needing to make a choice on how to get to her. There is never any way to know how bad a seizure will be. In situations like this, there's always a judgment call. I have to make split-second decisions and just react, hoping I'm making the right choice given the circumstances. Luckily, this seizure passed without convulsions or Christina needing her Diastat. I was thankful that Anna knew what to do and how to get help for her sister.

As the adrenaline subsided and I was gradually able to start noticing everything else around us—life-threatening emergencies have a way of blocking out everything else while they are happening—I noticed the same first aid responder who had helped Maria earlier in the day. He smiled and told me that we needed to fill out another accident report. Since I had dressed all three girls in matching mint-green swimsuits to make them easier for me to track in the crowd, he could clearly tell that Anna was also my daughter. He nodded toward her and jokingly said, "Well, I guess we only have one more accident report to fill out today."

I laughed and replied, "No, we won't need to fill any out for her."

Right about then, I looked around and realized that Maria hadn't come down the ride yet. This didn't seem right because she should've been within the next couple of people to come down the slide. I didn't realize that the operators had stopped all the slides while Christina was being treated. Maria had not been allowed to get on the slide. Just as I started to worry about her being stranded at the top of the stairs, I saw a lifeguard walking her over to me. Apparently, right after I left, Maria told the lifeguard at the top of the slide that her sister had had a seizure. The lifeguard picked up on her green swimsuit and, having noticed the matching suits of Christina and Anna below, pieced together that they were all sisters. She led Maria back down the stairs to where we were.

The commotion died down. We knew Christina was going to be fine, but she needed to rest. She said she was hungry, so we found a place to have lunch. I found a place for Christina to lie down and sleep while Maria and Anna went on some more rides. The lounge chairs by the pool were all occupied; fortunately, Christina can sleep just about anywhere. I made her a makeshift bed and shade cover off to the side. We were there for about a half hour when a stranger realized that Christina wasn't feeling well. In an act of kindness, she offered to move so we could have some space in the shade. Another couple went in search of lounge chairs for us; it turned out that they had raised an epileptic daughter and had plenty of firsthand experience with seizures. I'm always amazed at how nice people are to us and how many interesting people I meet.

Christina slept for about an hour and a half. When she woke up, she was ready to go home. I was too. The day had been eventful and exhausting. We went to find Maria and Anna at a pool where five different slides converge. Within a few minutes, they each emerged from a slide, one after the other, smiling and having fun. Anna came over and told me they had been on four of the five slides. She asked they could please just take one more turn so they could ride all five. I didn't want to press it with Christina, but she was looking much better. I asked her if she felt okay to wait. She surprised me by saying that she wanted to go on the ride too. I thought about it for a moment and decided it would be nice to end the day on a high note for all of us.

Instead of splitting up to go on separate rides this time, we all went up together. We were at the top and waiting for our turn when Christina started looking like a she was going into another seizure. All I could think about was having to get out of there. This time, going down the slide was not an option. We had to go back down the stairs and around the pool the long way; I couldn't risk crossing through the pool the way we had come in case Christina started seizing when we were in the water. I told the girls that we needed to go. They didn't complain. They know that Christina's health supersedes everything else when she goes into seizure territory. We left the water park not on the high note of that last ride but thankful for the fun we managed to have despite a day of seizures and accident reports.

The fear of seizures never goes away. We've learned to minimize it so it doesn't overrun life, but it is always there. Even recently, years after that first crisis, Jeff and I prepared to go for our regular early morning walk. Christina hadn't been feeling well the day before, and as we were leaving, it occurred to me I hadn't seen her yet that morning. I asked Jeff if he had. When he said no, I felt an overwhelming need to check on her before we got started. I just needed to see her to make sure she was okay. There was nothing else to prompt that intense reaction except the fear. She was fine—just sleeping a little later than usual. The fear never leaves you.

Before Christina had her very first seizure, she'd had a wonderful day. She'd spent the day in the pool; Jeff had been working with her on swimming various lengths across the pool both on the surface and under the water. She was so proud of herself afterward that she even insisted on bathing herself without my help before bed. At dinner that night, she was able to hold her fork correctly and manipulate it to eat her macaroni. This was an accomplishment that came on the heels of a major breakthrough in her speech therapy earlier in the week where she was finally able to make her tongue move at will to both sides of her mouth.

With all her successes, we had no reason to suspect that she was on the verge of crisis. When I put her to bed that night, I knew she was tired and needed rest. She was so proud of her achievements that day, and we were proud for her. It had been a great day. I tucked her in like any other night, not knowing how close we would nearly come to that being the last time I would ever get to kiss her good night.

Before that day, I didn't think about how life can turn on a dime. One day everything is fine, the next nothing is. We don't see it coming. We can't do anything to prevent or change it, although as parents we have a tendency to want to blame ourselves. I was surprised to hear Jeff admit he felt like Christina's seizures were his fault for allowing her to overdo it in the pool the day before. How could he have known at the time? The fear and grief that parents feel when a medical crisis occurs is hard enough; we have to allow ourselves to let go of the guilt. Guilt does not help us or our children with the challenges that lay ahead. All we can do is try our best to survive the new challenges, one moment, one hour, and one day at a time, being grateful for each moment we have to hold, love, and enjoy our most treasured gifts.

Tracking Seizures

Whenever a child experiences any kind of medical trauma, especially with something like seizures, it is important to keep accurate records of the time each symptom occurred and what medications where given, including exact dosages and times. I wear a stopwatch around the house so that when Christina has seizures, I can accurately record when they happen and how long they lasted. Whenever she has any kind of seizure-related symptom, I record it. Her symptoms may last for a period of days, so it can be hard to backtrack and remember specifics that aren't written down. When we call 911 or end up in the emergency room, the first thing medical responders want to know is what happened, what drugs were given, and when. Because Christina's medications are so strong, it's imperative that everyone involved knows exactly what she has already had. An overdose could lead to respiratory failure. That's a risk we can't afford to take, and it's easily preventable with a piece of paper and a stopwatch.

Suppositories

Chances are that most parents have encountered the unpleasant task of giving a young child a suppository at some point. When doing it during a medical crisis, however, there are a couple of differences. The child may be older, perhaps physically full grown, and they may be stronger, meaning they are that much harder to overpower if they resist. During a seizure situation, the child does not have control over his or her body and is often in the midst of deep convulsions, making the task extremely difficult.

During the midst of a crisis, everything changes. Things that seem normal become chaotic and sometimes confusing. This is not the time to try reading instructions to figure out what to do. When you receive a prescribed suppository for your child, it is absolutely imperative that you take the time to become familiar with the dosage marking, the applicator, and how to use it properly. You don't want to lose precious seconds fumbling with the applicator for the first time when you need it most.

While it's helpful if two adults are available, this may not always be the case. Both parents need to know how to administer the medicine quickly. Most important, parents need to overcome their hesitancy; your child's life may depend on you being able to act swiftly and without queasiness. Many applicators come with a premeasured dosage stop tab, so you can press the plunger and know it will stop when the correct amount of medicine has been released. Hopefully, the process is clean, but even if it isn't, the parent needs to expect to stay at the child's side until the crisis is over. There will be time to wash up later. As unpleasant as the task is, it does become easier over time. The more you can do to prepare yourself beforehand, the easier it will be during those first experiences.

Our Disney Vacation

After years of hoping, we finally found ourselves preparing for the biggest trip of all—Disney World! For us, being able to take the girls to the most magical place on earth meant more than just taking them on what many consider to be the ultimate family vacation; it was also symbolic that our girls were doing okay. There was a time in life when I doubted whether or not we'd ever be able to take such a trip. To me, it was like a small miracle for our family.

Before planning our Disney trip, we had already been able to take the girls on a few short, one-day outings to places like the zoo and the aquarium. We knew that Disney World would be filled with more people and excitement, which in turn would mean increased anxiety for Maria and Christina. To prepare for the big trip, we decided to gradually build up to it by going to places with greater levels of stimulation. We bought season passes to Busch Gardens and took the girls on three different occasions over the course of a year.

During our first outing, Maria was going through a stage of extreme anxiety; it was so high, in fact, she needed to wear gloves to stop her from picking her cuticles to the point of bleeding. We had a slight incident with her that first day. Fortunately, we avoided having a major episode. With each successive trip, the girls handled the stimuli better, and as Maria moved out of her "glove" phase, we felt more confident about going forward with our Disney plans. When we thought the girls were ready, we made reservations at the Disney Resort for the following week, but we decided not to tell the girls about our plans until the morning of the trip. Our fear was the anticipation would be too much for them and would force us to cancel the whole thing. We even waited to start packing until they were asleep the night before leaving.

Christina and Maria were the first to wake up and find the matching outfits I had laid out for them. When they woke up Anna and discovered she, too, had a matching outfit, the excitement really began to escalate. They knew something was going on, but they didn't know what. Then they saw the suitcases near the door. We finally told them the big news: "We are going to Disney World!" I'm sure it comes as no surprise that the girls were overjoyed and didn't waste any time getting ready that morning. We were on our way before seven o'clock and pulled up at Disney's Beach Resort just over an hour later. For the duration of the drive, Jeff and I shared an unspoken gratefulness that the trip was finally happening. Christina vomited once on the way there, which thankfully seemed to be a result of overexcitement. With her, we never know if hyperventilation-induced vomiting is a prelude to a seizure. I remained on high alert until the episode passed, and she returned to normal.

The decision to stay at one of the Disney Resort hotels was a practical one—we wanted to be able to return to our room quickly if Christina were to get sick or if Maria had a meltdown. We also liked knowing we'd have an hour of early access to the park before it became too crowded. The amazing Disney Resort pools would provide plenty of low-stress fun during our downtime from the park. Since we arrived early in the morning, we had plenty of time to visit the Magic Kingdom before checking in to our room that afternoon. I don't think I've ever seen the girls more excited than on that first shuttle ride toward the park entrance.

After a quick stop at City Hall, we went to Fantasyland, where we had an amazing time experiencing the rides, seeing the characters, and listening to Story Time with Belle. That day, we were able to ride on Dumbo, Cinderella's Golden Carousel, It's a Small World, Peter Pan's Flight, Snow White's Scary Adventure, and the Many Adventures of Pooh. Every ride, every new site was a glorious event for the girls. On our second day, we enjoyed riding on Mad Hatter's Tea Party, Indy Speedway, Magic Carpets of Aladdin, Swiss Family Tree House, Pirates of the Caribbean, and the Jungle Cruise. The girls did great with just about every attraction, although we did decide to bypass rides that we thought might be too much for them, like Haunted Mansion and Space Mountain.

Since I had brought their IEPs along, Disney accommodated the girls' dietary needs by allowing us to bring in our own food, and they provided special fast passes so we wouldn't have to wait in line for rides. I was glad to know we had passes if we needed them, but admittedly, I felt guilty about using them and only did so once. Of course, I was also prepared with essentials like Christina's seizure medicine and the accoutrements, like band aids, that can help bring Maria back from an OCD crisis. Luckily, we only had a few minor incidents with Christina feeling nauseous, and we made it through both days in the park without incident.

Spacing the rides out between two days helped ensure a successful trip. We didn't want the girls, especially Christina, to become overtired, so we limited ourselves to about six hours in the park on the first day. Around midafternoon, we took them back to the hotel to rest. Unfortunately, the sandy beach pool with its colossal three-story waterslide outside our window was like a flashing neon beacon to the girls, meaning naps clearly were not going to happen. We allowed them to change into their swimsuits so we could go play in the water. The sand was like an invisible fence for Christina at first, but she overcame her reluctance to walk through it, and we were able to situate ourselves in a spot near the slides. Soon enough, we were climbing the stairs to one of the best waterslides we've ever been on. Surprisingly, Anna was the only one to protest going down the first time, but after a momentary hesitation, she was fine. We all had a wonderful afternoon in the pool, rounding out our perfect family excursion at Disney World—where the dreams of three little girls finally came true.

Society

Everyday Life
Anything but Average

As every new parent learns, life with children is unpredictable. Gone are the days of quiet and calm. Instead, households are filled with the energy and exuberance of childhood. Irrational behavior and emotions replace the relative sanity of adulthood. In a home with a special needs child, the emotional reactions are harder to predict, and behaviors require more tolerance to endure, but the innocence and joys of childhood are equally prevalent. If anything, we learn to appreciate the good moments and treasure small accomplishments even more. For most parents, snuggling with their young child is a special part of the day that is simply expected, maybe even taken for granted. But when a parent of an autistic child receives that child's first sign of affection or voluntary hug at two years old, that is a moment the parent will never forget.

While having children with special needs may have taken our lives in an unexpected direction, it doesn't mean we've stopped living. We still go through the usual events of day-to-day life: church, school, shopping, field trips, dinners, birthday parties, and family outings. We still want to have a family life that is enriched with special memories and experiences. The difference is we can't always count on things going as planned. We have learned to never take a good day for granted and are (almost) always prepared to make impromptu changes to best meet the needs of our children. We have grown accustomed to expecting the unexpected, and to keep trying, even when progress seems impossible. We do our best to plan ahead for possible problems and to anticipate the limit on how much can be expected of them on any given day. As we promised in our marriage vows, we are in it for better or for worse; we give thanks on every good day, and we struggle but get through the bad days.

Out and About

Running everyday errands presents unique challenges. Simply being out in public means dealing with external issues beyond our control. At home, we have created an environment and routine that includes rules and expectations designed to help the girls manage their anxiety and behavioral issues. Being out of the house means having to deal with unexpected situations at any given time and cope with the added pressure of having an audience of strangers. Anna once whispered to me that someone was staring, to which I replied, "Anna, people always stare at us."

Having the girls attract attention is something I've grown to accept over the years. I try not to let it bother me. I can't let a stranger affect how I react to whatever situation I may be dealing with. If either of the girls goes into distress while we are out, I have enough on my hands just trying to diffuse the problem without worrying about other people's impressions. Yes, there have been times when I've felt embarrassed but not because of my girls. When negative thoughts creep in, it's because I don't want people thinking poorly of me as a mother. No mother does. Fortunately, the vast majority of people we meet are very kind, helpful, and nice to us.

As a stay-at-home mother, I always had the girls with me when they were little. Now I have the window of their school day to run errands, but they aren't always in school. Jeff is at work sometimes twelve hours a day and usually on Saturdays; I can't wait for him to be home to watch the girls so I can go shopping alone. I have to go to the grocery store or the post office whether they are with me or not. Even when Christina was going through her rough period of seizures, I needed to go grocery shopping. We still needed food in the house.

When I do have to take them with me on errands, I try to find times that are the least crowded so the trip will be faster and easier on the girls (and me!).

When they were little, I always had to pack milk and the particular food that they would eat since they didn't eat regular food. If they got hungry, I was able to just hand them something instead of trying to go through a drive-thru and find something they might eat. As long as I had a cooler with milk, they would be okay until we could get back home. I still keep a cooler with us on days we are out of the house for any length of time. Now that they are older, they like going to play in the tunnels at fast-food restaurants. Not only do they enjoy this, but it also gives us all a break to decompress a little between errands or after a long medical appointment. Having an outlet like this helps reduce the number of times I have to cut the day short and go home before I've finished everything on my list.

Clothing stores are difficult, but if I know exactly what I'm looking for, I can usually get in and out quickly enough. If I need to try something on them, we all go into the largest available dressing room; they usually entertain themselves with the mirrors, but they still don't last long. Grocery stores, on the other hand, are very difficult for individuals with anxiety or sensory issues. The rows of products combined with the lights, sounds, and movement of other shoppers is more stimulation than many special needs children can handle. I had a friend whose child refused to go through the automated doors at the grocery store. It can take a long time for children to learn the coping skills they need to get through what seems to us a common task. I do my best to minimize meltdowns, but they aren't always avoidable. When a shopping trip ends poorly, I just try to regroup, analyze what might have been done differently for a better outcome, and continue on.

Getting them into or out of the car can easily add fifteen minutes to each stop. Since there is always a limit to the amount of time we can be out of the house or number of stops we can make, the one-stop superstores have been a lifesaver. When they were small enough, I would find a cart in the parking lot to put them all in and push them into the store. This was much easier and faster than trying to walk or carry all of them across the parking lot, especially in poor weather (I rejoiced the day they finally learned to work the seatbelts and I no longer had to run around the van in the rain getting them situated and buckled).

Today, I still have Christina ride in the shopping cart when she isn't feeling well. She carries a plastic bag in case she needs to throw up, but she's still small enough to ride in the cart and keeping her from walking and exerting that energy enables us to get through the store without her lapsing into seizures. The hardest part is when one of them needs to use the restroom at a store. Obviously, I can't leave any of them unattended, so if one has to go to the bathroom...we all do.

One day, I took the girls to Walmart to get book bags; they were very excited at the prospect of picking out new book bags. On our way through the aisles, Christina said she needed to use the restroom, so we made a detour to the other side of the store. We all went into the bathroom together, and Christina promptly vomited into the plastic bag she was carrying. She was very worked up, and it took me nearly five minutes to calm her down. Meanwhile, Maria became increasingly agitated because of the delay and anticipation of getting the book bags. So there we are: Christina in the cart going through her contortions, Maria standing next to the cart moaning and stim-ming, and Anna waiting impatiently while I tried to restore calm in the other two. Of course, plenty of customers were staring from afar.

We finally made it to the aisle with the book bags. Christina and Anna each picked out a bag, but Maria agonized over her decision. It took her fifteen minutes before she finally made a selection. Moments later, Maria changed her mind, and we had to go back and let her switch for a bag identical to Christina's. By this time, Anna had started complaining that her feet hurt from standing so long, Maria's temperament was touch-and-go, and Christina looked very weak and peaked from all the commotion. I still hadn't started with the normal grocery shopping part of our trip, and the girls were already spent.

By the time we reached the checkout lane, I was worried about Christina having a seizure. Maria slipped behind the register and began talking nonstop to one of the cashiers we knew. I dropped a yogurt, which splattered all over the floor. Another employee came to my aid and helped me clean it up while the cashier helped load my groceries back into the cart. What started out as a simple trip to Walmart for a few groceries and book bags ended up lasting over two hours. It was exhausting.

On another more recent trip for groceries, we made it through without incident until we reached the checkout lane. That's when Maria realized she had forgotten her yogurt. From where I was standing at the register, I could look down the aisle and see the yogurt case. I had already unloaded my groceries and was in the process of checking out. I couldn't leave the girls alone, and since there wasn't anyone behind us in line, I told Maria she could go get the yogurt. I didn't want a meltdown because she didn't have it, so I made a decision to let her go get it.

When Maria reached the yogurt display, she became overwhelmed by having to make a decision between the different brands and flavors. I had forgotten about that part. Decisions are very stressful for her. She screamed for me to come help her. I had to leave Anna, Christina, and our partially checked-out groceries to sprint down the aisle for the yogurt. As the event unfolded, a few more people had gotten in line behind us. I've never liked being the person holding up the line, but I've gotten used to the unpleasant looks from impatient people behind me. With special needs children, even the simplest tasks take longer. There were many times, especially when they were little, that I'd see people who had checked out well after me drive away as I continued wrestling with loading the girls and the groceries into the van.

As the girls have gotten older, it has become more apparent that they have special needs, which does help. When they were little and had breakdowns, it was more embarrassing for me because I felt like people were judging my parenting abilities. Now bystanders are more helpful than judgmental. Sometimes, I feel really bad when I am so caught up in the moment that I snap at questions from well-intentioned bystanders. For example, after hearing Maria's deep, raspy voice, a cashier asked if Maria had a cold. I was too focused on dealing with the girls, and I curtly replied, "No, that's just her voice." I knew she was trying to be nice; I didn't take her comment the wrong way, but as soon as I answered, I realized she might have thought I had. I then felt compelled to explain that Maria was autistic, and the deeper voice was normal for her.

All in all, people are usually really nice to me, and I always try to expect the best of people. We live in an urban area where there is plenty of crime, yet that hasn't jaded the good people of our community. People are kind and thoughtful wherever we go. Maria went through a phase of going around the cash register to hug the cashier. I used to apologize for that, but I have learned that people are more okay with these actions than one would think. It is such a bright spot in my day whenever I see the goodness in the people we meet.

When we were trying to sell our last house, we decided to update the kitchen to make the home more marketable. Going to the cabinet store was an adventure; it took two visits to accomplish one goal because of the distraction of Maria's bumbling, repetitive comments, and unending questions, and Christina's loud precise statements and huffing. They finally busied themselves with some toys the store had available. When they were out of earshot, I explained to the salesperson who had been helping us that they had special needs and had high-anxiety issues. She complimented me on how cute they were, to which I agreed. She then commented on how quickly they responded and how well they cleaned up the toy area when it was time to leave. Apparently, most of their customers' children would leave a mess. I appreciated the compliment. Our girls are cute, well-mannered, and chaotic, all at the same time. We've just become adept at working around their stress and anxiety issues.

Because the girls had such difficulty at mealtime, for many years, we avoided going as a family to a sit-down restaurant. But not forever. After Jeff had moved his mother to an assisted care facility, we decided to take her out, as a family, for a Mother's Day breakfast. It went surprisingly well. Christina was able to eat macaroni off the menu, and I brought Maria's food with us. Since Anna could take care of herself, we sat her between her sisters. Jeff is better at controlling Christina's hyperventilation, so we put her next to him, and

Maria sat next to me. I found the experience refreshing. After so many years, it was wonderful to be able to sit down in a restaurant as a family.

After that first breakfast outing, we have continued taking the girls out with us. We favor family-friendly restaurants that aren't too loud and try to go during off hours when the noise level is minimized. Many restaurants have television sets playing and when crowded, the volume gets turned up; a blaring TV is too much for Christina and no help for Maria.

After Anna's First Communion, we went to a frilly tea room to celebrate. When I called to make the reservations, I made sure they knew that two of the girls had special needs and required their own food. I didn't want an uncomfortable situation to unfold after we arrived. This was a very nice, quaint establishment, and I wanted them to know ahead of time. I've always felt bad about bringing our own food to a restaurant; I understand that we are taking up two seats without ordering. It's an awkward situation, so I like to give the management the courtesy of knowing what to expect.

Going out to eat is easier when it's just our family. I know what each of my girls need to be happy. Planning birthday parties is a completely different story, especially when most of the kids on the guest list also have developmental challenges. The first birthday party we held that was outside of our home was at a fast-food restaurant with a play area. Again, I talked to the manager ahead of time, explaining that I would pay for all the kids' meals, even if they didn't eat. With special needs children, there are so many dietary restrictions that vary from child to child; we weren't planning on going for the meal as much as we were going for the play tunnels. I always find it best to communicate with management ahead of time.

For Maria's "sweet sixteen," we wanted to do something a little more special. My first choice was a pool party. We wanted to invite all the students in Maria's class. Since all of the guests would be children with varying degrees of developmental challenges, we were concerned about putting ourselves in a position of supervising all of them in the water. I was concerned too many of the parents would just drop their child off, leaving us with the responsibility of watching them. I was especially concerned since I never know when I might have to leave the group to handle a seizure emergency. In the end, Jeff and I decided the risk was too great. We had no way of ensuring that parents would stay to watch out for their own child's safety in the pool. Instead, we had a gymnastics party, which worked out very well, and was a great way to celebrate Maria's special birthday.

Making—and Changing—Plans

As carefully as we plan outings and try to minimize anxiety triggers, we've also learned that the only plan we can ever count on is being ready to change plans if one of the girls goes into distress. We just never know what challenges the day might bring. And while Jeff and I need to remain flexible and switch gears, we also understand that Maria and Christina don't have the coping mechanisms to deal with sudden change. If I tell them we will do something that day, I need to be very certain I'll be able to follow through. Once they have it in their minds to do something, "no" is no longer in the equation.

If I do have to change our plans, I have to do it creatively. Usually, I can assuage their disappointment by telling them we can do later, whatever they were planning on. They can cope with delaying, much better than canceling, plans. Hopefully, the delay provides enough time for them to refocus their attention and forget about the original plan. With Maria, this isn't always the case. Because of her OCD, she can hold on to an idea for a very long time and won't be at ease until it is completed.

For instance, when Maria bought a new doll with her holiday money, she decided we needed to make a jacket for it. By Saturday morning, all she could think about was making a jacket for the doll. We were getting ready to leave for soccer, but she was becoming more and more upset. First, she hid in her closet, something she often does. When that didn't work and we called to her to come to the car, she ran outside and into the playhouse and refused to come out for several minutes. When she finally came to the car, she was highly stressed, and her eyes were twitching. Not being able to make the jacket was the source of all her anxiety at that moment. I assured her that we could make the jacket after soccer. That helped with enabling us to get to soccer, but Maria continued obsessing and would not let go of the doll the entire time.

Luckily, we still made it through soccer that day. However, there have been countless times we've had to cancel lessons or appointments because either Maria or Christina was too ill or out of sorts. Christina's health is always a concern, and she can deteriorate on a dime in certain circumstances; overstimulation is a major catalyst. Not long ago, the girls had a field trip to see the Disney Earth Day movie at a theater. Everything started out fine; both girls were excited for the outing and the movie. As usual, I was there as a chaperone, just in case. Then the previews came on at a deafening volume that both girls had trouble tolerating. It was even hurting my ears. At last, the movie started at a much more normal volume. Maria bounced back all right, but Christina went downhill quickly. She lasted about fifteen minutes into the film before I had to take her out of the theater. We spent the rest of the field trip in the lobby, with Christina resting on a bench. It took her several days to get back to normal.

We had a similar experience during Christina's first school dance. Maria absolutely loved her first dance, but Christina found the noise and lights overwhelming. Instead of being the fun night she had been looking forward to, she spent most of the evening in the hallway, covering her ears to combat the sensory overload, while Maria danced and cavorted inside. I did not want to end Maria's evening since she was having fun. Instead, I waited outside with Christina, making sure she was able to rest while we waited for Maria to finish her first school dance.

We just never know when one of the girls will throw a curveball at us. There we were, at a go-cart track for the first time ever; Jeff was purchasing our admission tickets while I waited nearby with the girls. Maria was getting all worked up because of her OCD: she didn't like the way one of Christina's sleeves was turned up, and she was carrying on about Anna's pink shirt. When Jeff returned with the tickets, we started to follow him out of the building to the event grounds. But suddenly, Maria refused to come. She was making an odd expression that I hadn't seen in a long while, and she simply refused to walk with me. Nothing I tried worked. She stood with feet planted, swaying, moaning, and staring at the ground. I ran and caught up with Jeff and told him he needed to go back in and get Maria. In just a few moments, they came walking out together, nearly back to normal. I asked incredulously, "What did you do?" He simply smiled and made a reference to the actor Paul Hogan's technique for communicating with a crazed water buffalo in the movie *Crocodile Dundee*. We both laughed hilariously and breathed a sigh of relief that the day was not ruined. He confessed later that she was just ready to come on her own. Sometimes, there is no rhyme or reason behind what sets off a behavior.

Maria's OCD plays a major role in her rapid mood changes. When we took them to the circus, the trip was almost over before we made it across the parking lot because Maria became fixated with a string on Anna's shirt. She can't stand it if anything is out of order. She's constantly trying to pull bits of fuzz out of her sisters' hair. This drives Anna crazy because Maria is too aggressive. If Anna retaliates, the tension between the two can escalate out of control and sometimes last for days. Maria has recently learned to refrain from touching Anna and instead will ask me to fix Anna's hair. This still upsets Anna, but she tolerates it, knowing that her sister can't stop obsessing until the "problem" is resolved.

A couple of years ago, we took the girls to their first county fair. We surprised them with this treat on a weekday when Jeff normally would have been at work. He took a day off and explained to them that we were having a "Fair Day" as a reward for how well they'd been behaving. Overall, the day was everything we had hoped for—an exciting and whimsical time for childhood fun. Christina couldn't tolerate the live animal smells for very long, but they were enthralled with watching the equestrian exhibition. Later, all three had a chance to ride a pony. I was hoping Maria would enjoy this new experience since she had never ridden a pony. Unfortunately, only Christina and Anna would ride the ponies. Anna explained "something about ponies scare Maria even though she likes them." Maria's apprehension was probably sensory related. I'm not surprised that she didn't ride a pony at the fair.

One year, Jeff's Rotary Club received a community citizenship award, and the members were invited to lead the Fourth of July parade. Families were invited to march with the group. The girls looked adorable in their matching outfits and big strawhats, and since we were the only Rotary family with young kids, they were getting a lot of attention as the parade was about to get underway. The excitement was too much for them, however. Christina became ill and vomited on the grass while Maria started shushing. I knew we weren't going to make it through the parade. Jeff didn't say anything, but I could tell he was disappointed to have to go without them. It struck me that he was experiencing a moment like I did after their First Communion. There's always that moment for special needs parents when they, just for once, want to feel like they have a normal family—but realize it will never be.

Everyday Madness

As crazy as things can get out in public, life at home isn't always easy, either. Some days are good, some not so good, and others bring a unique blend of chaos that can only be looked back upon as comical. Although, I'll be the first to admit, most of these events weren't funny at the time. As with everything in life, maintaining good humor and being able to take things in stride can make all the difference.

Mornings are always hard because I never know how the girls will wake up: happy and flexible or stressed and struggling. To make our morning routine as simple as possible, I have them shower before bed, lay all their clothes out the night before, and make sure their morning medications are properly dosed out and ready for them. Maria has to take her medicine thirty minutes before she can eat breakfast, so I have taught her to do that as soon as she wakes up. Some mornings, however, she finds endless distractions, and I have to constantly stay on top of her until she takes it.

Christina is generally much more methodical in her morning routine and will get up, get dressed, and take her medication without reminder. She struggles more with becoming agitated in the process of getting ready. Just trying to put the toothpaste on the toothbrush can cause her to start huffing. If one becomes upset, the other is likely to follow suit. Then if Anna's attitude is uncooperative, in addition to Christina's huffing and Maria's bumbling, we are lucky to get out of the house at all.

There are times in the morning when I just want to read the paper for a few minutes. I know I'm supposed to be on top of things, that I should be responding as soon as they call to me, but I also just need a few minutes to myself. Being able to enjoy a quick cup of coffee without interruption can be a lifesaver for the rest of the day. Maria is finally old enough to understand the concept that Mommy needs quiet time once in a while—not a lot but sometimes. Maria talks a lot, so it was a relief when she grasped that I wasn't necessarily angry with her, that I just needed a minute or two of quiet. My husband teases me that Maria's continual chatter is my payback for all my talking to him. Despite the teasing, he does understand how strenuous and tedious our mornings really are.

As much as I enjoy those quiet moments, they rarely happen. Instead, I end up contending with a myriad of emergencies from the dog getting sick and one of the girls tracking it through the house, to soiled bed linens, flooding bathrooms, and even a broken toilet lid during one morning's chain of bathroom catastrophes. I've cleaned up more messes and dealt with more plumbing emergencies than I care to count. Once, Christina flooded the entire house because she unrolled all the toilet paper rolls trying to get the cardboard tubes. She stuffed all the paper into the toilet and flushed. I didn't know this when we left the house. By the time we returned hours later, water was all the way out to the garage. That was a disastrous event that required expensive cleanup. From then on, I banned them from playing with all toilet paper and paper towel tubes.

That wasn't our only flooding incident, either. When Anna was much younger, she plugged the toilet in the guest bathroom before bedtime. The bowl flushed all right, but the toilet was running slow afterward. I was tired from a long day and decided to let it wait until morning. Of course, that happened to be a night that Christina would awaken me covered in vomit. She had it everywhere, on her bedding, her nightgown, and even in her hair. I cleaned her up and made a dry bed for her on the floor. I took her quilt to the bathroom to rinse it out in the tub, which must be why Christina, later in the predawn hours, decided to use the slow-running guest toilet instead of her own. This time, the water did not go down when the toilet was flushed. Instead, the blue water spilled over the bowl and flooded the floor. By the time I realized what had happened, we had nearly an inch of water covering the bathroom floor. And all of this happened before we would normally even be up to start our day.

Special needs parents become very accustomed to cleaning up messes. As much as we want to be supermoms, it's okay to accept help when it's offered. With Christina, vomit is a normal part of life, and I've cleaned up more than my share. If we are out of the house when this happens, I take her to the nearest restroom and help her wash her face and rinse out her mouth. If it is in her hair, I try to rinse that out first so the mess doesn't spread. Then we do our best to wipe off her clothes. When Christina is sick, even when she goes through rough patches that last for weeks, I am usually very patient; the only times I become frustrated or short-tempered when dealing with the messes is when she has the ability to control herself from becoming overexcited but does not try. These are moments when I believe she could stop herself from getting sick if she wanted to. When she is truly ill, the circumstances are different. She is a frail little girl who is very dependent on my enduring compassion and care.

As accustomed as I've become to it all, I still have my moments when Christina's vomiting can make me gag. Usually, this is when we are in a confined space, like the car, and the smell becomes overpowering. When I see that she's about the throw up, I try to pull over to let her out. But this isn't always possible, especially if we happen to be on a crowded expressway. All I can do in those circumstances is try my best to talk her through regaining control of her breathing before she gets sick and hope she gets it all into the bag when she does vomit.

Getting her to stop huffing is the hardest part because I can't take my focus off the road. Jeff reminds me that I need to work harder at controlling her huffing at home. In the car, it's too late. There's nothing I can do. To compound the situation, quite often, Maria's anxiety becomes heightened while Christina is huffing in the car. She'll begin shushing or, if we are on the way to school, compulsively telling me again and again that we are late, a fact I'm usually very well aware of, anyway.

Sometimes, when Christina wakes up early, she wants to come in and snuggle with me in my bed. One particular night, I had already been up with her when she wet her bed. I made her a dry bed on the floor, and she went back to sleep for a couple of hours. About a half hour before we'd normally get up, she wanted to snuggle, so I invited her in and told her to rest. Within moments, she vomited on my bed. I faced that day with two beds in the house trashed. I knew Christina would have to stay home that day, but I still needed to get Maria to school. This involved getting all three girls in the car on time. As we pulled to our usual drop-off place, I told Maria to unbuckle. For some reason, Anna thought she would go to school and take Christina's place that day, so she unbuckled too. I couldn't understand how she arrived at that conclusion since she was homeschooling at the time and was used to staying in the car while I dropped her sisters off each morning. It took a couple of minutes to resolve the confusion and get Maria out and on her way into the school. Just another morning of being "that mom" holding up the carpool lane.

Now that the girls are older, things are getting easier. They can usually bathe themselves. I help them during their periods, but otherwise, they can pretty well manage on their own. Because they have coordination challenges, I buy soap, shampoo, and conditioner with pumps that are easy for them to use. Maria has trouble getting the water started, so Christina will take her shower and leave the water running for Maria to get in after her. When they were little, I dreaded the evening bath ritual. I was typically tired from a long day and knew I was still facing hours of bedtime chaos. In an attempt to lessen the burden, I'd bathe them and have them come out and watch

TV while I dried them, cleaned their ears, and put lotion on them. One evening, Jeff came in, saw what was going on, and said, "What's with the spa? Just turn the TV off and bathe them. You are prolonging your agony."

His point was that I needed to take a more proactive approach. By allowing the distraction, I was actually stretching out the very task I dreaded doing. As parents, we have to be proactive or these daily rituals can overrun us. I started looking at how to take control and speed up the bath-time process, among other things. I set a goal of having baths done in time to have them all in bed at an hour that still allowed me time to relax. That was a great lesson for me to learn. Setting attainable goals for everyday tasks helps restore balance and, when I'm lucky, provides me with some much-needed downtime at the end of the day.

Parenting Mistakes 101

Try as I might to be patient, logical, and rational in the midst of various crises, I am the first to admit that I've made my share of mistakes. I call them my "bad mother award" moments. These can range from being short-tempered to having occasional lapses of judgment. We all have those times when we think we are doing our best and then realize afterward we could have (and perhaps should have) done something different. Parenting doesn't come with an instruction manual; all we can do is try our best each day and learn from our mistakes. And we will inevitably make mistakes. Here are a few of my more memorable ones.

As you can tell by now, Christina is always sick. Throughout her whole life, she's always been sick, sometimes worse than others. We can get so caught up in dealing with her being sick that we forget to take a step back and look at the larger picture. On one of her sick days, I realized that I was doing just that; I was so focused on just getting her through the day that I had stopped considering other factors that could be contributing to her health. Namely, her diet. Jeff and I suddenly realized that all she had eaten for days had been carbohydrates. Her diet consisted of nothing but pasta. "No wonder she's sick," we agreed.

We talked about how the pasta may be too much for her system. We also considered the possibility of her being allergic to gluten; if that were the case, then all that pasta was contributing to her aggravated state of illness. I thought back to how we'd slipped into such a high-carb diet with her. I had been feeding her yogurt for protein, but when the store discontinued her favorite brand, I hadn't searched hard enough to find a replacement. Giving her something I knew she would eat, like macaroni, was simpler than trying to get her to try something new. Looking further, we discovered she was only eating French fries for lunch at school every day. She was getting absolutely zero protein in her diet.

We put an end to it that day. Jeff went to the grocery store and bought several brands and flavors of yogurt. When he came home, we conducted a blind taste test with all three kids to see which ones they liked. We spent nearly the entire day doing this, but we were able to find some new alternatives that helped get Christina's nutritional needs back on track. That Monday, I began packing lunches of yogurt, fruit, and vegetable juice for her to take to school. I also started keeping a chart in the kitchen to help balance her macronutrient intake throughout the week.

Most of my parenting regrets come from moments when I've lost my patience. I'd like to think that I'm good at rising above those moments that can try my nerves, but in truth, I can become irritable at times, too, especially if I haven't had my morning coffee. I remember once when we were away from home and not on a regular schedule and the lack of caffeine had triggered a massive headache. I thought I was doing a decent job of keeping my spirits up despite the pain until Anna called me "Mrs. Grumpy-pants." Apparently, I wasn't hiding my irritability very well that day. We were supposed to be having a fun family day; I felt bad that I was giving off that vibe.

With Maria and Christina, I try very hard to be consistent with my moods. They don't understand if Mommy is having a bad day, and in order to maintain their moods, mine has to be predictable. I also want them to learn from my example that not every little problem warrants a dramatic reaction. I do have bad days, however. But I try not to let those get the better of my mood. When I slip up, all it usually takes is a quick reminder to help me shake off a bad mood. Unfortunately, Anna is often the one to provide those reminders; unlike her sisters, she is very sensitive to minor shifts in my mood.

One such occasion happened during Maria's clumsy phase. She was constantly dropping and spilling things, and I was constantly cleaning up messes and stains. One afternoon, we were all in Anna's room cleaning. Maria was holding a bottle of Windex when the sprayer somehow detached from the bottle. As the bottle fell and blue liquid doused Anna's bedspread and windowsill, Maria was left standing there with just the sprayer top in her hands. *How does that even happen?* I thought to myself. The words that came out, however, were a little harsher. "Why do you always do things like this?" I said in exasperation. I caught how wrong that sounded when I saw the condemning look Anna was giving me. I regained my composure, cleaned up the mess, and reminded myself to do better next time.

We all have bad parenting moments when we are tired, but sometimes, they can sneak up on us when we are having good days too. For instance, Jeff and I sometimes allow the girls to have a lollipop after dinner. One night we told them they could each pick a lollipop. Maria poured the bag out to sort through for the color she wanted. She took a long time deciding but finally settled on purple. Jeff and I were lingering in the kitchen conversing after dinner. We watched Maria go through this elaborate process of unwrapping the lollipop and adjusting the wrapper, so it was neatly flattened and in line with the edge of the counter. Maria suddenly remembered she needed to turn off the TV in the other room. While she was out of the room, we decided to have a little fun with her by replacing her purple lollipop with a green one. We relished a moment of rebellion and retribution for having to put up with her endless OCD behavior. We should have known better.

The expression on her face was priceless when she discovered our switch. Not to be fooled so easily, she immediately found where I had hidden her purple lollipop, and everything seemed fine. Although, she went to great lengths to make sure the green lollipop was rewrapped and put back in the bag correctly. But later that same night, Anna touched Maria's hair while they were all in the bathroom brushing teeth and preparing for bed. Maria ran out of the bathroom screaming with indignation, "She pulled my hair!" Even though Anna had only touched her hair, not pulled it as charged, I had to send Anna to her room just to diffuse the situation. The outburst sparked Christina's anxiety, so then I needed to intercede to stop her huffing and help her finish brushing her teeth.

I was at last able to calm everyone down and get them settled in bed, but the night was not going to end so easily. As I was tucking Maria in, I gave her the American Girl doll she sleeps with. This reminded her of a Barbie-style doll she had been playing with earlier. It was a cheaply made doll, and the leg broke while she was playing. An OCD child can't tolerate something not being right, so I had to repair the doll right away when the incident occurred earlier in the day. I was concerned that if it broke again just as I was trying to get Maria to go to sleep, she would have a meltdown even worse than she'd had in the bathroom. I showed her the doll was okay but was reluctant to let her touch it. Satisfied with seeing the doll's leg fixed, she asked me to put it back in its correct storage place. She needed all those details attended to before she was able to rest her mind and go to sleep.

Jeff and I decided afterward that our little joke, something that seemed so harmless at the time, had sparked the entire sequence of events. We had no idea we were pushing her OCD buttons that far and causing her such anguish. We thought we were having some good-natured fun with her; we certainly were not trying to be mean or cause her distress. I guess I can only chalk it up to learning yet another parenting lesson the hard way.

Vacations

When we lived in Virginia, we occasionally took the girls on weekend drives for brief family getaways. After moving to Florida, however, the girls' needs became more acute, and we stopped trying to take them out of town for several years. Car trips were difficult, and flying was out of the question. It would be three years before we finally ventured out for a weekend trip to Key West. We prepared for the drive by bringing along plenty of food, milk, and a portable TV. We hoped that being able to watch their favorite videos on the way would lessen the strain of a long ride, but the six-hour drive was still too much for them. Both Maria and Christina went through their anxiety behaviors—shushing, moaning, huffing—for the majority of the ride. Maria's anxiety was heightened by her need to use the bathroom. With no rest stops in sight, we had to stop on the roadside. I had to hold her arms, supporting her in a semiseated-semistanding position, while trying to provide some privacy from passing traffic so she could relieve herself along the side of the road. With her transitional issues, these roadside stops added considerable time to our drive.

Finally, we reached the hotel. The girls were beside themselves with excitement. Not having any recollection of being away from home before, everything was an adventure for them. Like all kids, they were excited about the pool. They enjoyed the breakfast buffet more for the novelty than for the food, of course. We were able to do a little sightseeing but with mixed results. What I had hoped would be a highpoint attraction—reef watching on a glass-bottomed boat—didn't turn out so well for me. The viewing glass was on the lower, enclosed deck, and the ocean was choppy that day. The back-and-forth lurching as we floated over the murky reef ended up sending me to the rail for fresh air. Our other attempts at tourist attractions ended in similarly lackluster ways.

Today, the girls remember the trip as an adventure; Jeff and I remember it as being long and stressful. By the time we left Key West, our only goal was to make it through the drive home without incident. Neither of us wanted to endure their stimming behaviors the entire way home. Jeff was so anxious to get the drive over with that he earned his first speeding ticket in years. It would be another three summers before we attempted to travel with them again.

Jeff attends an industry conference in Ponte Vedra each year. Since I have an engineering background, I enjoy going to this conference with him. It's become our annual trip and welcome break. But the year Christina started having seizures, I was very concerned that she might have an attack while we were gone. Ponte Vedra is a three-hour drive from home. In a seizure situation, that is too long. We decided to take her with us, which meant taking Maria and Anna as well. We also hired a babysitter we knew very well to come with us to watch the girls while Jeff and I were at the conference during the day.

The sitter watched the girls and helped feed them while Jeff and I went to dinner, but we didn't want her taking them to the hotel pool by herself. The pool was too large, and there were too many people around for her to be able to safely monitor all three girls. Instead, we all went together when the conference had concluded for the day. Even with Jeff, the babysitter, and me watching over them, we still had a close call with Christina losing her bearings in deep water after coming off the waterslide. At home, she knows exactly where the shallow water safety mark is, but we were in an unfamiliar pool. Instead of swimming toward the shallow end, she headed for the deeper water and quickly became exhausted. Jeff saw her struggling and was right there, pulling her to safety, within seconds. The exertion of the event took a toll on her stamina. The next day, she was sick and needed rest. Afterward, however, she bounced back and did much better for the remainder of the trip.

Unlike our trip to Key West, this trip went well enough that we decided to take the girls again the following year. They've been back with us every year since. I think about how good things can come from bad situations. If Christina had not gotten sick, I wonder how long it might have been before we dared attempt another road trip, following the Key West fiasco. So far, the convention trips have all been a success.

One year, Christina decided before we left home that she wasn't going to go on the beach. She had suddenly decided that she didn't like the feel of sand. Anna was very upset at the idea of not going to the beach. I reminded Christina that she'd had said she liked sand after playing in a sand table at therapy, and we got her a pair of beach shoes just as a precaution against any tactile defensive disasters. When we got there, she was fine. She had a great time on the beach and even let Jeff teach her how to ride the waves in an inflatable raft.

The only disappointing trip was our most recent one. It rained the entire time, and we couldn't go to the beach at all. The hotel was supposed to have ponies to ride on the beach, and the kids were really looking forward to that. It was not easy for them to accept that the pony rides were cancelled. Still, we managed to get the girls settled for the evening before going to dinner. To our shock, while Jeff and I were at the restaurant, we saw the ponies outside. Apparently, they had not been cancelled. I felt so bad and was tempted to go back to the room and get the kids but thought better of it. Thirty minutes later, it started raining again; we would have missed the ponies even if I had gone and gotten them up. We did learn from that—to avoid telling them too far ahead of time about events that could be cancelled. They had been so excited; I hated having to disappoint them.

Ten years after moving to Florida, we decided to take the girls to see snow. They were too young when we moved from Virginia to remember the cold, blustery northeastern winters. We planned a weeklong trip that would be our longest and farthest from home. Aside from all of us having colds and Christina having one slight seizure, it was surprisingly successful. The trip was filled with fun new experiences, like tubing, building snowmen, and swimming in a nice warm indoor pool after a freezing day outside. We even found a pond with Canadian geese to feed. Being gone so long was difficult at times, but we brought home many fond memories.

The hardest part of being away from home is finding ways to accommodate their dietary needs. Christina only wants macaroni, and Maria struggles with anything solid. I have to either bring or buy what they need for each meal. When we go into restaurants, I always feel bad asking them to heat something that I've brought in. I explain why the girls can't order from the menu, but I'm still aware of the burden. Some establishments won't allow outside food; most have been helpful when they understand the reasons. Of course, away from home, everyone is hungry, so we are always pressed to find an alternative that will satisfy all our needs. More often than not, we end up at fast-food restaurants simply for the convenience and because the management does not care as much if we are using extra seats without ordering.

For me, the best part of our trip north was being able to visit my *alma mater* on the way home. I had not been back since graduating and had not attended any of the class reunions. We walked around the campus and took the girls to the fountain at the student center. Sometimes, I wonder what my path in life would have been if I'd chosen career over family. On that day, however, watching my girls play on the Georgia Tech campus, I felt truly blessed and successful with the way my life has turned out, even if it wasn't according to my original plan.

Celebrate the Little Things

The first year we took the girls trick-or-treating, we felt like we'd hit a huge milestone. Part of the joy of having kids is celebrating the holidays with them. There was a time when I wondered if we would ever be able to do this traditionally child-centered tradition with them. Finally, in 2004, we were able to walk through the entire neighborhood, and we made it through the evening without incident. Maria and Christina don't eat chewable candy, but they had a wonderful time collecting it. After receiving candy at each house, Christina would call out excitedly, "Another house!" It was a wonderful evening that reminds us to take joy in the small accomplishments.

Potty Breaks

Using public restrooms is never pleasant but always a necessity. I try to have everyone use the bathroom before we leave the house, but they don't really understand the concept of having to hold it for any length of time. We've been working on that, especially at church where we discovered that going to the bathroom was becoming a little adventure when they were tired of sitting through mass. Making them wait at church has helped, but if we are on the road or in a store, I don't usually have much of a window to get them to the nearest restroom. We have a forty-five-minute drive to school each day, and there have been numerous times that I've had to pull off the road and find the nearest gas station or open restaurant.

Maria's transition process in the bathroom can take up to fifteen minutes. She does a lot of stimming and shushing to cope with having to undress and then redress. For her, this is a major source of stress. And because she is primarily on a liquid diet, she is the one that most often needs to stop. If one of the others needs to go, I always make sure Maria goes too. Otherwise, I know we will have to make a second stop before long.

Family bathrooms were wonderful for being able to have them all together so I could help one while keeping track of the others when they were younger. Handicapped stalls were the next best option for us. As Maria and Christina have become more independent, they've started using separate stalls. I still need to be nearby in case they need me, so I spend a lot of time standing in public bathrooms waiting on them. Handwashing is always a long ordeal that would take forever if I left them to do it on their own. Whenever I become frustrated with the amount of time I spend in bathrooms, I remind myself of the positive parts of how much they can do autonomously now. I know many other parents have it much worse in this regard. It helps to keep perspective and focus on their abilities rather than their disabilities.

Infamous Oatmeal Disaster

The morning of the incident, forever since known as the Infamous Oatmeal Disaster, began relatively well. We were actually running ahead of schedule. Maria had finished her oatmeal and was taking her bowl to the sink. She accidentally bumped the bowl onto the edge of the counter; she must have hit it just right, because the bowl fell and shattered all over the tile floor. In spite of being startled by the noise, I reacted with surprising calm. I told Maria that I would clean it up. She sweetly reminded me that everyone makes mistakes. I smiled and agreed. Then I asked her to leave the kitchen so I could clean up.

Before I could finish sweeping up the broken bits of glass, I heard a second crash. Christina had dropped her bowl, still full of oatmeal, on the floor, sending shards of glass and sticky oatmeal everywhere. Mommy was not so calm that time. Christina had already refused her oatmeal once, but I had given it back to her and had told her to finish it. She had taken a couple more bites and decided she was done. As she got up to take the bowl to the sink, she had started huffing—a common reaction when she is excited, stressed, or just not happy. This time, it was because she didn't want to finish her oatmeal, and it was because of her huffing that she dropped the bowl.

I believe that on some level she dropped it intentionally. She hadn't wanted it to begin with, and what better way to get rid of it? After all, Maria didn't have any consequences when she broke her bowl. I sent the girls to get their things and go to the car. I reheated my now-cold breakfast and took five minutes to gather my thoughts while I wolfed down a bite of food and a cup of coffee in silence.

A few days after the oatmeal incident, I was putting on my coat and noticed blood. I couldn't figure out why my finger had started bleeding. Then I remembered. My coat had been hanging on the back of a kitchen chair that morning. Sure enough, a glass shard had gotten embedded in the fabric.

A Difficult Day

Some days just seem like they will never end. I had one of these days on the date of a consultation appointment with a highly recommended reading tutorial service that I'd waited weeks to see. The morning of the appointment started out great. It was the girls' first Monday back to school after a break, and I was looking forward to being able to go to the gym without having them in tow. I dropped them off and went to the gym as planned. When I got home an hour later, I received a message from the school nurse that Maria was running a slight fever and was complaining of not feeling well. I thought it was odd since Maria had been fine when I dropped her off earlier.

I jumped back in the car, still sweaty from my workout, and went to pick Maria up from school. When I got there, Maria was in emotional crisis mode. Even later when we got home, it was still hit-and-miss on how she was going to behave from moment to moment. I tried everything in my parenting arsenal to placate her, but nothing worked. I had my hands full with Maria and was now up against the clock for picking Anna up from preschool. She was at an age where she panicked if I was late. I didn't need two children falling to pieces on me that day. I got Anna home and then called the tutorial service, explained the situation, and told them I wouldn't be able to make it.

Maria had already been home for a couple of hours, but I hadn't been able to get her to calm down. Nor had I been able to shower; I remember thinking if I could just bathe life would be good. But that was not in the cards. Maria was in full crisis mode. She wouldn't eat or drink. She was walking around the house aimlessly, crying and moaning. By eleven, I was starving and finally managed to get my first bite of food.

Finally, Maria started coming back around to her normal self. I realized I could still make the appointment if I hurried, so I called the clinic and told them we were on our way. I got Maria and Anna in the car and rushed to the appointment. I told them we would go to Chick-fil-A later if they were good while I was talking to the tutor. Sometimes, bribery is just easier. Afterward, I took them to Chick-fil-A as promised, even though I really didn't want to go. But I had to uphold my end of the bargain since they had behaved.

I got Maria and Anna settled with their milkshakes and lunch (Maria's food was packed from home, of course). Maria was talking nonstop in a very loud voice; Anna was agitated with her because Maria was dominating the conversation. I just wanted to be alone for five minutes to eat my sandwich in peace and enjoy a cup of coffee. The morning had been so hectic, and I'd barely had time for a sip of coffee before the chaos started. By this point in the day, I had a raging headache from the lack of caffeine, and I still craved a shower and felt very uncomfortable being out in public in my workout clothes. I told myself it would only be a little while longer until Christina got home from school, and then, just maybe, the three would cooperate so I could bathe.

By five o'clock, my only goal was to make it to bedtime. The day had been long and stressful. I heated frozen chicken nuggets for dinner, allowed the girls to skip their baths, and put them to bed early. I knew the morning would bring new challenges, but this day, at last, was finally over.

Puberty

Puberty on Steroids

Sometimes, it can seem so unfair that girls with cognitive developmental delays still have to go through puberty. Adolescence is a confusing time for all young girls, but with special needs children whose emotional maturity is often years behind their physical maturity, their changing bodies bring a host of new challenges. Not only can these changes be scary, but girls with autism may not have the ability to communicate what they are experiencing or to understand the erratic mood swings of hormone fluctuations or the cramps and discomfort of menstruation the same as most girls can.

Special needs children are blessed with the gift of innocence that brightens days and brings joy to those around them, yet it is this same innocence that makes puberty seems so unjust in the eyes of parents. We know our daughters aren't mature enough to fully comprehend what they are going through, but biology, not emotional readiness, drives the onset of puberty. Parents have the added challenge of trying to explain the physical aspects of puberty in a way that will make sense, often having to reexplain it many times over—each day may seem like starting over—as the child slowly begins to adjust to her developing body.

Christina was only ten when her pediatric endocrinologist confirmed that she was already starting puberty. I was devastated. It was one of the rare moments when I was not able to fight back my emotions. There I sat with my delicate, barely four-foot-tall daughter curled up in my lap, listening to the doctor tell me she would start having periods within the next two years. She was just too small, too young. In my mind, she was still just a baby. I couldn't see her being ready for such a traumatic physical change. I didn't want Christina knowing I was upset, so with watering eyes, I tried to talk in code to express my reaction to the doctor. He picked up on my cue and played along.

The doctor went on to explain that if I truly wanted to slow her biological development, we had an option of giving her shots to delay the start of her periods. Some parents, he continued, also put their special needs daughters on birth control pills to regulate periods and lessen the severity. I wasn't interested in introducing any new drugs or chemically altering her physiology, so I resigned myself to accept the inevitable—and to prepare for it. On the upside, at least I knew I would have about two years to get her mentally ready. When it comes down to it, all parents really can do for their kids is try to prepare them for what's to come. We support, love, nurture, and educate them in hopes that they will be ready for whatever life brings. Handling puberty is just another transition along that path. All parents go through it; but with special needs kids, there will always be some unique considerations and situations that occur along the way.

Our Little Girls Are Growing Up

One summer evening, when Maria was fourteen and Christina was twelve, the five of us were sitting together at the dinner table. Jeff and I happened to look at Maria at the same time. The light must have been just right because we both noticed the first tiny bumps on her peaches and cream cheeks. We looked at each other and smiled knowingly: puberty. Our first baby was growing up. It was a tender moment at a time when the combination of hormones and medication were wreaking havoc on our eldest daughter's disposition. Her behavior had been so extreme that I even went so far as to film her tantrums to show the psychiatrist. In a way, the sight of those first pimples—those dreaded badges of adolescence—was a visual reminder that Maria's radical mood swings were, at least in part, normal for her age. Her body chemistry was changing, and she was struggling with moods and emotions she wasn't equipped to express.

Changes in behavior and complexion weren't the only symptoms we'd noticed as the girls neared their teens. Both started wearing bras before entering middle school. Maria had a habit of pulling her shirt up when shushing, which was a behavior I worked fervently to stop because I did not want her being labeled or teased for doing that in school. The last thing she needed as a special education child in middle school was to expose herself, even if it was accidental or part of a compulsive behavior. She would never live that down. We successfully broke her of this habit, but I decided it would be best for her to have a bra on just in case she regressed.

Since Christina started puberty early, her breasts were already developing by the end of fifth grade. I remember the sadness that weighed on me during her elementary school graduation ceremony. Knowing she was physically changing and that her period would be starting soon, the ceremony almost seemed like a formal end to her childhood. I knew I had to get her accustomed to wearing a bra over the summer, and she was not happy about it. She'd say, "No want to," or "No like bra." I explained to her that she was a big girl now and that Maria started wearing a bra in sixth grade too. Christina was not very cooperative at first, but in my mind, the issue was nonnegotiable. As special needs girls, they are already at a higher risk for sexual abuse. I need them to be dressed appropriately for their physical development so they don't attract unwelcome attention. Wardrobe changes can be tricky for tactile defensive kids, and school breaks are a good time to take on these battles. Not all changes can be preplanned to utilize school vacations for transitions, but when it comes to something like wearing a bra, starting early is better than waiting until it's too late and something potentially embarrassing or harmful happens at school. We eventually prevailed over her resistance.

Even though Maria is two years older than Christina, both girls have gone through many of their changes at nearly the same time. In a way, this has made the transitions easier for them. But as with all sisters, there is also a bit of competition. Before Maria's thirteenth birthday, she excitedly bragged to her younger sisters that she was going to be old enough to ride her bike on the streets in our neighborhood—a milestone privilege that allowed her to assert her position as the oldest. Not long afterward, Jeff and I overheard Christina tell Maria, "Mine are bigger than yours," in reference to her breasts. We couldn't stop laughing, but it also reminded us that despite their challenges, they are each acutely aware of how they compare to one another.

They know when one is ahead of the other, so it's important for us to remember to find ways to make each feel accomplished and proud of her abilities and specialness. We don't want to fuel a sibling rivalry; this sometimes requires finding creative ways to give each child her own chance to shine. As Anna has gotten older, this has become even more pronounced. She has started surpassing her older sisters' abilities when it comes to swimming and gymnastics—activities they've typically shared—and I worry that Maria notices this and compares herself to Anna. We know that Maria sometimes feels down about herself when she sees Anna excelling at an activity or when she silently notices that Christina is "winning the puberty contest" of breast development. She can't express that something is bothering her, but we sense it. During these times, Jeff and I will make a conscious effort to give Maria tasks that she can do well, like folding laundry or setting the table. She feels so proud of herself for her accomplishments, and her mood always brightens afterward.

Managing Menstrual Cycles

Knowing their periods were going to be starting soon, I decided to have a talk with all three girls so they would be more prepared. Anna was still young, but I knew that she would see everything her sisters were going to go through. As a result, I've had to explain some things to her earlier than I probably would have. Her sisters didn't need to know more than the basics about physical development, so I felt all right including Anna at that time. Several years later, I talked with Anna again, to explain in more detail, about the facts of life. That wasn't a topic I needed to discuss with her sisters, so I was able to wait until Anna was old enough to go over that more sensitive material. Maria and Christina only needed to know about their changing bodies. To help them, I bought an *American Girl* book that explained these changes fairly simply and had illustrations that weren't overly graphic. I removed the pages that would create unnecessary questions on topics such as sex and tampons, and then the girls and I went through the book together.

We had a good discussion, and although it can be hard to measure how much Maria or Christina retained or grasped right away, I found out later that my early efforts paid off. The day Maria started her first period, when I tucked her in bed that night and asked if she knew it was her period, she said yes. I then asked her if she was glad I had told her about it already. She smiled sweetly and said yes. I was glad to know I'd been able to save her some anxiety by preparing her beforehand.

Maria started her first period on a Friday evening while Jeff and I were out at dinner just a couple of blocks from our house. The girls had gone to bed around 8:00 p.m., but when we got home an hour later, Maria and Anna were still awake. I said good night and then went to the kitchen to finish cleaning up. Within a few minutes, they appeared in the doorway. Anna said, "Maria keeps getting blood on her underwear." I soon learned that she had gone through five pair of underwear while we were at dinner. Of course, I knew what that meant, so I took Maria into the bathroom and showed her how to open the pad and position it to her underwear. I also showed her how to clean herself properly. I tried to show her that I was excited for her and how she was growing up, but I also kept it low-key so she wouldn't get too worked up.

Christina slept through it all that first evening, but Anna was very intrigued. She wanted a pad too—not to wear but just to have because her sister had one. I told her no, but the pleading look in her eyes told me she was feeling left out of the excitement and attention her sister was getting. The next morning, Anna decided to start wearing her training bra. Apparently, Maria had upped the ante by starting her period. Having read the *American Girl* book many times, Anna also enjoyed asserting herself into a more dominant role by trying to tell Maria how long her period would last. "Three to eight days," Anna said knowingly when Maria asked. I had to assure Maria it wouldn't be as bad as Anna made it sound.

In the morning, I showed Maria how to remove and discard her pad, and then put on a new one. Luckily, her first period was very light and only lasted three days. Christina started menstruating a couple of months later. Although she didn't seem very interested when it was happening to Maria, it was clear that she had learned from her older sister's experience and knew what to expect when it happened to her.

When Maria and Christina would first begin their periods, they would call me every time they went to the bathroom, day or night. And they were constantly going to the bathroom to check their pads. They would insist that I come and see, every time, even if there was only a spot or two. The first several months were exhausting and frustrating for me. It wouldn't be unusual for me to get up three or four times a night to help them, even when I knew they didn't actually need my help. It made them feel better just to have me there. This is something we've had to work on over the years; I know they need to feel confident enough to manage on their own eventually.

Over time, they have gotten better and can change their pads and clean themselves pretty well on their own now, but in the early days, their cycles meant relentless bathroom duty for me. For example, it was not uncommon for Christina to wake me at 4:00 a.m. I would help her with everything she needed to do in the bathroom. By the time we were finished, it would be time to get started with the day. I'd go back into my bathroom to get ready, which only takes me about fifteen minutes, but without fail, either Maria or Christina would be calling for me again before I could finish. On those days, they couldn't make it through ten minutes without a bathroom check. The voice calling for me would not stop, even if I was in the bathroom and could not come right away. They don't have any cognition that Mommy is busy, needs a shower, or can't come to their aid immediately. It was no different than a newborn crying from hunger. It was exhausting for me.

When Maria first started menstruating, she also had heightened anxiety issues. She was off-the-charts shushing and stimming. It was getting harder and harder for her to stop. She would fall on the ground, crying at home and in class. Going to the bathroom has always been a challenge for her. She goes through a long transitional process to cope with getting undressed and redressed every time. On a good day, it may take up to fifteen minutes for her to use the bathroom. It doesn't matter if we are in public or at home; she still needs to go through the same process. In public, I feel the pressure of knowing other people may be waiting for us. At home, however, I know she's just in the bathroom doing her thing. I can hear her, so if she needs my help, she will call to me. Usually, she can manage on her own, but when she was having her first periods, between the newness and the heightened anxiety, she really had a difficult time. This meant I had a more difficult time too.

There was a time when I became so utterly frustrated with having to help in the bathroom that I just didn't have the patience to tolerate it. I remember one night when Maria was relentlessly calling out to me for help, but I couldn't work up the energy to go in and deal with it all again. I didn't respond very nicely. I was tired and aggravated, and in my frustration, I responded with an exaggerated, "Maria! What do you want?" I feel bad about it now, but getting up multiple times a night and never being allowed a break to catch up does wear on a person's (even a mother's) nerves.

Regardless of the reason, my attitude toward her just wasn't positive or patient at the time. And Jeff called me on it. "How do you think that makes her feel? What effect is that having on her self-esteem?" he asked. His comments helped me see things in the proper perspective. It didn't matter how tired I was or whether or not I wanted to help her change yet another pad. I needed to remember that our primary objective is to build confidence within our girls so they can someday take care of themselves. Maria needed me to be supportive and encouraging. This was a scary time for her. And when you first start your period, the image of that experience and the way you perceive it can have a long-lasting impact on how you feel about being female.

On my good days, when Maria is shushing and stimming from the anxiety of changing her pad, I remind her that she knows what she's doing and is good at doing the task at hand. I try to calm her down and build her confidence. "You don't need me to help you," I'll reassure her. "You know what you are doing." If she still does not settle down, I leave the bathroom, but I'll make sure she knows I'm not upset with her about her period. She needs to understand it's because of her shushing behavior that I'm leaving and that when she pulls herself back together, I will return to help her.

Today, the girls have an easier time managing their periods, but we still aren't to the point where they can handle their cycles independently. They know how to align the pads and only occasionally put them on incorrectly. They no longer need my help every time they go to the bathroom, although they continue having moments of high anxiety. Maria shushes, and Christina hyperventilates. With Maria, I can say, "Do you want my help or not?" and she will usually regain her self-control. With Christina, sometimes flicking water droplets on her will distract her from the stress of changing her pad. It annoys her but also switches her focus, which allows her to calm down enough to stop hyperventilating. Once I get her attention, I can help her stop huffing by having her count to ten or by hugging her tightly. The combination of stress caused by her period and uncontrollable hyperventilation is a recipe for a seizure, especially if she's already weakened from not feeling well.

Fortunately, neither of them have had severe cramps. Once, early on, I picked Maria up from school and could tell she was experiencing some cramping by the way she was balled up in the seat. She had had a hard day at school and told me she was in pain. I explained to her that cramps were sometimes part of having periods and then told her that when she got home, she could put on her pajamas and lie down on the couch to watch TV and rest. I gave her some pain reliever, and she perked back up. I was glad the medicine worked; she had been so upset. I think the pain concerned her because it was a new, unknown kind of pain.

I'm always concerned about them when they go to school during their periods. I make sure they wear longer shirts to cover their bottoms. They both constantly pull at their pads to readjust them, and my hope is that the longer shirts make this habit less obvious. They frequently have accidents and need to change their clothes at school, and I worry this will happen in the lunchroom or gym when they are outside of the relative safety of their special ed classrooms.

They know not to talk to boys about their periods, which has been interesting when they've had male teachers. The school makes sure there is a female aide in the class to handle these types of issues, but I think the situation can still be awkward at times. This came up one time when I volunteered to help out on a class field trip. The kids were separated into groups, and I was assigned to supervise two children in addition to my own. One of the girls in my group was having her period. The male teacher couldn't help her in the bathroom, and the female assistant was not on the field trip that day. I'm fairly certain that's why the teacher asked me to take her in my group, although he wasn't able to expressly communicate that upfront. That would've been a violation of student privacy.

I wasn't necessarily prepared to handle this scenario; it's one thing to help your own child, but helping someone else's child presents a whole new set of personal boundary issues. Luckily, I knew the girl and happened to have her mother's phone number in my cell phone, so I was able to call and talk to the mother before putting myself in an uncomfortable situation. And thankfully, the girl was fairly independent in this regard and didn't need my help.

At home, hygiene is always a concern. Maria and Christina know to have me help them in the morning. I want to make sure they are clean before they go to school and again each night before they sleep. I have them wipe themselves first, but I usually need to follow with a more thorough cleaning. I don't know if they realize that they will feel better, because they are more clean and dry. Considering their tactile defensive sensory issues, I can only imagine how the discomfort must be exaggerated. Not only do I want them to be more comfortable, but I need to make sure we are keeping them clean and preventing other potential problems from developing. It's interesting that they also want my help bathing during their periods, even though they can usually shower on their own. They need that extra step-by-step instruction for getting out of the shower, drying off, and immediately putting a pad back on. This process continues to cause them anxiety, so they manage better if I'm there.

Christina is typically very organized and obsessed with tracking dates on the calendar. Once she started learning about menstrual cycles, she started wanting to know about mine. "Have you had your period yet? When is it coming?" I give her simple but honest answers. She's very curious. When they were little, I didn't try to hide it, but I didn't tell them, either. Now that they are having their own, I try to be open with them and satisfy their curiosity.

Their cycles are not yet predictable, so we don't necessarily plan family activities around them. But there have been times when their periods have limited our recreation. The most noticeable has been restricting water activities on those days. If one happens to be on their period while we are on vacation, we can't spend any time in the water as we normally would. At home, Anna sometimes gets frustrated when her sisters can't swim in the pool with her. She asked me why I didn't teach them how to use tampons so they could still swim. My immediate thought was, "I would have to do that. I'm not ready for that."

As it is now, I still monitor when they need their pads changed and then help them clean themselves. My concern with introducing tampons is that I'd have to track when they had one in and remember to take it out. I wouldn't know when it was ready to be changed. And if it became too uncomfortable for them, they would fight me. I might have to physically overpower them to take it out. I don't want that kind of negativity associated with their periods; they're hard enough already. I mentioned the idea of teaching Maria and Christina to use tampons to a friend of mine. Her response was right on target: "You are just now trying to teach them to put food in their mouths." So true. I'm going to do *that*? I'm still teaching them to chew food.

The idea of helping them clean up and washing them at this age didn't necessarily come easy. Most mothers don't anticipate having to physically help their daughters with toileting during periods. At first, the prospect was very distasteful in my mind, as well. Having no choice but to do it has lessened the chore over time. In a way, it's like changing diapers or cleaning up vomit; these are things mothers just adapt to and do. It's not my choice, but they need the help, and it has become the norm. I don't know if I could ever become comfortable with helping them insert and remove tampons, however, especially if there is no need to cross that line.

Maria doesn't change her pads unless she's told to. Christina is better about this, but Maria, for some reason, doesn't notice when it needs to be changed or simply doesn't want to be bothered with it. Many times, I pick her up from school, and her pants will be stained. I always send them with spare clothes. To help minimize accidents, I have them wear nighttime pads all the time. Since I know Maria is reluctant to change her pad, I should have been more wary one recent morning when she was up and ready unusually early. Mornings are always difficult whether they are having their periods or not. Maria usually takes forever to get dressed; yet on this morning, she had done her hair (usually I help position her ponytail), made her lunch, made her bed, brushed her teeth, and eaten breakfast. She wanted to play on the computer, so I ran through everything to make sure she had done it all before giving her permission to play.

I didn't think about her period, because I knew it should be finishing, and she hadn't called for me to help her. They always call for every little thing. If they don't need me, there is nothing there. On the way to school, however, I decided to ask, "Maria, is your period over? Did you check your pad this morning?" She said no. I asked if she noticed when she went to the bathroom if her pad was soiled or not. Again, she said no. She simply didn't notice it.

Needless to say, this created a fair amount of stress. We have a long drive to school that passes through some sketchy neighborhoods. I didn't want them to be late, but neither did I want her having an embarrassing episode at school. Making matters worse, since I thought her period was over, I didn't pack extra clothes in her book bag. My only option was to stop at the next decent-looking place I could find, which happened to be a doughnut shop I'd never noticed before that day, and have her change her pad.

I shuttled them into the bathroom and prepared to wait as Maria began her shushing and transitional process. I sighed and thought how I could really use an iced coffee. Buying something would make me feel less guilty about coming in to use the bathroom, I rationalized, so I had Christina lock the door while I went to the counter (in sight of the bathroom) and treated myself to a coffee. Maria was just finishing up when I returned. We were able to get back in the car and somehow make it to school on time despite the added stop. I knew the mistake was mine for forgetting to check; but sometimes little things, like getting an iced coffee, can make a big difference in an otherwise chaotic situation. We do the best we can.

Looking toward the Future

One day, I picked Maria up from school without Christina or Anna in the car. We went to the store so she could use her own money to buy a notebook she wanted. On the way, she asked me if she would be able to drive someday. I didn't want to tell her no, so I said we would see. Leaving it open satisfied her and enabled her to share more about her plans for her future. She wants to work at Toys R Us when she grows up. She isn't so sure about leaving home and asks me from time to time if she will be able to stay with us. I always assure her that she can.

Another time, Maria pointed to an elderly couple at church and wanted to know where their kids were. I explained that their children were probably grown up and did not need to be with their parents. She looked up at me with her big brown eyes and asked if I would always be her mommy and if Daddy would always be her daddy. I said, "Yes. Always." I also gave her the example of how Grammy is always my mother even though she lives in a different house. I could tell Maria was still trying to work out how this was going to affect her as an adult, so I added that she would not have to leave home. She thought another minute and asked, "Will I still be able to go to the treasure basket on Sundays?" When I told her yes, she could still get a treat from our treasure basket each week, she was once again at ease.

Maria often expresses concern about her future, and sometimes, it comes up in different ways. When she first started realizing that she was growing up, she asked me about having a baby. I explained if she wanted to have a baby, she could get married and ask God to give her a baby. Her next question was, "If I don't get married, can I stay with you and Daddy?" I enjoy having these moments with her; I can see in her that she's realizing she is growing up and wants to find her place in the world.

As the girls get older, we overhear them talking with each other from time to time about their futures. They ask each other if they want to have babies or get married. Usually, the answer is no, at least for Maria and Christina. Anna wants to have children someday, but she is always concerned about her sisters' well-being too. Of course, we'll never know how their wants and desires will change when they become adults, but for now, I find great warmth in knowing that they all see themselves fitting in each other's lives. Maria and Christina inherently seem to know that they will be living together and taking care of each other and that they most likely won't have children of their own and that Anna will. Of course, there is also sadness about this reality on my part, but that grief is a burden I will gladly bear for them if it means they are safe and happy.

It's probably a blessing that they don't want children; if they dreamed of becoming mothers, the discussions and moral decisions we'd be faced with would be a lot harder than they already are, at least in terms how those choices blend with their emotional happiness. Jeff and I know that we may have to make some difficult decisions regarding birth control at some point, but we are in agreement about having them stay as close to biologically natural as possible for as long as possible. As a parent, the idea of birth control with a special needs daughter always turns your stomach. More often than not, the discussion turns to sexual abuse, which is a sickening thought. Sadly, it is a statistical reality that cannot be ignored. As horrific as the act of abuse would be for a special needs teenage girl or woman, I can only imagine what trauma a pregnancy would bring.

I wish I knew that I could put them on a pill that would ensure everything would be okay, that they'd be protected from becoming pregnant and would not have to manage periods when I'm not there to help. But I don't. Our history with medications has proven otherwise. Drugs may help for a while, but then they can turn disastrous. We don't and won't ever know the full scope of the damage that's been done because of negative effects of medications they've already taken. I can't fathom the idea of adding one more drug into their systems, and I know there are medical procedures available to stop menstruation either temporarily or permanently. When I hear doctors say that girls don't need to have periods anymore if they don't want them, that's scary to me. Sterilization, even temporarily, seems so unnatural.

Jeff and I have talked about this in depth. Our conclusion is that much of this debate about birth control comes from the idea that girls are having sex outside of marriage. In regard to our girls, if they have their own place someday and have company coming and going, then yes, we'll want to look at options. But as far as them living here at home, birth control is not necessary. Until then, our goal is to continue teaching them the skills of managing their periods and keeping themselves clean so that someday, when they are living independently, they can handle it on their own.

Puberty does have its challenges. Emotions can run high, anxiety-related behaviors are exacerbated, and mothers of special needs girls may need to take on some undesirable tasks. But it isn't all bad. There are so many special and tender moments that come during these years, often when we least expect it. They constantly surprise us with new ways they see the world expanding around them. They've crossed new milestones both at home and at school, and we've applauded their accomplishments along the way. As a mother, I've enjoyed special moments with my daughters teaching them to dress, sit, and carry themselves like young ladies. From birth to adulthood, they are my precious children, and I cherish each moment of watching their personalities develop as they blossom into young women.

Discipline

Fine Line between Discipline and Devastation
Parenting Special Needs Children

According to *Random House Webster's*, the word *discipline* has multiple meanings. The one Jeff and I endeavor to parent by is this: "to bring to a state of order and obedience by training and control." This includes blending nuances of instruction, repetition, rules, and when needed, correction. People often confuse discipline with punishment. Punishment may be a piece of the equation; but true discipline—or order—is only achieved when punishment is used appropriately and in conjunction with providing the children an opportunity to learn, practice, and master the skills necessary to live according to the expectations we set forth. Discipline starts with us, the parents. It's up to us to define the order by which we want our family to live. While this may sound easy enough, any parent knows that when dealing with children, even the best laid plans can be difficult to achieve. It takes persistence, patience, and consistency.

With special needs children, the endeavor is even more difficult. They often lack the coping skills to handle disappointment, change, or tension of any kind. They may have very limited ability to remember what is expected of them, from one day to the next—without continual reinforcement from the parents. The need to establish the difference between right and wrong behavior is a given; coping with children who are emotionally ill-equipped to handle the disappointment of being told "No!" is quite another matter. When they have such difficulty just transitioning from one activity to the next, how seemingly impossible must it be for them to be denied in total—simply, to have to accept the word *no.*

A single parental misstep can lead to an emotional unraveling, and chaos can ensue within moments. Some days, when the kids aren't feeling well or if we've allowed ourselves to become lax in our efforts, the entire day can be like walking a tightrope, tiptoeing a fine line between discipline and devastation.

Creating a United Front

The only effective way to instill discipline is for both parents to be working together. There must be cooperation and agreement between the adults in order to have any effect on the children. Not only do the kids need to know what is expected of them and what the consequences are for not behaving in a way that upholds those expectations, but they also need to know that both Mom and Dad have the same set of rules. Kids need to know that what one parent says comes from both of them. Conversely, parents need to communicate with each other to make sure they continue working together toward the common goal of raising children according to their shared beliefs and values.

This is often easier said than done, especially in homes with one parent working and one staying at home. Since I am with them all day, there have been times when I find myself feeling like it will never get better and that the constant effort will never pay off. We go through phases when each day feels like starting over, and the cycle just seems to go on forever. For me, this becomes discouraging, and I'll find myself becoming lax in my disciplinary efforts. Sometimes, I just want to make it through the day and can lose sight of the larger goal. Of course, as I begin to pull back, the burden shifts to Jeff, who hasn't had the benefit of being able to nip behaviors in the bud throughout the day. Instead of being proactive during these times and taking control to handle situations as they arise, I overlook some of the minor infractions throughout the day, sending mixed messages to the girls and allowing the minor issues to escalate over a period of days until we have larger challenges to contend with.

Rather than tuning out the nuisance behaviors because I don't want to deal with correcting them at that moment, I should be intervening immediately to let the girls know I am always in control. Jeff can see when I'm letting them get away with things I shouldn't, and he reminds me that when I don't act like I'm in charge 100 percent of the time, I am unintentionally negating my authority. And the kids are quick to pick up on that. They simply don't respond the same. They become more difficult; I try to avoid further conflict by intervening less, but as a result, the bad behaviors quickly spin out of control. Jeff is more consistent with his parenting style (being at work during the day and catching a break from the kids, no doubt, helps); but expecting him to right the listing ship each day, the moment he gets home from work, is not the answer.

If I am not in charge, things don't happen the way they should. At the risk of sounding antifeminist, the kitchen is my kingdom, and in order to establish discipline and control, it's important that I embrace it as such. Mornings are the hardest part of the day, and the kitchen is the epicenter. From there, I oversee the progress and preparations for getting out of the house on time. In military terms, it's my command center, and I'm responsible for making sure everything goes according to plan. That's because I'm always here. When Jeff comes through on his way to work or on the weekend, it's like the general showing up. The general can and will pick up the slack, but when operations are running smoothly, he doesn't need to.

When Jeff has to become more disciplinarian than Dad, the relationship between the girls and their father changes. We noticed this happening with Anna for a while when I had become lax with her. Jeff was always the one correcting her, and because she was getting away with certain behaviors around me, there were more behaviors for him to correct. Anna started feeling like she was always in trouble with him, which made her cautious of him when he was home. We want our daughters to respect, not fear us, so this was something we needed to correct in order to eliminate the strain it was putting on their relationship. I had to be more firm and consistent with Anna throughout the day so she would understand the rules were coming from both of us, not just Jeff.

Conversely, we had an opposite experience with Christina. When Maria and Christina were very little, we made the mistake of allowing Maria to become Jeff's baby and Christina to become my baby. We loved them both equally, but we let them bond with us separately. Maria followed Jeff everywhere; she was his little shadow. We didn't question that Maria did this or why Christina didn't until one day when Christina was grabbing and pulling on the vertical blinds. Jeff told her to stop and swatted her on her diaper. She gave him a look of complete shock, like she was thinking, "Who is this person?" Jeff and I both saw her expression; it was as if he was a stranger to her. That's when we realized that she hadn't been bonding with him the same as Maria. Christina wasn't connecting him with what was happening to her in her life. We had to immediately make changes to eliminate those disconnects.

In order for my disciplinary efforts to work, I have to remember to communicate with Jeff so that he knows what challenges I am experiencing with the girls on any given day. For instance, when Maria misbehaves all day, refuses to eat, snots her nose continuously, and has not responded to any of my reprimands, I only have one opportunity left to make an impression on her that day—bedtime. She loves the special attention she receives during our nightly bedtime ritual. I have learned that this can also be a highly effective tool for making her understand when I've been displeased with her behavior throughout the day. I say good night and tuck her in, but I don't linger and give her the special attention she wants. Usually, this has positive results, and the next day, she will try to behave better. However, if I fail to tell Jeff that I have reached that point with her and he goes in and tells her good night as if everything is fine, all of my efforts throughout the day are lost. The result—we are back to square one the next day.

Order from Chaos

As parents, we are the leaders of our family. We have to have standards that define how we will parent, or lead, our children as they grow up. Good leadership includes instilling discipline that is just, predictable, and balanced with love. Kids have a keen sense of justice; they always know whether something is fair or not. When the girls start acting up, our goal is to react swiftly with a clear message: under no circumstances will the undesired behavior be allowed. We believe that discipline needs to be clear and consistent. The kids need to understand the reason, the expected behavior, and the consequences for misbehavior.

We do not believe in excusing our special needs children from having self-discipline just because of their challenges. We do, however, realize that the expectations we set forth for them must be within their ability to achieve. As the girls grow and improve their skills, we increase our expectations accordingly. This means that we might be working on different issues with each of the girls at any given time. Regardless of any given stage we may be going through with them, we also have house rules that they all need to follow, such as keeping their rooms clean, picking up after themselves, and doing what they are told. The rules are meant not only to keep order but also to build character and independence.

When we start having problems with their behavior, we can usually look back and see that the problem stemmed from a lack of predictability on our part. Jeff is consistent in his disciplinary efforts with the girls, and they usually respond to him. For instance, for him, all it takes is a word and sometimes just a look, and Christina will stop huffing. For me, though, it takes me a lot more effort and sometimes physical intervention to help her regain control of her breathing. When I get tired, I am more prone to letting certain behaviors slide. This, in turn, means my reactions aren't quite as consistent or predictable as Jeff's. The girls will take advantage of that and will act up even more around me. Then when I've finally had enough and try to regain control, my reactions aren't as just or fair as they should be, because the expected consequences were not clear, consistent, or predictable. That is my continual struggle: to remain balanced and predictable day in and day out, regardless of the tedium.

In order to achieve order and calm in our home, we know that we must train the girls to behave according to our expectations. This includes cleaning up after themselves without being told, taking their school bags to their rooms when they get home instead of dropping them at the door, and doing chores or homework without continually being told to stay on task. When parents are having a problem with their child, they should first determine if it's due to a training problem, a lack of discipline, or some other issue. In my case, sometimes it's my inconsistency, sometimes it's their high anxiety, and sometimes it is a training problem.

Training is essential for encouraging the positive behaviors we want to instill in the girls, but first, we have to have the discipline in place for it to be effective. As an example, when we wanted to move Maria and Christina forward with their diets, we first needed to look at our family's mealtime routine. Anna and I were eating on the same schedule, but with the other two needing liquids or special diets, I was allowing them to eat separately at the kitchen bar or drink their nutrition shakes in front of the TV. There wasn't any structure in the way we approached meals. But in order to get them to eat different foods (which was the hard part), they needed to have a structured mealtime with a group dynamic. When we sit and eat as a family, each child benefits. If one is good, the others hear those praises. Just as when one is bad, the others see those consequences. Simply sitting together creates an atmosphere that allows them to better understand the expectations. That piece needed to be in place before we could even begin working with them to eat new foods.

When things get chaotic, we have to come down hard to regain control, or else one will feed off the other and the chaotic behavior will continue escalating. We use a variety of techniques to get their attention because what works one day may not be effective the next. Time-outs worked well when they were young, and while these still work on occasion, taking something away that they want works much better now that they are older. For example, if toys are not picked up, I will put everything that hasn't been put away into a trash bag; they can earn those items back after a period of good behavior. When time-outs and deprivation fail, the laborious task of writing a short sentence multiple times has been effective. This is difficult for Christina because of her fine motor challenges. Maria writes well, but the task takes her a very long time. It usually makes an impression on them.

For Maria, nominal rewards, such as paper stickers, are very good incentives. On one difficult morning, I was giving her eggs and oatmeal, and she asked if she could eat her oatmeal before her eggs. She only wanted the oatmeal, so by allowing her to eat it first, I lost my leverage for being able to get her to eat the eggs she didn't want. She completely refused to touch them, and I had nothing left to use as motivation.

Sometimes, the best course of action I can take is to just remove myself from the area when they start acting out. For instance, Maria likes to come into my bathroom while I'm getting ready. If she starts shushing and spitting, instead of scolding her, I simply walk out of the bathroom and crouch down on the other side of my bed where she can't see me. She comes out, doesn't see anyone, and leaves the room. The point we are trying to drive home with her is that people don't want to be around her when she behaves that way. We want her to learn to control it.

There are some behaviors that we won't tolerate for any reason, such as talking back. That's one of those behaviors that may not seem like a big deal when kids are little, but the idea of a sarcastic, disrespectful teen is less than appealing. Everyone knows that the teenage years can be difficult. Why would we want to make it worse by adding that into the mix? Parents need to look past the cuteness of the little kid and envision them as teens. If that foundation isn't there and those early negative behaviors aren't nipped in the bud, adolescence will be extremely difficult. There's only a limited window of being able to teach children those lessons. Once they are older, it's too late.

Once when Maria was younger, she lay down on the floor at the grocery store and refused to get up. I was terribly embarrassed and did not want to create a scene. Of course, knowing that people were watching and security cameras were recording everything, I felt even more pressure to end the standoff without incident. Here's this cute little girl, all dressed up with her hair done, lying on the floor, not minding me—her mother—when I told her to get up. Instead of doing anything dramatic that would have made the situation worse, I quietly leaned down and whispered to her, "If you don't get up, I'm going to paddle you." She jumped right up without a sound. I was relieved because I didn't really intend on spanking her, but I needed her to respond without causing a scene. Luckily, it worked. If she had had no regard or respect for my authority, who knows how long I would've struggled to get her off the floor? Just as with trying to prevent creating a petulant, back-talking teen, when the usually adorable child is lying on the floor testing her boundaries, it is too late to expect results if discipline hasn't been instilled. That piece already needs to be in place so the child knows that when Mom or Dad says something, they mean it.

Even after children learn to respect parental authority, they will still push limits every so often. During these times, it is important to react swiftly and not to make empty threats. Parents always need to be prepared to back up their words with action, even if it means the child will be disappointed or miss out on something he or she has been looking forward to. When Anna was habitually slacking on her schoolwork, I decided against allowing her to audition for a play. I didn't want her feeling entitled to things simply because she wanted them. I also wanted her to learn that privileges, like participating in a play, must be earned through good behavior and initiative.

On another occasion, Maria and Christina were to start swimming lessons and were scheduled to test for the right level one day after school. They'd been looking forward to their "tryouts" all week. I had picked the girls up from school and told them we could go through the Chick-fil-A drive-thru on the way home. Maria decided she wanted to go to Burger King; everyone else still wanted Chick-fil-A, so that's where I took them. Maria became upset the minute I said we weren't going to Burger King. She started shushing and wouldn't stop. She was holding the ice cream cone I bought her but wouldn't stop shushing to eat it. As we were driving home, I told her in a very firm voice, "Maria, if you keep shushing and drop that ice cream, I will not take you to try out for swim class today."

When we got home, Maria defiantly dumped the ice cream into the kitchen sink. She clutched the dripping cone in her tight little fist. I pried the messy cone from her fist and sent her out of the kitchen. As frustrating as that was, I still wanted to salvage the afternoon by finding a way to give Maria a way out without undermining my own authority in the process. I scooped the ice cream that was left inside the cone into a bowl and told her that if she ate it, she could still go to the tryouts that day. Meanwhile, Christina was in her room, excitedly changing into her swimsuit. I fixed Christina's hair and gave Maria a final opportunity to eat those few bites of ice cream. Still, she refused. At that point, I had already told her the expectations and the consequences, so I had no choice but to follow through. I left her home and took Christina to the pool.

As it turned out, the instructor advised me to put Christina in the lowest level. There was no need for Maria to return to try out for a higher level since her swimming was comparable to Christina's. When we got home, I explained to Maria that the instructor did not need to see her swim and that she would start in the same class with Christina. I had really wanted for Maria to be able to go to the tryouts, but I had to hold firm and take that away from her as a punishment for her behavior. She felt an immediate consequence, but it was not excessive to the point of excluding altogether the upcoming lessons. Christina, meanwhile, was beaming with pride for her "successful" tryout. I had wished for the same for Maria, but it was not to be.

In order for discipline to be effective, the punishment needs to fit the crime. It's also important for parents to isolate the exact behavior that is being punished. We've all had those days when our kids seem to be doing everything they can to try our patience. Usually, they do something that displeases us, and before long, they can't seem to do anything right. However, when we stop to think about it, there is really only that first issue at the heart of the problem. The rest fall under a phenomenon Jeff and I call "stacking the charges." When a parent is irritated with one behavior, it's very easy to find many other behaviors to add to the list. This not only creates a situation where it's nearly impossible for the child to do anything right, but the consequences for the main infraction are more severe than necessary because of all these other faults added in; and unless the punishment is fair, specific, and timely, the child may not associate the consequences with the bad behavior.

Also key to instilling discipline is maintaining the right level of positive reinforcement for expected outcomes. When I was trying to potty train Anna, I offered her a tangible reward, displayed on the kitchen counter, for the purpose of reminding and motivating her. It didn't work. After several days, Jeff said that it was representing failure more than a possible reward, so we took it away. We also realized, at that point, that Anna was no longer motivated to please me or perform to my expectations. I had erred in being too liberal with my affection. In retrospect, I was spoiling her at that time; I was struggling with the realization that my last baby was growing up. In showering her with affection, whether she had earned it or not, I had let things get out of balance. That was not in her best interest, and it took some discipline on my part to get things back on track. In contrast, now when I ask the girls to unload the dishwasher, all three try their hardest to do a good job to help me so they will receive the praise afterward.

Sometimes, I give them little treats when they complete a specific task. Beads, stickers, pennies, check marks on a chart—mostly anything will work. These rewards are great motivators, and the girls enjoy receiving them; however, material rewards never take the place of the emotional reward that comes with parental approval. At the end of the day, praise for good behavior and for trying to achieve the goals we set for them is the best reward. When we've created a fair and balanced environment, the girls thrive from knowing they're earning our approval and meeting our expectations.

Approval is not to be confused with love. They know we love them unconditionally. Praise and approval are earned through their efforts, which, in turn, build their confidence and self-esteem as they learn that controlling their behavior brings favorable reactions from the world around them. Likewise, they need to understand that other people don't have to, or want to, tolerate bad behavior. For Maria and Christina, learning self-control is paramount for them to be independent and hold jobs as adults. Not teaching them this now does them a huge disservice later.

When Maria started a wailing phase a few years ago, she made life very hard both at home and at school. The teacher called me to discuss it. I remember her saying, "That's a real showstopper, Mrs. Ames." Jeff and I explained to Maria that this was unacceptable. She knew wailing would get her in trouble, but she continued doing it. Finally, Jeff told her that the teacher did not have to put up with that behavior and that if she didn't stop wailing she might be sent to a different school. Maria also knew that a classmate had recently been moved to a different school because of a behavior issue. Her eyes got real big; we could tell she was putting the pieces together. She did not want to go a different school and stopped wailing after that conversation.

Once when Christina lost a tooth and was expecting to receive a visit from the tooth fairy, we took the opportunity to use it as a teaching moment. She had been in trouble most of the day because she refused to stop huffing. When she awoke the next morning, she was disappointed not to find money under her pillow. We told her the tooth fairy knew about her behavior the day before and that she'd visit after Christina proved she could control her huffing. That day, Christina did a much better job and was rewarded with a visit from the tooth fairy, reinforcing that both negative and positive behaviors have consequences.

Discouragement

Perhaps one of the greatest challenges in establishing discipline for our special needs children is their inability to understand the emotional nuances of those around them. Unlike Anna, who knows she's done something wrong just by the expression on my face, Maria and Christina are impervious to our moods. They are like Teflon— they are tough emotionally and tough physically. They lack the comprehension to know that Mom's had a bad day or that the rules may be different because of some other variance in the routine. Anna can understand that if something is going on and the rules are lax one day, that doesn't mean they no longer exist. Christina and Maria don't see that. With them, if they get away with something one day, they should be able to get away with it the next.

Conversely, there are many behaviors we struggle to correct day after day after day. Every day is like starting over. It's as if we are Bill Murray in the movie *Groundhog Day*, reliving the same day, over and over. Even though we acknowledge there have been times we haven't handled things perfectly, Jeff and I also know how many times we've put them in the corner for the same thing. We know how many times we've corrected them. Yet we still can't expect that they won't repeat the same behavior again the next day. For us, sitting there exhausted at the end of a long day, it is sad to realize that they simply don't understand.

As much as I try to keep my spirits up, I have times when the endless repetition becomes too discouraging. I look at them and think it's hopeless, that we'll never get there. Of course, allowing myself to have those thoughts doesn't help. Between Christina's refusal to eat and Maria's continual stubbornness, we have something we have dubbed our own version of the war on terror—a mission that will never be over regardless of the small victories. It can sometimes become just too much to take.

In 2004, Christina flatly refused to eat anything other than her beloved SpaghettiOs. We did everything we could think of to get her to eat something, anything, else. We were worried about her nutrition, her chewing and swallowing development, and her future ability to adjust socially. To top it all, a nutritionist we knew well firmly believed that Christina's issues, including her seizures, were born of a gluten intolerance, which we were knowingly aggravating with the diet of SpaghettiOs. After months of this battle, I broke. I cried for three days straight. I was overwhelmed by the sheer hopelessness of the situation. At that point in time, I truly believed that nothing I would ever do was going to help them. I couldn't see beyond the struggles and failures. I couldn't see the things we had done right or the ways they were improving.

It was during that same period of time that I temporarily stopped working with them on their schoolwork. Jeff and I talked about it, and he encouraged me to try to figure out why I had let that piece of our routine slip away. In reflection, I realized that some part of me had given up because I couldn't see the progress. It wasn't an intentional giving up so much as a gradual discouragement that weighed my spirit down. After much soul-searching and a break to re-charge my resolve, I vowed to focus on the small victories to better keep the bigger picture in perspective.

We still struggle with the same issues but are now able to look at them from a different, more positive, angle. For instance, every week or so, Maria will backslide and lay down the gauntlet. For a long time, this was so tiring and overwhelmed me with feelings of failure and discouragement. It helped immensely, one day, to go back and reread Dr. Dobson's *The Strong-Willed Child* and be reminded that her stubbornness was normal and was not a personality deficiency. It is part of who she is and will be there always. Instead of trying to change her personality, I have gradually learned to work with it. I have learned to be more aggressive and not coddle or negotiate with her. The minute she starts to snot her nose (this is her primary act of rebellion), I take immediate disciplinary action. It's typically off with the TV, away with her favorite toy, or off she goes to the corner, to contemplate her misbehavior. With Maria, especially, swift and consistent reaction is our best tool to curb the undesirable behaviors; stickers and rewards are the best approach for encouraging the behaviors we want.

Potty training was extremely difficult. Maria seemed to be unable to grasp the concept of what I wanted. I tried different types of training pants to no avail. She eventually would sit on the training toilet but only to pee through her pants. The only way I made any progress was by using a reward system. I bought a huge set of plastic food, that she loved to play with, and gave her a piece each time she used the potty correctly. The training process took forever, and Maria was not fully potty-trained until after we moved to Florida, and she was more than six years old.

Christina was a little easier to potty-train, but the process was still tedious. Stickers were a better reward for her, so I put a bowlful in the bathroom. When she used the toilet, she was allowed to pick a sticker for her chart. Looking back, this was our first indication of

Christina's methodical, orderly personality; it would take her forever to pick out a sticker. Jeff joked, "If she's anything like you, she's in there collating and processing." In a way, she was doing something very similar. She was making sure she had one of each type of sticker. Eventually, I learned to put fewer choices in the bowl, and the decision-making process, at least, picked up a little speed.

While discipline and behavior training are essential to keeping order in our home, they are also integral to proper social interaction. While Maria can be maddeningly stubborn, she is also a gregarious, loving little girl. She is very affectionate with people we meet and can quickly become the center of attention. We are reluctant to discourage her social nature but know we must also work with her to temper how she displays it, especially as she gets bigger and stronger. She can hug too hard, and at church, she might grab a person's hand and not let go, even if she's shushing and stimming. I sometimes must pry her fingers loose to release her grip, and I must always guard against the danger this can pose for a frail, elderly person. Christina, too, is prone to attract attention when we are out and about. She can quickly dominate any conversation with her repetitive questions and insistence on responses. Improving their socialization skills and self-discipline is a never-ending endeavor.

Money

Part of discipline includes teaching our children how to earn, save, and manage money. As a conceptual theory, this will be difficult to teach to Maria and Christina, but it's important that they come to understand it. To accomplish this, we provide them with opportunities to earn, save, and spend money on a regular basis.

All three girls receive an allowance each week. They each have a special place to keep their money. We encourage them to put half of what they earn toward savings; the other half is theirs to save or spend. When they want to earn extra money, we provide ways to do that through extra chores or by having yard sales. We allow them to keep the proceeds from any of their belongings they sell. If the yard sale is a bust, we donate their things to charity, and I pay them the going "yard sale" rate.

When they've saved enough or have received money as a gift, I take them to a store so they can buy something for themselves. Each of the girls has a different approach to spending money. At the extremes, Maria spends all of hers right away while Anna saves and saves. If one spends all her money, the others will usually tease her about not having any left, which can create some tension. Occasionally, one or another will become upset later if she loses interest in her purchase (usually because she's out of money and then sees her sisters buying something else), but allowing them to experience that regret is part of the learning process. I'd rather them grasp this now with toys than later as adults, when mishandling money creates larger problems.

While we like giving them an opportunity to earn money for doing certain chores, we also want them to know that money isn't the only reason for helping out around the house. Sometimes, things just need to be done, and everyone needs to help. One such lesson occurred during an afternoon when I'd asked all three of them to help clean up outside by sweeping the deck and bagging up leaves and debris on the lawn. Maria and Christina were working hard—hoping for an opportunity to earn extra money. Anna, on the other hand, wasn't helping at all. She had decided she'd rather watch TV. She wasn't interested in earning money. I sent her out to help, anyway. Reluctantly, Anna joined her sisters but exerted minimal effort while they finished up. I was not happy with her attitude, so when the job was done, I sent her to the corner while her sisters relaxed and watched TV.

When Jeff arrived home from work, I told him of the day's events. He tried to talk to Anna during dinner, but she wasn't listening and, instead, asked to be excused from the table to go watch TV. Jeff sent her to room, instead. When I tucked Anna in that evening, I tried to explain how her behavior had been selfish and uncaring of others, which we don't tolerate in our home. I could tell that the message still wasn't getting through. So Jeff went in and spoke to her. He reminded her of the time she met him in the driveway, coming home from work, pleading for him to fix her broken squirrel feeder. There she was, asking for help with something she wanted, and he had not yet even had a chance to come inside and put his things down after a long hard day at work. He reminded her how he had willingly helped her, simply because she had asked him, even though he was tired and would've preferred to do something else.

Jeff went on to explain how he chose to help her and put her desires before his own. Then he brought it around to how when Mommy asks for her help, Anna (or Maria or Christina) needs to be willing to help even if she doesn't feel like it at the time. Each member of the family has a responsibility to contribute. Money is only one element. It is a nice reward, but each of the girls also needs to understand that the best reward is being part of a family that loves and respects one another.

When it comes to discipline, our ultimate goals are to train the girls, instill self-discipline and initiative, and teach them to take responsibility for themselves. If we tell them we expect for them to complete a set of regular chores, we want to get to the point where they will do those chores without being told. We also know that the only way these goals will be accomplished is if we are diligent about following up on the rules and expectations we've established. If we don't hold them accountable, they will not learn to be responsible adults. I also have to hold myself accountable in the process. For me, it helps to visualize having a rope attached between us. If I asked them to clean up their rooms, I must follow from my imaginary end of the rope to make sure the job has been done.

When I become tired or discouraged, I have to stop and remind myself of the greater purpose. I don't want to find myself sitting up late worrying about Anna when she's missed curfew as a teenager because I failed to raise her to be dependable. With Maria and Christina, my fear is not teaching them to be independent enough to hold a job. By thinking beyond the moment, the day, or any given difficult phase, I remember how important the tasks of discipline and training are. Yes, the process is tiresome, frustrating, discouraging, and relentless. But if Jeff and I remain steadfast in our principles as we work to achieve our parental goals, one day, we will be able to look at them as adults and take pride in their characteristics of self-discipline, initiative, and responsibility. I will smile to myself and know what I have accomplished and how worthwhile the effort was.

Crossing the Devastation Line

Chaos had gradually crept into our home again. It didn't happen overnight, but there we found ourselves again: none of the girls were minding us, and each one was getting up and coming out of her bedroom repeatedly after being sent to bed. Maria was rallying to stay home from school the next day by trying to convince us she wasn't feeling well. Christina and Anna found a Silly Bandz on Christina's floor and became obsessed with figuring out whose it was. I had been giving them Silly Bandz—fun little stretchy bracelets that come in lots of different shapes—instead of stickers as rewards for getting ready for school on time. The Silly Bandz were a good incentive, and the girls were enjoying collecting them. This particular evening, however, my Silly Bandz strategy backfired on me.

Christina and Anna had started on their investigative mission to find the owner of the wayward octopus-shaped Silly Bandz. They asked Maria if she was missing any of hers. She said no. They wanted to know how many octopi Maria had in her collection. She said two, both of which were accounted for. All three girls then came to see me. I told them we would figure it out later and to go back to bed. Maria was in an emotional crisis by this point. She had already been agitated and whining all evening, so the unaccounted-for Silly Bandz sent her into OCD meltdown mode. I tucked Maria and Christina back into bed, but Anna was dawdling and taking her time to change, something that she'd been doing more and more often that was making me increasingly irritated with her. I decided to go to my room for a breather while I waited for Anna to finish getting into bed so I could tuck her in.

In the meantime, Maria had gotten out of bed again and went out to the living room whining to Jeff about the Silly

Bandz. In retrospect, part of the problem was that he didn't know what they were or why the girls had them. It wasn't that he would have objected or disagreed with using them as a reward, but he was caught off guard and didn't understand why they were making such a big deal over something that seemed so trivial. He confiscated Maria's box of Silly Bandz and told her she couldn't have it back until morning because she kept getting out of bed. This caused her to become extremely distressed; she cried out for me in a panic about her Silly Bandz collection. Jeff was upset because he didn't know what all the fuss was about. I explained the reward system and told him I thought with-holding Maria's collection from her was excessive—taking away something that meant so much to her wasn't fair, especially considering her personality and need to have everything in its place.

By the time the evening was over and I had placated Maria, calmed Christina, who feeds off Maria's emotions, and finally got Anna to bed, Jeff and I were as agitated with each other as we were with them. The evening had been a vicious cycle of chasing one child after another to diffuse the mounting chaos. I agreed in hindsight that Maria was overreacting more than usual that evening, but in the heat of the moment, with all three girls pushing our buttons, we both reached our tolerance limits. This, in turn, added to their escalating emotional crises. And what triggered it all? A tiny plastic pink octopus. Sometimes, the best way to stop the chaos is to step back and figure out what is at its center. We had gradually lost control of all discipline at that bewitching hour of bedtime.

Lady

The girls have wanted a dog for many years. Neither Jeff nor I have had a dog since leaving our childhood homes. Neither of us felt a need to get another one. For a while, we satisfied their yearnings for a canine companion with mechanical toy dogs. Then when we bought our current home, Jeff finally agreed that when Maria turned fifteen, we could get a dog. This gave them two years to work on their behavior, do their chores, and prove they could take care of a dog (and, as we secretly hoped, maybe lose interest in the idea). Even though they still had to wait two years, they were so excited they sat down and came up with the name Lady, just like the adorable cocker spaniel in Disney's *Lady and the Tramp*. They also wanted to show us how well they would take care of their future puppy by divvying up the tasks: Maria would take Lady outside to potty, Christina would feed her, and Anna would be responsible for bathing her.

When Maria turned fifteen, the girls had not forgotten Daddy's promise. I have to admit that I was not too anxious for the new addition, but they were so excited about getting the pet they had begged and pleaded for and worked to earn that we could not go back on our word. To prove their commitment, all three saved money, combined allowances and birthday and holiday money, and had a yard sale to come up with enough money to buy the dog. Altogether, they came up with an impressive $365. The search was on.

Knowing what a commitment a dog is and not wanting to get one that wouldn't work with our family, we carefully researched breeds and temperaments. I have pet allergies, so we narrowed our search to a breed that didn't shed and had hair rather than the fur, which would trigger my allergies. When I pictured having a dog in the house, I imagined my friend's tiny Yorkshire terrier. However, we soon learned that a larger breed would be more suitable. Because Maria and Christina don't always realize how rough they are, the dog needed to be large enough to withstand their affection. Early in our search, the owner of one pet store was very adamant that he would not sell us a dog too delicate for our family. I was a bit surprised at just how forceful he was in his position, but I was not offended, and we heeded his warning by seeking a slightly larger breed than the toy-sized puppy we had first fallen for in his shop.

During our search, we met with a breeder who had a black poodle that I bonded with right away. For weeks, I couldn't stop thinking about this sweet little dog. I thought it might be "the one" until we went back and learned that this particular dog had heart problems; it was going to require more tests and specialized treatments throughout its life. I was in shock. Needless to say, the odds of having two special needs children and then finding a special needs dog seemed unimaginable. I thought back to how quickly the dog had bonded to me; it must have sensed I had the ability to take care of it. Realistically, however, Jeff and I both knew that bringing a dog with known health issues into the home wasn't the best choice.

We added our name to the wait list at shelters (young, smaller, nonshedding dogs are the highest in demand). We saw puppies that the girls couldn't afford and others they could but didn't bond with. Then one day, we stopped to play with the puppies at a pet store after getting family photos taken at the mall. That's when we finally found our Lady. She was in a cage alone, a black shedless "peek-a-poo," which is a nice sturdy cross between a Pekinese and a poodle. She was adorable and playful. Even Christina touched her, which was something she hadn't really done with any of the other puppies we'd seen. I knew this might be the one, so I called Jeff as he was leaving work and asked him to come by the pet store. Jeff saw the puppy, confirmed the health guarantee, and gave his approval. We told Anna, and then watched in delight as she told her sisters.

Loaded with all the new-puppy accoutrements, we brought our little Lady home. Over the next few weeks, we worked on training her to ring a bell near the door when she needed to go outside to potty. We gradually transitioned her from a crate to a bed and, when she was ready, gave her full run of the house. We posted a schedule assigning each of the girls a shift for making sure Lady was taken outside to potty and had food and water in her bowl. If Lady had an accident in the house, whoever was responsible for potty duty during that time had to clean up the mess.

As is to be expected with a new puppy, the training wasn't always easy, and we had plenty of accidents to clean up. Likewise, as is also to be expected with children, scooping poop and cleaning up after the puppy soon lost its appeal. I'll admit, Jeff and I shared a few heated discussions about our new addition and the girls' lack of participation during those first few weeks. Then one afternoon, I looked outside and saw all three girls, walking in shoulder-to-shoulder formation, carrying bags and small shovels, back and forth across the lawn. Jeff had them scour every inch of the yard for Lady's waste. The sight reminded me of watching sailors inspect the deck of an aircraft carrier for the tiniest pieces of debris before allowing the jets to take off. The military-style drill worked; ever since that day, the girls have been much better about cleaning up after Lady.

Despite the early training challenges, having Lady has been a wonderful experience. We all had to adjust to the new dynamic of having a pet in our home. Ultimately, Lady has taught each of the girls a lot about responsibility, caring for another living creature, and how to behave around animals. In the beginning, Maria always wanted to hold her too tight, almost confining Lady in her lap. As much as we told her not to, Lady was the one that taught Maria to be gentler by issuing a warning nip one day when she'd had enough.

Similarly, Christina loves playing tug-of-war with Lady. At first, Christina was determined to win, and no matter how hard Lady tugged, Christina always tugged harder, sometimes lifting Lady off the ground and even flinging her a few feet when Lady finally let go. We explained how that hurt Lady and that she would stop playing if it wasn't fun for her. Christina finally understood that in order for the game to be fun for Lady, Lady needed to win too.

Of course, Lady has her moments and needs reprimanding. When she has an accident, she receives a timeout. My father was visiting one day when Lady was put in timeout. He looked at me inquisitively for an explanation, so I told him that since the girls are sent to timeout when they misbehave, we started doing it with the dog too. It's effective, and the girls understand it. My father found it comical; of course, we never had timeouts for either dogs or us kids when I was growing up.

The girls have grown very fond of Lady, and she of them. She is very protective of them and will growl if they are sleeping on the couch and Jeff or I start to rouse them to their beds. Christina is intrigued with Lady's little black nose. She likes to touch it gently and say, "Boop." This little endearment has caught on, and now all of us, except Jeff, have started doing it too.

At one point, they decided they wanted her to be a show dog. I explained that she wouldn't make a good show dog because she has an underbite, adding that this is also what makes her more special to us and reaffirming that we wouldn't want her to be any different. Maria was sitting on the kitchen floor, holding Lady at the time. I could tell she took this to heart. Lady's underbite holds a special significance for her now. In some small way, this helped Maria understand that love is not dependent on perfection. We love others for who they are, and it's the imperfections that make them unique and special.

We adore Lady and are glad to have made the decision to bring her into our lives. I'm also glad for the timing of when we decided to get her. If we had given in and gotten the girls a dog sooner, the results probably would not have been so positive. By making them wait and earn her, they were ready.

Diffusing Sibling Rivalry

Maria, Christina, and Anna love each other dearly and are best friends most of the time. But like all sisters, they have their spats, which are typically sparked by a sense of competition with one another. When they start fighting, if we can't resolve the disagreement within a few minutes, I send each of the participants to her room. From that point, they know they have to solve their own problems. There is always a tendency for a parent to feel like we know who is right and who is wrong, but I want them to learn to resolve their own difficulties instead of relying on me to be there as a referee. I get in the crossfire once in a while, but for the most part, they manage to work things out on their own. The best thing I can do is separate them until they regain control of their tempers. From there, they find a way to make peace with each other, even if it takes a couple of days. I will intervene, however, if I catch one intentionally antagonizing her sister, because that goes against our family rule of treating each other with kindness.

Part 4

Family and Spirituality

Siblings

Saint Anna (Mostly)

Having two children with developmental delays, that went undiagnosed during early childhood, created a somewhat skewed perception for me of what parenting small children was supposed to be like. It wasn't until we had Anna that I began to realize how much I had missed out on, with Maria and Christina. The way Anna was able to communicate her feelings and express her emotions and imagination as a toddler and preschooler induced mixed feelings. I was simultaneously elated and grieving. I delighted in every moment of watching Anna discover the world around her during those magical years; yet with each new experience, I was reminded of just how much I had been robbed of with my older two daughters.

Over the years, the differences between Anna and her sisters have manifested in a variety of ways. After we learned about Maria's and Christina's genetic anomalies, we were better able to understand why there was such a difference between them and Anna. And as we adjusted to the diagnosis, we came to understand that parenting each of our daughters was going to require a different approach. With Anna, we have to be constantly aware of making sure her needs are being met in balance with the heightened demands of her sisters' needs. We also have to remain committed to our ideals of raising Anna in a way that allows her to reach her potential without letting her be swallowed up in the identity of being the sister of two girls with special needs. This can go both ways. The challenge comes with finding the right balance.

With Anna, we need to set the bar high enough for her to reach her fullest potential, but those expectations also have to be realistic for her. As our only regular-education child, it could be very easy to either spoil her or place too much pressure on her to attain the successes that her sisters will not be able to achieve. But that wouldn't be fair to Anna. We cannot overcompensate by placing all our hopes and expectations that we felt were taken from us with Maria and Christina onto Anna, nor do we want to create a dynamic that causes Anna to resent her sisters for any reason. In many ways, even though she is our youngest, with Anna we experience each stage of development as if it were our first time. She is a beautiful, talented, intelligent, strong-willed girl—sometimes with an attitude to match—who keeps us on our parental toes yet always amazes us with her curiosity and compassion.

Anna and Her Sisters

Anna adores her sisters as they do her. As is expected, they have their conflicts and moments of tension, but overall, the three girls share a strong sisterly bond. It didn't happen instantly. As a newborn, Maria and Christina mostly just tolerated Anna as this new being in the house. Other than the actual homecoming, when Maria was excited to wear her "I'm the big sister" tee shirt that we told her was a gift from Anna, neither of the girls wanted much to do with her until after she started walking. In retrospect, I think Maria remained cautious about Anna, because on some level she remembered how difficult it was when we first brought Christina home. Mostly, however, I think that since the two older girls had each other, they didn't have any reason to be interested in Anna—at least not until she was mobile and was able to play with them.

Finally, when she was about ten months old, they discovered Anna as a new playmate. Anna pulled herself up and was standing at the coffee table next to where her sisters were playing. She slapped the table. This caught their attention, so they slapped the table in response. Anna laughed, causing them to laugh. The game continued back and forth: Maria and Christina were clearly thrilled to realize that she was a new source of entertainment for them.

As they've grown older, their relationship has changed. Despite being the youngest, Anna has surpassed them developmentally. This presents unique challenges, especially when it comes to sibling competitiveness, but for the most part, they all seem to have an inherent understanding of their roles, abilities, and limitations. For example, one day when the three girls were playing house, Anna was playing the role of the mother. I overheard Maria saying that maybe Anna could be the mother when she was older too. Anna replied that even if she was the mother, Maria would always be the big sister. Maria seemed to intuitively know that Anna will be able to take care of them, yet Anna knew then and continues now to respect that Maria's identity as the big sister is important to her, even if Anna eventually does become the caretaker.

The reality of Anna's role as their eventual guardian is never far from our thoughts. We know that a day will come when we may not be able to physically care for Maria and Christina. It is our hope and expectation that Anna will be able to assume the role of guardian when that time comes. Of course, we never want her sisters to be a burden on her, so we are trying to take the necessary steps to ensure Maria and Christina will be as independent as possible. This includes teaching them how to care for themselves on a daily basis so they can live together on their own. We also need to make sure we have the financial piece in place, too, so Anna's primary role as guardian will only need to be that of protector and executor of their accounts rather than provider.

Anna isn't old enough yet to fully understand how her sisters will depend on her in the future, but she has recently started asking questions. The conversation started with her asking if her cousins would come live with us if anything ever happened to my brother and his wife. This gave me the opportunity to tell her about how children need to have adult guardians until they are eighteen. I was then able to explain that Maria and Christina will always need to have a guardian, even after they become adults. Anna wanted to know what would happen if I died. I told her that I would need to find someone else to take on the role of guardian after I am no longer capable. She then asked if she could be their guardian, to which I said yes. I did not tell her we had already planned on that someday, but it warmed my heart to hear her ask on her own.

A few days later, Anna asked if she had to be nice to Maria and Christina because of their special needs. I think she was trying to come to terms with what special needs really means and the implications it could have on her relationship with them. I told her no, that they are her sisters and she needs to treat them like sisters first and foremost. Of course, treating them differently would have been hard for her to imagine. We've never believed in special treatment—just fair treatment for everyone. Certainly, it was a relief for Anna to know that the boundaries of the sisterly relationship they had already established did not need to change.

Today, Anna's role in the relationship sways from friend and defender to competitor and antagonist. As she gets older and wants to assert her own independence, she is learning the balance between tolerating some of her sisters' more irritating behaviors, such as Maria constantly trying to fix Anna's hair and redefining the lines of what she will or won't tolerate from them. Being a preteen (as of this writing), she has limited tools for asserting those new boundaries and often sways between handling situations with maturity or childishness. For example, she is often the first to recognize if I've reacted impatiently or unwittingly created an injustice, yet she is still learning coping skills for times when she's directly involved in the conflict.

While Anna is very tolerant of her sisters, she also has a strong personality and is still learning the art of walking away when something is bothering her. For example, one day she did something that irritated Christina. Christina responded by saying, "Thanks a lot." Instead of that being the end of it, Christina decided she liked the way it sounded and said the phrase repeatedly for days afterward. This drove Anna completely nuts because the phrase had originated during a moment of conflict, so she felt like Christina was still directing it at her. I reminded Anna that autistic kids often do this repetitive type of vocalization as a way of practicing phraseology. Of course, that didn't make it any easier for Anna to tolerate, and as hard as she tried, she couldn't find anything that would bother Christina enough to make her stop. Finally, Anna came up with, "You're a boy." Hearing this annoyed Christina so much that she told Anna to stop. Anna, in turn, was pleased with herself for finding something that irritated Christina as much as the "thanks a lot" phrase had irritated her. She looked at Christina and said, "You're a boy. You're a boy. You're a boy." And then she looked at me and said, "I'm practicing."

No, I don't condone Anna purposefully goading her sisters. But I do understand that the situation is not always easy for her. There are many times when she has to act mature beyond her years. She has also become accustomed to the disappointment of having to cancel plans or skip lessons, activities, and even her choir performances on a moment's notice because of Christina's health issues. When these situations arise, Anna rarely complains, whines, or pouts. She displays remarkable empathy and understanding for her sisters.

During Anna's last birthday party (eleven years old), Maria decided to sit in the van instead of participating with the other kids. The party was outdoors, and the van was parked very close so I could easily keep an eye on her with the van doors open. When it came time to open Maria's gift, Anna left her friends and took the present over to the van so Maria could watch her open it. Anna knew that Maria had been very excited about the gift; Maria had wrapped it at least a dozen times trying to get it just right. Anna didn't need for me to tell her to include her sister in that way.

This is just one example of the small acts of kindness, selflessness, and thoughtfulness that Anna does on her own initiative, because she wants her sisters to be happy. She finds many small ways to make her sisters feel valued. Recently, Maria came to me beaming about how she had beaten Anna in a game of checkers. I congratulated her, then later, when Maria was not listening, asked Anna if Maria had really beaten her. Anna confessed that she had discreetly added Maria's pieces back to the board when she wasn't looking so Maria could win. For Anna, giving Maria the chance to be excited about winning the game was more important than winning it herself.

Occasionally, Anna has had to contend with negative comments from other kids at school or in the neighborhood. This is never easy for her, because she doesn't want to hear anyone speak ill of her sisters, and she is quick to defend them in such situations. Just as she knows what to say to get under her sisters' skin, she also knows how to make them feel better when other kids say mean things. Once when they were all outside playing, a neighbor girl told Anna that Maria and Christina were weird. Of course, Anna said they weren't, making sure her sisters heard her refute the insult. When she relayed the story to me, I knew my response was equally as important because Maria and Christina were listening. I replied to Anna, "Doesn't she have an attitude?" Anna knew that having an attitude was something they'd been taught was a negative quality, so she was quick to agree that this girl did, indeed, have an attitude. That was all her sisters needed to hear. Once they thought the other girl had "an attitude," they no longer cared what her opinion was.

Dealing with issues outside the home is always more difficult, even for Anna. She holds her own against other kids, but she isn't immune to being embarrassed by her sisters' behavior in public. About a year ago, we were in a large grocery store, trying our best to get through our regular shopping trip. Maria was already out of sorts because she had hurt her hand by shutting her finger in a desk drawer earlier in the day. It had taken me most of the day to calm her down enough so we could go to the store; waiting another day wasn't an option. We finally made it to the store and were in the frozen food section when Anna accidentally closed one of the freezer doors on Maria's hand—the same hand she'd already hurt.

I don't think the door pinched her hand hard enough to actually hurt it, but the shock was enough to send Maria back into crisis mode. She started screaming, "She did it! Anna did this!" over and over again. I knew that everyone in the store could hear her. Anna did too. She was terribly upset about how Maria was carrying on and blaming her to everyone in the entire store. I knew our shopping trip was over. I had the few essentials we needed, so we started making our way toward the register. Christina was in the cart, hyperventilating from the stress. Maria was relentless. Anna was horrified.

I did my best to keep it together and get us out of the store without added drama; however, Maria didn't stop until well after we were home. Later, Anna told me how embarrassed she was with Maria saying her name in the store. I reassured her that no one knew who "Anna" was. "The way Christina was hyperventilating," I told her, "people most likely assumed she was Anna." That helped a little. Anna needed a coping mechanism to get through that moment; allowing her to create this veil of anonymity, believing that no one else necessarily knew she was Anna or that her sister was blaming her, as opposed to Christina, gave her a way to avoid feeling so embarrassed about being the center of unwanted public attention.

Other times, however, Anna has expressed that she feels overshadowed by her sisters, especially Maria. I discovered this when asking her why she was so fond of the *Little House on the Prairie* books. Anna's responded that she felt a connection to the main character Laura. When I asked her to explain, she told me that people in the stories were always complimenting Laura's big sister, Mary, on her curls of gold. Then she said, "Everywhere I go, Maria gets all the attention because she hugs everyone." I thought that was an interesting analogy because even though I know Maria has a way of drawing people to her, I hadn't thought about how Anna might feel left out.

Through it all—the competition, the challenges, the understanding, and even moments when Anna likes to torment her sisters (like the time she hid outside the glass patio door with the remote and kept turning the TV off while Maria was trying to watch it)—Anna and her sisters share a sisterly bond and love that I know will last throughout their lives. She understands them in ways that even I sometimes cannot. She is proud of them and wants them to be happy. She used to draw pictures of Maria in a wedding gown, hoping that her sister would one day be able to get married and have babies. She now understands that this isn't likely. Anna vacillates between wanting and not wanting to have her own children (but we know this is mostly due to her young age and gradual awareness of the facts of life). When Christina's seizures occur, Anna becomes very anxious and worried, even confiding to me her fears of Christina dying during an episode. That's a lot of worry for a young girl to shoulder, and although I try my best to alleviate those concerns, we can't pretend they aren't justified.

Perhaps Anna's feelings for her sisters are best expressed in the opening lines from a Thanksgiving Day essay she wrote in kindergarten: "I am thankful for everything because I love everyone in my family. Every minute I think about my wonderful sisters Maria and Christina because I love them." To Anna, her sisters are not special because they have special needs. They are special because they are her big sisters.

Fighting Favoritism

For a long time, it never occurred to me that people might favor Maria and Christina over Anna; however, when I evaluate social situations objectively, I see that they tend to get more attention than Anna. This is especially true with Maria. It's not that Maria does anything wrong or intentionally tries to be the center of attention. She's so outgoing and uninhibited about talking to people that they naturally pay more attention to her. Christina doesn't notice, but Anna does. I can see that for Anna it must feel like Maria simply sucks all the air out of the room. Then add in the amount of attention Christina receives because of her fragile health and petite, doll-like appearance, and it's easy to see how Anna can easily slip into the background if she doesn't demand to be noticed.

Within our home, we've tried to create an environment of equality among the three girls. We love them all equally and wouldn't ever want one of them to feel as if they weren't just as special to us. We put a lot of effort into making sure each child has her moment to shine and that they all receive the same amount of attention from us. However, this isn't always easy. Just as Maria and Christina can become the center of our attention for behavioral or health issues, it's also easy for me to slip into giving Anna more one-on-one time because she's so inquisitive and communicative. Bedtime is a quiet time when Anna likes to ask questions or talk about things that are troubling her; I can easily spend a long time having a conversation with her. But I try to be mindful of then spending the same amount of time with the other two, so no one feels slighted. I don't want my actions or how I share my time with them to imply any one of them is more or less special or important.

Jeff and I have the advantage of perspective and maturity to help us balance the emotional needs of all three girls. They, however, are not quite as capable of doing the same for each other. Even if they aren't behaving with intent to hurt one another, the effect is still the same. As a parent or grandparent, it can be painful to watch one child be made to feel lesser by the others. Unfortunately, the situation is not always preventable, but when it happens, our first concern is to make it stop.

For instance, when Maria practices reading her words, we "count" it with a check mark if she gets it right the first time. I never make her feel bad if she doesn't get a word right, and I'll encourage her to keep trying. The check marks are in recognition of getting it right on her first attempt. Once when my mother was helping, she checked every word as correct, even if it took Maria several attempts to get it right. Both Christina and Anna kept chiming in that Maria shouldn't get credit for those. It wasn't that they wanted Maria to feel bad, but in their eyes, Grammy was being too lenient by counting all the words as correct. The more they objected, the more Maria wilted because she knew they were pointing out her mistakes. Grammy, of course, felt horrible about seeing Maria's reaction and frustrated because Christina and Anna were unwittingly counteracting her intentions of boosting Maria's esteem.

It's easy to think that Anna would be the one to receive preferential treatment, but in truth, we have to be careful about her being subjected to reverse discrimination. Over the years, she has complained about Maria and Christina being favored by sitters because they are special education. In a way, the preceding was also an example of that. It is normal for people to hold Anna to higher standards and accountability while giving Maria or Christina passes because they have so many other challenges. The difficulty comes with helping Anna understand that this has nothing to do with the other two being favored or loved over her. For a young girl, that can be hard to understand, especially when it involves people closest to her; Grammy's worry about the two with disabilities can be interpreted by Anna that Grammy loves them more. This, of course, is patently untrue.

On one occasion, Anna claimed that I didn't tell her I love her as often as I told Maria and Christina. I thought this was odd. How could I tell one child I loved her more often than another? I thought about it for quite some time, only to realize that I do tell Anna very often that I love her. So I asked her what made her think that I didn't. She reminded me how Christina routinely tells me she loves me, and then after I respond, she loops around the room and comes back to say it again, eliciting yet another response from me. Something as innocent as Christina's game of affection is not missed by the acutely receptive feelings of her younger sister.

Anna is both observant and sensitive to the moods and actions of others, traits that help keep me on my toes. She lets me know when I am correcting bad behavior if I am less harsh on Maria and Christina than I am with her. But then she'll also tell me when I'm overreacting or being too hard on her sisters. In that regard, we help keep each other in check during the day. If she lapses and starts teasing her sisters or making them feel bad, all I have to do is give her a disapproving look. She immediately realizes the error of her ways, feeling upset not only about getting in trouble but also with herself for her lack of judgment.

Additionally, we want Anna to understand that she should not feel guilty because her sisters have challenges and she does not. This wasn't something we would have necessarily thought would be a problem, but we saw signs of it beginning around the same time that Anna started becoming aware that she could perform tasks more easily than her sisters. She started doing little things to compensate and level the playing field between them, such as drawing with her left hand even though she's right-handed so her picture would look similar to Christina's.

When I see these behaviors, I remind her that God expects each of us to perform at our own level, and I reinforce the message I've told them each since they were very young—that they have each been blessed with their own gifts. Anna never needs to feel bad that she is at a higher level than her sisters, but it's also important for her to understand that she can't brag to them or make them feel inferior. Fortunately, she is compassionate and understands this, and resists the temptation (most of the time!).

Education and Expectations

Our goal is for Anna to take pride in all her efforts and tasks, including schoolwork. The prize for a job well done is receiving an A on a test. We want her to learn to have the self-discipline to achieve success based on the merits of her efforts. Anna is bright and talented and can pursue any level of academia or career path she chooses if she internalizes these values early. Certainly, we have high hopes and expectations for her, but we do have to balance those expectations. Accepting that Maria and Christina won't reach certain milestones, like college, was very difficult at first. And yes, we are grateful we will still be able to experience those things with Anna; however, our primary goal is to make sure Anna lives up to her own potential and is not living under the shadow of having to compensate for her sisters.

The difference between Anna and her sisters as far as school goes was evident early on. In kindergarten, Anna's teacher commented on how she was one of the best writers in the class. In comparison to my earlier experiences with teachers giving me bad news, I was thrilled to hear such accolades about her at this early age. While her sisters struggle with formulating words and verbalizing their thoughts, language has come easily for Anna. I remember one time, when she was a young five or six, she recognized that an adult speaker had made a grammatical error. She told me later that although she didn't say anything at the time, the error had really bothered her. I used the opportunity to tell her I was proud of her for recognizing the error and for knowing that it would be disrespectful to correct an adult. We talked about the importance of continuing to use proper grammar even when she hears others using incorrect phrasing. This lesson reinforced our message that she always needs to strive to do her best and work at her own ability regardless of what others—peers, adults, or her sisters—are doing.

For most of her elementary school years, we decided to enroll her in the academically challenging K12 online charter school program. I attempted homeschooling Maria and Christina when they were preschool and kindergarten age. However, the challenges (undiagnosed at the time) made the task so difficult that I often felt like I was a failure. Now we understand that we simply could not have provided Maria and Christina with everything they needed; my homeschooling endeavor with them was doomed before it began.

With Anna, it was different. I could successfully teach her, although it wasn't always easy. Having the structure that K12 provided helped. If anything, the rigorous schedule proved challenging to keep up with. Anna often felt as if she had to do more work in virtual school than her friends in traditional school were doing. Of course, we also experienced many days to the contrary, days filled with distractions. In order to stay current with assignments, we definitely had to set and follow a daily work schedule.

The need to put Anna back in regular school became evident over the course of our third year of homeschooling, which was fifth grade. Much of our decision came from her increasing agitation of her sisters, especially in the morning. They needed to get ready to leave the house for school while she did not, creating a difficult dynamic. Every time either Maria or Christina needed to stay home or go to the doctor, the disruption to routine created yet another distraction and excuse for Anna to not do her work. This, in turn, meant more strain to catch up the following day so she wouldn't fall behind in the curriculum.

The turning point came one day during the middle of the school year. We had had a very difficult morning. Anna and Maria were fighting more than usual, both causing the other to spiral out of control—Maria with her obsessive behaviors and Anna with her indignant attitude. Maria had a feeding therapy appointment that morning, and since she was so distraught because of the conflict with Anna, she wasn't able to finish getting herself dressed. I had to take Christina to school, so I told Maria to lie down and rest, hoping she could calm down while I was gone.

When I returned, Maria was in her room, and Anna was messing around instead of doing her morning assignments. I went to help Maria finish dressing and found a note on her bedroom floor. Apparently, Maria had written it as a message telling Anna to stay out of her room. Despite the content, I was impressed with Maria's writing on the note, writing being a particularly difficult task for her, so I told her she had done a good job with it. Anna overheard and became envious, recognizing that this was a benchmark in Maria's development. Because she was still upset from the events of the morning and did not want her sister to receive the recognition, Anna claimed the note was hers and tried to take it away. This caused Maria to become distressed; she had done something well, and her sister was trying to take that away from her. Fighting over ownership of the note escalated to the point where I decided it needed to be thrown away.

Throughout all of this, I was still trying to get Maria ready for her therapy appointment, and Anna was supposed to be quietly working. By the time we were ready to leave the house, Maria was still distressed and moving very slowly. It took nearly five minutes to get her into the car. I left Anna to do her schoolwork. Just as we were pulling out of the driveway, I looked up to see Anna standing in the doorway waving a piece of paper—the note retrieved from the trash. Maria couldn't believe her eyes. She was too exhausted from all the stress of the morning to react. She sat frozen, staring in disbelief and shock. It was very unfair of Anna to do that, and I made sure to let her know later in the day. That's when it became clear to me that allowing Anna to be home all the time was giving her an unfair advantage over her sisters.

Jeff and I had already been thinking about enrolling her in a traditional school, so we began researching schools and preparing for her to transition at the start of sixth grade. Even if the "note incident" had never happened, the likelihood was high that we would have moved toward traditional schooling that year anyhow. It was exhausting for me to teach Anna all day and then still work with Maria and Christina at night. And there were times when I would have difficulty getting Anna to focus—I'd catch her listening to kid CDs or watching shows on the computer when she was supposed to be studying. It was becoming clear that she would benefit from the structure of a classroom.

Having Anna at home and Maria and Christina in school presented other challenges at times. During the summer, Maria and Christina would go to special summer school classes so they could continue making progress and not lose hard-won skills. When they all became old enough to realize that they were going to school and Anna wasn't, they had questions. We explained to Anna that her sisters weren't in an actual grade that stopped in the spring and changed in the fall. And for the benefit of all three—so Maria and Christina didn't perceive Anna as having vacation time while they didn't, and so Anna didn't simply get a pass during the summer months—I implemented a practice of having Anna study and learn something new, like Spanish. This seemed to appease everybody.

With Anna, we have to teach concepts with more depth, which is something that always brings new experiences when she reaches new developmental milestones. Where her sisters will take an explanation at face value, process it, and move on, Anna wants to understand why. She asks questions that her sisters would never ask. She is curious and loves to delve into issues, read about them at length, and digest them fully.

We encourage her to embrace learning and hobbies; however, she knows she must earn privileges, such as music lessons. We do not want to raise a prima donna. Simply because she excels in certain areas does not mean we will allow her to believe she is entitled to rewards without working for them. If her study habits become lacking or if she stops showing enough commitment to practicing, we don't hesitate to drop extracurricular activities.

Our primary goal in parenting Anna is to encourage her to excel without losing sight of her values. Pride, selfishness, ego, and judgment—these are character traits that her sisters may never fully grasp, in the innocence of their childlike understanding. Anna, on the other hand, needs to learn how to make decisions regarding ethics and morality; we want her to grow into a charitable, gracious, and respectable young lady who remembers to pray and keep faith in her life.

Santa Is Watching You

Strong-willed with an equally strong attitude at times— that's Anna. In one of her younger displays of wit, Anna tried outsmarting us when we told her she needed to behave or Santa wouldn't bring her any presents. Anna's quick reply was she had already spoken to Santa, and he knew what she wanted and that she had been good. She was quite certain she had nothing to worry about.

Jeff and I had to find some way to put the doubt back, so we told her that Daddy had also spoken to Santa when he drove him to the children's neighborhood party. Santa comes every year with the volunteer fire department. That year they were called to respond to a fire, and since Santa has such a busy schedule, Jeff offered to drive him to the party. While they were together, Daddy had a chance to tell Santa about Anna. Jeff informed Anna that she was not free and clear with Santa yet. She still needed to behave well if she wanted to get presents at Christmas. This worked, this time. She decided that Santa was still watching her and improved her behavior accordingly.

If nothing else, Anna knows how to challenge our parental creativity with her sharp intellect and strong attitude.

Faith

The Ties that Bind
Marriage, Faith, and a Family
Touched by Grace

Jeff and I were very fortunate to have been married nine years before having children. These years gave us the opportunity to work through many issues, including some of my own ill-conceived ideas of love that evolved as a result of my own parents' divorce. My husband came to our marriage with a better understanding of how a good marriage should work. The year we were married, his parents celebrated their thirty-eighth anniversary, while mine were still harboring mutual anger and resentment toward each other. Only two years had passed since the divorce, and the wounds were still fresh.

Unfortunately, at the time I didn't realize just how much the dissolution of my parents' love for each other had damaged me emotionally. Their divorce left me with the belief that nothing lasts forever. On some level, I also resented God for not fixing things, although I did not realize this until years later. I prayed many prayers for my parents during those days without fully realizing how much I needed God's help too. My parents, along with those who loved them, survived the ordeal of their relationship *but* barely.

Love was a difficult concept for me. I knew Jeff loved me then, but I didn't trust that he would love me always. My idea of love was lifted from the old movies: the act of falling in love, the romance, and the magnetic attraction. I believed that as long as both partners kept acting in this overtly romantic manner, the relationship would last. But in a marriage, that just isn't reality.

Our honeymoon phase lasted for about a year, and everything was fine that first year. I remember the day I realized that the honeymoon was over. It was just after our first anniversary. We were visiting his parents, and Jeff was helping them take care of some home repairs. Watching him working outside, it struck me that our relationship had changed; I was no longer his sole priority. This would have been the normal progression of a healthy marriage. Instead, I saw it as our marriage being doomed. I thought I had made a mistake. Even worse, I started looking for reasons our marriage wouldn't work. Of course, I found them. Before I knew it, we were constantly arguing, and the tension didn't break until I went to visit my family during the holidays. That's when Jeff decided to read a book called *The Joy of Committed Love* by Gary Smalley that we'd received as an anniversary gift from my mother a couple of months earlier. When I got home, he suggested that I read it too.

The book was very helpful for both of us, but especially for me. It helped me realize that love was not a feeling but a commitment. I began to learn how to communicate, which was something I had not done during our first year of marriage. Not being able to express my real and perceived grievances created a buildup of anger that I was then directing at Jeff. I was too consumed with my own pain and anger to see that I was the one with the problem, not him. My anger at Jeff then turned into anger at God, causing a period of great darkness and despair for me. The one thing I wanted was a good marriage, and I felt this had eluded me. All I could see was negativity, turning what should have been a healthy growth stage of a relationship into a hellish period for me, Jeff, and our marriage. Jeff was devastated. He was deeply sorry for any pain he had caused me, but in fairness to him, the sweet woman he had married had seemingly disappeared, and he didn't know why. In one heated moment of frustration, he said, "I didn't know I was marrying an emotional cripple." I had no comeback. He was right; I was an emotional cripple.

The saddest part was that we both felt helpless. I so badly wanted to please him, and he wanted to help me. At one point, I was reading a book called *Healing the Child Within* and learned that it can take anywhere from two to five years to overcome emotional wounds once we identify them and begin the recovery process. By this point, we both knew I had wounds that needed to heal. I showed Jeff the book; he skimmed it and acknowledged the two-to-five-year healing period. He then assured me he was committed to me and our marriage and that he wasn't going anywhere. During those next few years, he remained true to his word and helped me by becoming a master of tough love and the Socratic Method, asking me questions until I reached the logical conclusions of my own thoughts. This gave me the ability to examine my beliefs from the simple to the complex.

By the time we reached our seventh anniversary, after five years of healing, we were a happily married couple. I remember telling everyone it was *my* anniversary instead of *our* anniversary. I was so excited to be married. Me! Happily married! Everything in our life was going well, so we started thinking there needed to be something more. That's when we decided to try to have a child. Jeff had always wanted a family. I was not confident in my ability to raise children, but I knew that with his help, we could have an emotionally healthy family. It was amazing to realize that I would be able to give our future children what I didn't have growing up—a peaceful home.

The irony is that my past emotional weakness has become one of my greatest strengths—I am at peace with God. I became thankful for my life, and I could see beauty and goodness again. When someone asks how long we have been married, I will playfully say, "Twenty-six years and happily for twenty-one." The math is simple: the number of years we have been married minus the five it took for me to heal the child within.

Today, our marriage has progressed way past the honeymoon phase. I understand that love is a commitment. You make a decision to commit your life and your love to another person, and then you make it right through your actions. Jeff and I have a mature love. One of Anna's songs for singing class is "So This Is Love" (The Cinderella Waltz). It is nice to sing the song and know that I have what I dreamed of finding one day. The last line of the song is even truer now than it was the day of our wedding: *So this is the miracle that I've been dreaming of. So this is love.* Now I understand love—not the Disney version but the tried and true kind.

Our Marriage with Children

When Maria was born in our ninth year of marriage, Jeff and I had solved so many issues, we both knew we were committed for the long haul. I believe that, as a couple, we were able to weather the unique challenges presented by our children because of our previous challenges. When Jeff agreed to see things through with me in those early years, I knew he wasn't going to leave, regardless of what the future would bring.

Having two children with special needs has certainly come with its own set of challenges. Fortunately, Jeff and I have been able to stay connected to our faith and our relationship, both of which have helped us through the unexpected. When I was dealing with the guilt of knowing Maria and Christina inherited their genetic conditions from me, Jeff didn't waver in his love for them or for me. He never blamed me, even when I was blaming myself. At first, I struggled with feeling a sense of inequality in the relationship because of that guilt, but over time, I came to terms with the fact that those feelings were self-imposed. I was the same in Jeff's eyes as I had always been, and his love for Maria and Christina has always been completely unconditional. He would never trade them for anything in the world.

As solid as our relationship is, we aren't immune to having differences of opinion or to the tolls everyday stress can take. I am fortunate because he is a very supportive husband. I couldn't do this without him. Sometimes, his challenge is having to go through me to influence how our kids are raised and taught. This can be frustrating for him because he wants to know they are accomplishing the things they need for their proper development. I think this is true for any family where the husband works and the mother stays home. The reality is that the working parent isn't around for a lot of the hands-on moment-to-moment teaching opportunities that come up during the day. Jeff has to trust that I'm optimizing those moments to teach the kids in a way that fits with his vision too.

Sure, Jeff helps me and engages with the kids when he's home, but at the same time, as a stay-at-home mom, I'm the primary person dealing with the children. It can be easy to lose sight of the implications that come with that at times. In my mind, I agree with him when we have discussions about how to the handle certain situations that come up. However, if I'm not fully onboard for implementing what he's talking about, this can cause all kinds of problems. Essentially, a dynamic is created in which I'm asking him for help, he offers a suggestion or advice, but I may or may not follow it. This is frustrating for him, because he's used to solving problems. From my perspective, I may simply want to have a conversation about whatever issue is going on at the time. He's listening with the intent of solving the problem. His goal is to fix the situation in order to make me happy. Then when I bring up the same topic again because I just want to discuss it again, he feels like I'm not listening to his input. This can cause frustration and tension because we both love the children equally, and while he's doing everything he can while he's around them, we both know I'm the parent who's with them for the majority of each day.

Here's an example. We've been going around and around for a couple of years about how much I'm doing (or not doing) to make sure Maria and Christina learn life skills they will need to become independent. Am I taking the time to have them fold their clothes and do some of the cleaning, or am I doing it myself because it's easier and faster? I've gotten better about making sure they do their chores, but I like my home orderly, and I'm at home all day. I've always been the type who handles stress by cleaning up, but the double-edged sword of this is that while doing the chore myself may seem easier than taking the time and having the patience to teach or allow them to practice it, I'm wearing myself down further by not delegating the tasks out.

During one semi-heated discussion on the matter, Jeff wanted me to name three things I had done in the previous week to encourage their independence. Being put on the spot, I was forced to really think about what I had been doing in this regard. And yes, I was able to come up with three things: Christina had vacuumed the whole house, Maria had learned to make her own milkshakes, and they had all gone through their rooms and decided what they were ready to donate to Goodwill. The last item was a process they had to do on their own, each making their own selections and bringing those items to me when they were finished. Jeff was impressed, but this also demonstrates how the working parent can become disconnected. I hadn't shared those achievements, so he was left to feel concern about whether or not the girls were making progress. His point was that as the one who's with them all the time, I need to be proactive about remembering on a daily basis the larger goals we have for them. I'm sure most moms will agree this is not always easy to do.

In any marriage, there's a part where each partner has to protect their own psyche from their spouse, especially when it involves discussions like I just described. That's important. When we were first married, I didn't know where to draw the line in discussions or when I needed a hug. Learning how to recognize my own needs, as well as to express them, has helped me safeguard my emotions during challenging situations. For instance, if we are having a discussion about something I'm struggling with, Jeff may logically be correct with his assertions, but for me (as it is with most women), that isn't always the main objective. Sometimes, we just need our frustrations to be heard. Sometimes, if he takes too logical of a stance, I become annoyed with him because what I really need at that moment is tenderness rather than solutions. Clearly, I can't expect him to read my mind or magically know what my needs are. However, if I'm able to tell him, he is happy to acquiesce. Then we both benefit from a more peaceful marriage.

And for the most part, our marriage is a peaceful one. We may have our disagreements from time to time, but we rarely fight. Only once, several years ago when the kids were little, did we have a fight big enough to even hint at the idea of divorce. Neither of us ever wants to get a divorce, but in the heat of the moment, Jeff asked me if we were going to make it to our fifteenth anniversary. I remember having this little light bulb go off in my head when he said that. My first thought wasn't about our marriage being in trouble (probably because I knew that it wasn't), but instead I thought, "Hmm, that means he would take the kids half the week." As expected, we both cooled off and were able to laugh about the idea of how I would want joint custody and he could be rid of my exercise equipment. Using humor is our way of releasing tension and putting things back in perspective.

One of the hardest times for Jeff was when he knew I was on the emotional brink after learning of the girls' genetic condition. He knew I was looking into the abyss and was on the verge of being consumed by the darkness I saw around me. One day during that dark, desperate period, Jeff turned to me and point-blank said, "You can't. You don't have the luxury to check out. Your children are depending on you." I could see in his expression and hear in his voice the firmness, concern, and dread of it all. The memory of that hellish period early in our marriage when I turned in on myself was still there—for both of us.

I never again wanted to be that soul that hurt so much it would doubt the beauty of its own life. I knew Jeff was right; I didn't want to go back there. At that moment, I was able to slowly begin my retreat from the darkness that was beginning to envelop me again. Having healed once made me stronger. This time I knew that with God's help, I could endure this challenge. This time, I did not turn my back on God, even in moments of tears and anger over Maria's and Christina's challenges. Sometimes, I've found myself wanting to put their problems on God; sometimes, I've needed to. And God has always responded with just the right people who have miraculously come into our lives at just the right time.

Taking care of Maria and Christina will never be over. They aren't going to grow up and fly the coop. We will always have to have resources for them. Even when they learn to live more on their own in a few years, they will continue needing our care. So in addition to the routine stress most married couples experience while raising children, Jeff and I have acknowledged that caring for our girls will never stop, not physically, emotionally, or financially. That reality creates added stress on our relationship, which is why communication is so important for helping us stay connected regardless of the pressures caring for two special needs daughters brings.

For the most part, I think we've done a good job at finding a balance to keep our relationship strong while handling the day-to-day stressors. Sometimes, however, the stress can take over, and we'll go through periods that are a little harder and more tedious than others. Holidays are a good example. I remember one Thanksgiving that was particularly rough. I had hardly slept from the long nights with Christina and her seizures. Jeff spent the day cooking the turkey, and my mother helped us prepare the meal and watched the girls as much as she could. But in the end, none of us were able to sit down and really enjoy the meal we'd worked so hard to make. And to further frustrate my fantasy of a Norman Rockwell Thanksgiving, the girls, with their eating challenges, all had to have their separate meals prepared and ate at different times too.

At one point in the day, Jeff went for a bike ride to catch a break. He admitted feeling the pressure of never getting any relief from the reality of our situation. I was equally as exhausted. Neither of us felt like keeping our annual tradition of putting up Christmas decorations that Thanksgiving weekend. The girls love to decorate the tree, but I never let them do it without supervision because we have too many special and breakable ornaments. Desperately tired, I decided to take a nap before we started decorating. I woke up to the sounds of Maria and Anna rummaging through the decoration boxes in the next room. I cringed to think of them handling the ornaments without me, but at that moment, I was too tired to move or care.

I was numb to the usual joys of the season that year. I think Jeff felt the same. It wasn't until Jeff had a helicopter crash that we truly felt our blessings again. He had been taking flying lessons, and this flight was one of his early solo night flights. The crash was the result of a mechanical failure, and he was lucky to walk away with only a small gash on his forehead. A fellow pilot took him to the hospital to be checked out, and when he came home with blood on his shirt, the gravity of the situation hit both of us hard. I realized how close I had come to becoming a widow that night, with three children—two with special needs—to raise on my own. We were so thankful. For the first time during a physically and emotionally grueling month, we felt the joy and spirit of the season.

Sometimes momentous events help us keep things in perspective; other times the little things do. Jeff summed up the simplicity by which we try to live our lives one evening during a discussion with a colleague at a Rotary event. The gentleman was telling us about how he and his wife had recently celebrated their anniversary at a posh steakhouse. Jeff laughed and told him that we would be more likely to go to McDonald's. This caught him by surprise, so Jeff explained that McDonald's was the first place we were ever able to eat together as a family. Jeff went on to explain the girls' feeding challenges and how Christina only recently ate her very first cheeseburger—a moment of true celebration for us. The gentleman asked Christina's age, and when Jeff told him she was twelve, he said, "It makes you want to cry." We agreed that yes, it does. And yes, McDonald's is our favorite restaurant because of what it represents to our family.

Acceptance and Discouragement

Growing up, succeeding in school, being considered the "most likely to" among my family and friends, and creating a successful career, I never expected the role I was destined for: mother of special needs children. Of all the labels I ever thought I'd have, that wasn't one of them. No one anticipates or plans for this path in life. Coming to terms with it is not always easy. My ability to balance the expectations I had for my life with the reality of it waxes and wanes.

Jeff sometimes thinks I'm depressed when rough patches come along and my energy drops; however, I've realized that discouragement more accurately describes these emotional lulls. These are times when I second-guess and wonder what life could have been if I hadn't let go of my career. Or I struggle with doubt about whether or not I'm following the right plan for my life. After all, I was extremely driven and career-minded, and those traits don't simply go away just because I'm at home raising children. They may become muted, but those characteristics are still part of me.

A few years ago, I was approached to run for a public office; I was devastated about having to decline, but I knew a campaign—let alone holding an office—would have been too hard on the girls. There's a part of me that still wants to be that woman with the career or who goes to graduate school, especially when I'm feeling like I need some external affirmation as a form of self-validation. But I know that, for now, the girls need me more than I need to fulfill personal pursuits. I also know that my self-worth should not be contingent upon having a title or degree hanging on the wall. That can be a difficult concept for me at times, because I envisioned my life with those pieces in it. In a way, accepting that responsibility of family over self came with a sense of relief—relief from knowing that I was able to make the mature decision and could overcome preconceived ideas of what makes a person successful.

Sometimes, the reality that life is not how I had anticipated it to be becomes overwhelming. God has blessed me with gifts and talents that I feel I'm not using. That's hard to accept at times. I struggle with feeling that there's so much more to life than just being here with the kids. At one point, when I was musing on the life I had once thought I would be living right now, I calculated the lost income from my career in terms of real dollars. But how does one really know the full measure of the loss beyond dollars? Then I remembered how happy I've been to be there with the girls and experience all those little moments with them. That's when I knew I had made the right decision. No regrets. There's always going to be that splinter of doubt, but doubt gives way to shades of discouragement that diminish with time. I try to embrace where I am now. In a broader scope, I know new opportunities are still out there for me. Sometimes, though, it can be hard to remember to enjoy today for today.

My lowest times were when the girls were younger: the genetic diagnosis, losing my fourth child, and Christina's seizures. These times all stand out as the hardest, most challenging periods. I was consumed with guilt, fear, and feelings of failure. Right after Christina started having seizures, I confided to Jeff about how upset I had truly become after the diagnosis and how I had briefly thought about leaving after my miscarriage. He responded,

"I could never do this without you. I'm glad you didn't just deposit them and leave."

The thought of leaving was fleeting, of course. And it stemmed from drowning in despair and helplessness. In all that mess, Anna was a bright spot because she was predictable. I thought about her and how I needed to be there for her. It'd be bad enough for Maria and Christina not to have a mom around, but what about Anna? She had a life full of challenges and triumphs ahead of her, and I needed to be there to help her navigate those.

One of my core values is the belief that every child deserves to have a loving mother. That is what keeps me in the game. I want all three of my girls to know they are loved beyond measure. When it comes to being a mother, it cannot be about me or my needs—it's about theirs.

For a long time, especially when they were little, it was very hard to picture the future. When they were first diagnosed, I worried a lot about a genetic unraveling. I don't think about this as much now as I did earlier, but we still have to accept that we really don't know what the future holds for them, medically. No one else has what they have, so not even the medical experts can predict what is in store. Early on, I had such a terrible time teaching them, and I remember thinking that if they weren't going to live a long time, I wish I knew so that we could just play and have fun. I didn't see a point in creating all this stress for me and for them if it was going to be to no end. My thoughts were that if they didn't have long to live, I would rather spend precious time with them doing fun things and making good memories. Finally, I realized that self-worth comes from one's ability to work and do things, regardless of IQ level. For them, there is great reward in going to school and accomplishing things. Even if they were to pass away at a young age, in their teens, there is still much to be gained by living a full life, including going to school. Looking at their journey in those terms helped me to stop agonizing over the unknown. At this point in my life and with where the girls are now, I have a good feel for where they are headed and what their abilities and limitations will be. Back then, I didn't have a clue, and that was a very distressing place for a mother-to-be.

Over the years, I've struggled off and on with figuring out what my purpose in life is and in defining, or possibly redefining, my perception of success along the way. My conclusion is that life is really about reaching our full potential. One of my favorite Bible verses says that at the end of your life, you hope God says, "Well done, good and faithful servant." That is what I want, to be the Lord's good and faithful servant.

I've realized that discouragement, especially the part that wonders if I'm missing out on all these other things (have I failed the potential of what I'm supposed to be?) is, at its root, a lack of faith. Yes, I'm faithful, but these thoughts and self-doubts are contrary to what God has tasked me to do—to raise these children. I have been given these children, and these children need me. That's where I am in my life right now. My future may hold something else, but today—this is my station in life. I've always drawn comfort from knowing that we are only expected to excel at our station in life, not someone else's. For instance, my station is a mother of three. As such, I'm not expected to pray as much as a nun who has devoted herself to a life of prayer. This is where I am supposed to be, and that brings me peace.

I believe it's a tragedy that too many mothers are torn and don't have this acceptance early in life when their kids are little. We should take peace and comfort in knowing we are doing the best we can and are making the right decisions at the time. Right now, I know I'm making the right decision. What's sad is what occurs when I reach those moments of discouragement or lack of faith or question my purpose in life. That uncertainty then bleeds over into every other aspect of my life. When negativity takes hold, it skews our perspective, making it easier to believe the worst parts of a situation and ignore the good parts. When we do this, we are believing a lie that will tear us down even further. We begin to resent our lives, our spouse, our kids; and we stop being a fun person to be around. By remembering to focus on the good, the bad will shrink to a realistic proportion.

When we get into those spells, that's when it's even more important to read the Bible and find a way to reconnect with the spirituality that fills us with peace and gratitude. What's the pur-pose in life? Love. Loving includes both what you have chosen to love, such as a spouse, and loving the things you've been given to love—your children. I truly believe that's what we'll be judged on. We all make sacrifices for our children, but those sacrifices are just a footnote on a choice made long ago to become a parent (a choice I would make again today). Feeling regret about those sacrifices stems from a lack of gratitude. So when I find myself woefully wondering what could have been, I have to stop and remember just how blessed my life truly is. I am grateful for my gifts from God. I am grateful He has tasked me with loving these beautiful children.

Through God's Grace

As I began writing this section on grace, I had a conversation with Anna. I told her that I lived a life of grace, and I asked what she had learned about grace at her Christian school. She said they always use the word but never explain it. She went on to ask me, "Doesn't everyone have grace?"

I had to stop and think about it before replying, "Yes, everyone who asks for it."

Learning to ask and to receive it, however, was the challenge I faced during my crises of faith: healing wounds of my youth and enduring the pain of loss I felt following the girls' diagnosis and my miscarriage. During those times, I wanted so badly to have God's presence in my life, but I didn't feel like he was there. I know now that he was, but those days were so dark that I didn't know it then.

My greatest fear has always been allowing myself to become bitter or jaded in a way that causes me to turn away from God. And there was a period when I felt that happening. Even during that time, when I was floundering emotionally and spiritually, Jeff and I continued going to church every week. To me, it felt like nothing more than going through the motions. Jeff would kneel to pray and take Communion, but I never had anything to say to God during those times. I remember thinking that Jeff was praying to God about me and about us. For me, praying was like placing a long-distance phone call.

Along with Jeff, my parents were instrumental in helping me through my darkest time following my miscarriage. In one discussion, my father talked about the idea of permissive will.[8] For instance, if a person runs a stop sign and gets in an accident, the wreck was part of the natural course of events. Since God could have stopped it but didn't, theoretically, God indirectly allowed the wreck to occur. Similarly, my situation with the miscarriage and disabled children was set in motion with my translocation. Since God did not prevent these developments, they are the result of his plan. Knowing this brought me comfort, because it meant I was not alone. Since these events were part of God's plan, he would be there with me throughout the journey.

In my attempt to understand where God was in my life and in our daughters' lives, I struggled with a couple of key concepts: Where is God concerning my children? How do I appeal my case? How does God make himself known in a person's life?

As a relatively new Catholic, I was intrigued with pilgrimages to holy places, which seems to be a practice embraced by Catholics. I wanted to know where this mountain was that I must climb to plead my case to God. I wanted to know how to get a healing for my children and where my children were in the Bible. I was willing to go around the world and climb the highest mountain for an opportunity to beg God to show his mercy and heal our girls. I wanted to be able to find God; and as disconcerting as coming face-to-face with him would be—the Bible says that the prophet Elisha was the only person recorded to see God, but even he was so scared by the encounter that he could only look at God's back after he passed by—I desperately wanted answers and healing for our girls.

I finally realized that I did not need to make a heroic pilgrimage to receive God's grace. He is here with our family every day. Not even the holy family had a roadmap to foretell or explain their journey. And just as they had guidance when they needed it, I came to

---

[8]   This discussion was based on the Presbyterian Catechism I grew up with.

understand that God would always be in my life and in the lives of my girls. His messages are subtle, but the guidance is clear when we choose to look. I truly believe through his grace, God participates in our lives. Answers and people have come to us so many times when we most needed them; I didn't make that happen—God brought them to us because we needed help.

As I returned to God, I discovered the Serenity Prayer most commonly used by Alcoholics Anonymous members. Although I am not an alcoholic, I've known others who are and how they traditionally use the first part as a daily prayer to help with recovery. But there's more to the prayer. It was the rest of the prayer that made the difference for me. It depicts faith and God's grace in action. I said it daily, and it helped me greatly during my time of healing.

> God grant me the Serenity
> to accept the things
> I cannot change,
> Courage to change the things
> I can, and the wisdom
> to know the difference.
> Living one day at a time:
> Enjoying one moment at a time;
> Accepting hardship as the
> pathway to peace.
> Taking as He did, this sinful world
> as it is, not as I would have it;
> Trusting that He will make all things
> right if I surrender to His will;
> That I may be reasonably happy
> in this life,
> And supremely happy with Him
> forever in the next.
>
> —Reinhold Niebuhr

The part about being reasonably happy in this life really spoke to me. Nothing is perfect. We have to learn acceptance and to live with the events that present themselves in our lives. Through this, I learned to stop being angry with God. If I embraced my life instead of resenting the circumstances of it, yes, I could be reasonably happy. We all have everything we need to be happy. God is always with us and will provide what we need, even if it isn't necessarily what we think we need at the time. Once we let go of trying to control life and accept living according to God's plan, not ours, we can find the happiness we, ourselves, cannot control or create.

I was not completely healed from the pain of my losses until the summer when Christina started having seizures. Authentic love is sacrificial, and since we do not live in an age of sacrifice, this truest form of love can take a long time to realize. With Christina's crisis, I lost myself only to be found. Her seizures were so serious and so consuming that all my attention and thoughts were on her, not on me. During this time, I was able to cut through the noise of all those whispers in my mind that taunted me—thoughts from the past, concern over how others perceived me, and even my own self-perception—and focus on what was really important. But I wasn't purposely focusing on anything. And that's the point. When I finally came up for air after the crisis, the noise was gone. I was able to finally see clearly.

Maria's and Christina's challenges continue to keep things real. Our life is based on basic values. Many people get caught up in things that don't matter, such as status or material possessions; but our girls help keep us centered on what's important in life. What's real? I suppose people with regular ed kids could say the same thing. The difference is that I am not forced to depend on God to help me with Anna. I know what a normal child's life is supposed to look like; I have traveled the same roadmap Anna is now traveling. With Maria and Christina, I am not so sure and am regularly left with no recourse but to seek divine guidance. That is what keeps our perspective in check.

Our special needs children have brought us all closer to God. The burden of raising them is too great to carry alone. While growing up, I was so afraid that I would one day leave God. I feared this because I didn't understand how people could turn their backs on what they know to be true and good or how they could abandon their Creator. What vulnerability of the soul allows that to happen? How could I be sure it wouldn't happen to me? My favorite hymn growing up was "Come Thou Fount." There is a verse that says, "Prone to wonder, Lord, I feel it. Prone to leave the God I love. Here's my heart. Oh, take and seal it, seal it for Thou courts above." I believe that our girls are the answer to my prayer that I would never turn my back on God.

God gave me this life for a reason, and I am grateful for it. I've heard assertions that God allows pain to teach others lessons. I don't believe this, and I don't believe that God creates a child with challenges as a means to frighten, punish, or make sure we trust in him. Are we victims of fate? Are our children to be pitied? No. Our children deserve our love, and they deserve for parents and society to expect—demand—the best of them. All human beings do. Through our actions, we determine what our child's life represents. Are we doing everything in our power to allow them to do their best and live a life of fulfillment?

I was recently reminded of the story about a boy throwing one of hundreds of beached starfish back into the ocean. An old man stopped him and said he was wasting his time, that he was not making a difference. The boy looked at him, threw another starfish back into the ocean, and said, "I made a difference to that starfish."

Yes, raising special needs children can be tedious and unending, but all of us who enter the life of a special needs child make a difference in that child's life. I often wonder if special needs teachers get discouraged, and I hope that all the special people in our children's lives know that they are making a difference. I truly believe God is going to judge me on how well I love my children. He gave them to me. They are his gift, and it is my responsibility to cherish and nurture them for him.

Several years ago, I had the privilege of hearing an elderly minister speak about his two children—a grown daughter and a son with special needs. Although his son had many unique gifts, the boy's challenges had been so great that the minister and his wife could not get sitters for him when he was young. Eventually, his son was able to take on a simple job that he took great pride in doing. The minister then told how his son had died in his sleep while only in his twenties. He went on to explain that he and his wife were old and that they had worried who would watch after their boy when they were gone. He was at peace with his son's death. The minister explained that he had lived a life of grace while his son was alive. He had so many people praying for his son and their family. Now that his son was gone, there was less grace in his life.

Hearing that story allowed me, for the first time, to put a name on what we were experiencing with our girls. We were experiencing grace. I also realized that my life had been rich with grace, even more so now with the girls. I once heard a sermon where the priest said there's something about the condition of severe human need that makes people receptive to the grace of God. They turn to God and are filled. Because of this, regardless of the state of wealth or health, a person can be happy.

James Ryle, a founding member of Promise Keepers, has suggested, "Grace is the empowering presence of God enabling you to be who He created you to be, and to do what He has called you to do." It was God's grace that led me to Jeff. I was so broken by my parents' divorce and the thought that nothing lasts forever that I thought finding a good, decent man to marry would elude me. Luckily, God had a different plan that included a husband who is loving, patient, and truly committed to our relationship. Together, our faith has helped us endure some very difficult times. But we both know we weren't and aren't alone. It wasn't enough that we met and fell in love; we were united in our love by our Creator. It is his love that has kept our love strong.

I now live a life of grace. *Grace* is a difficult word to explain. There are many definitions of the word, and many books have been written on the subject. To me, *grace* is the undeserved love and salvation God gives. Grace is God working in our lives, meeting our needs where we are. God works through people. This is why Christ says, "Whatever you do for the least of these, you do for me." Where does the ability to have the strength to press on come from when all things look hopeless? I believe it is God's grace.

Twenty-five years ago, I was an emotional cripple. It took me five years to become an emotionally healthy person. I learned to live in the present and not to dwell on the past or obsess about the future. I learned that the greatest part of love is forgiveness. I finally found peace. Years after I was healed, I pondered out loud to Jeff, "How do people with real problems (i.e., victims of abuse) heal themselves?"

Jeff answered, "What makes you think you healed yourself?"

His reply made me realize that it was God's grace that healed me. It was a relief to know that God's love can penetrate any life no matter how dark and hopeless things may seem. Things were very dark the day I sat reading the letter from the geneticist. My life as I knew it was turned upside down. Fortunately, I was already at peace with myself. This news would have been impossible for the younger woman I once was to handle. I don't know what the outcome would have been had I not had Jeff's love and God's grace in my life.

I used to look at life as some kind of sentence devoid of happiness—a gauntlet to be run with the hopes of being rewarded in heaven for my efforts here on earth. I had never considered the possibility of not existing at all; I was too busy feeling victimized by the imperfect world into which I had been born. Today, I no longer feel that way. I am thankful and eternally grateful to God to be part of this human experience, even with my translocation and the challenges it has brought me. I still do not know if my translocation is inherited or if I am the only one in my family to have this unique genetic condition, but I do know that I am at now at peace with it. One time, Anna asked me if I could get my translocation changed. I laughed and said, "No, I would no longer be me if it were changed."

And neither would Maria or Christina. For that—for the love, affection, strength, and grace they have brought into my life—I am truly blessed.

I can do everything through Him who gives me strength.
—Philippians 4:13

Attending Mass

Staying true to my faith has always been important to me. Both Jeff and I grew up in religious homes (his Catholic, mine Protestant), and we knew we wanted to live a life filled with spirituality. This included going to church each week and raising our children to have God in their lives. With special needs children, staying true to our convictions can be a challenge at times. Going to mass is an important part of staying connected to our faith, but rarely are we able to sit, as a family, through an entire sermon. Despite the difficulties, we continue going to church every Sunday, only missing mass under times of extreme crisis or illness.

Through the years, we've developed some preemptive coping strategies that have helped abate but not eradicate the girls' behavioral problems during mass. Christina wears headphones and goes to sleep. Without the headphones, the noise becomes too much for her to tolerate. For the most part, Maria stays occupied with coloring books or picture books, but she usually goes through multiple bouts of stimming and frequently wants to get up to use the restroom during the service.

When we can, we find seats near the back in case we have to slip out during the service if Maria's stimming becomes too severe or if Christina becomes overstimulated and begins hyperventilating. People around us don't always realize that our children have special needs, which occasionally makes me feel uneasy about drawing attention to ourselves when we have to leave early. Unfortunately, leaving is the only way to prevent causing an even greater disruption to the service.

There are days when having to leave affects me more than others. Jeff seems to handle the unpredictability that comes from week to week better than I do. When it wears me down, he can read the frustration and discouragement in my countenance. In his usual way, he says something that he knows I will find funny to help me bring things back into perspective.

The fatigue I feel on those days is no different at its root than many other aspects of parenting special needs children—my preconceived expectations for my life have not matched reality. Before having children, I pictured sitting in church as a family, awash in spirituality and leaving with a sense of fulfillment and peace each week. Never did I anticipate the behavioral issues that would make sitting through mass from beginning to end a struggle. But each week, we go and try, praying that our efforts are providing each of our children with a connection to God that will last their lifetimes.

First Communion

Although younger, Anna was ready to receive First Communion before her sisters. She worked very hard in her classes leading up to the big day, and we were all excited when it arrived. She had a beautiful dress and veil and lovely shoes lent to her by a neighbor. I had painstakingly curled and sprayed her hair to make her feel even more special. We attend a large church, so there were many children besides Anna involved in the ceremony that day, and Anna was to be one of the line leaders. It was all very exciting for her.

I was so proud of Anna and how hard she had worked that I wanted to be seated as close to the front as possible to share in her moment. We found a spot just a few rows behind the front rows reserved for the children in the ceremony. My mother was with us, and Jeff went to pick up his mother from the nursing home so she could participate in the day. Forty-five minutes later, Anna and the other children had made the procession into the church, Jeff was standing with his wheelchair-bound mother at the back of the church, and I was beginning to regret sitting in the front. Maria and Christina had to wait too long before the service started, and now they were becoming increasingly agitated with each transition between sitting, standing, and kneeling.

Both girls started acting up: Christina was huffing and hyperventilating, and Maria was doing a new burping thing she'd recently started. Christina's voice has a low, bellowing quality, and it was carrying throughout the church. People began turning and looking at us. Maria was struggling with her sinuses—I'd forgotten to give her a decongestant beforehand—and she blew her nose before I could get a tissue. I madly worked to clean up the mess while my mother tried her best to help bring the girls back under control. But without Jeff nearby, our efforts to diffuse the situation were ineffective.

Generally, when the girls' anxiety increases, mine does too. By the crescendo of the commotion, I was mortified. I was embarrassed and upset with my lack of judgment. This was supposed to be a beautiful, holy, family-shared experience; and here were my two oldest children, demonstrating the epitome of poor church behavior. I felt like I exemplified the role of the obtuse mother. All I could think of was of getting them to the cry room—it was clear that both girls had completely gone into another world and weren't going to calm down anytime soon.

I worried about not even being able to get them out of the pew, but somehow I managed to get them to the aisle. Since the center aisle was the closest, my embarrassment was only compounded by our inability to make a discreet exit. I led them to the rear doors and out to the cry room, sobbing in defeat. My mother followed us out while Jeff stayed back to watch Anna take her First Communion before coming to check on us. At least one of us was able to see and share in her big moment. By the time we reached the cry room, all I could do was sit and weep.

I've only had one other breakdown of this caliber out in public. The best way to explain it is as being swallowed by an overwhelming sense of being let down. *How could they do this to me on such an important day?* Logically, I know that they aren't to blame, but when emotions are high, logic and reason can be temporarily hindered. Sometimes when I think of Maria and Christina, the words "no mercy" come to mind. They have an

indomitable spirit, relentless energy; and through their complete lack of perception, they can create a situation that gives us,
as parents, no mercy. But some of these traits are also their most
endearing in day-to-day life.

Removed from the environmental stimuli and pressures
of the nave, they snapped out of their zones and returned to
normal behavior. They couldn't understand why I was so upset.
I began to regain my composure and went to the washroom to
freshen up. Jeff was waiting in the hallway. He stopped me and
said, "Go easy on them. They think they were being good." I
looked back toward the cry room, where my little angels were
smiling back at me through the window. He was right. They
had no idea of what transpired. And sadly, I know that the
entire situation probably could have been prevented by sitting
in our usual place at the back of the church.

Jeff suggested that I go back in and take Communion
with the rest of the congregation. I didn't want to, because I
felt embarrassed about being seen as "the woman with the rude
kids," but I knew it was my chance to see Anna and let her
know I was there. As I passed by her on the way to the altar, we
were able to exchange a small, respectful smile. Anna has never
liked feeling alone, so I hope that little exchange helped her
realize that we were all with her, regardless of anything else that
happened.

After the service, we decided to skip the party in the social
hall. We'd already had enough turmoil for one day. So we took
a few pictures and left for lunch with the grandmothers. I had
doubts about whether or not we should even attempt to carry
out those plans, but luckily, the rest of the day was uneventful. I
was able to relax a little and feel the joy of the occasion.

The chaos surrounding Anna's First Communion created a
bit of trepidation as the time drew near for Maria and Christina
to receive their First Communion and Confirmation. Because
they are special needs and were already older, they experienced
both rites at the same time. Unlike Anna's First Communion,
Maria and Christina did not have to go through the rigor of

preparatory coursework, nor were they part of a large processional of other children. Our priest worked with us to prepare the girls for their special day and to make the ceremony as easy on them as possible.

On the morning of the ceremony, we all arrived at the chapel ten minutes early. The congregation was already assembled and praying with the priest. I panicked with the thought of being late and was relieved to find that mass had not officially started yet. We were just hearing the recitation of morning prayers. We found our seats in the back row; Christina was already huffing, but Maria was on her best behavior.

The pressure of having this day go well was building—I was terrified about this special day being a repeat of Anna's. I remember fighting back the tears as I tried to stop Christina from hyperventilating, all the while trying to convince myself that everything would be okay. Our priest came and sat with us, assuring me that the girls were fine, their behavior was fine, and I did not need to feel distressed or anxious. His words helped put my mind at ease, which, in turn, allowed me to remain calm enough to help Christina.

The service went well, and when our priest welcomed me to bring the girls up for their Communion and Confirmation, I took them to the front while Jeff stayed back with Anna. Neither of the girls understood the baptismal questions, but luckily, since we had prepared them at home ahead of time, they accepted the priest putting oil on their foreheads. With their tactile defensive issues, I was concerned about an adverse reaction.

The priest said a beautiful prayer', and then asked the congregation to kneel in preparation for Communion. That's when another wave of panic washed over me; we were still in the front row without a kneeler. I had no idea how the girls were going to react to kneeling on the floor. They do not adapt to change well, and transitions always aggravate their anxiety level. At an opportune moment, I moved them around to the second pew and was able to avoid a potentially loud and disruptive scene.

Our next hurdle came with the sacrament of wine. Maria drank without incident, but Christina was hyperventilating again. I was concerned about her spilling the wine, which would have been bad in the religious context, not to mention ruining her lovely white dress. The priest was patient and kind, giving Christina a chance to regain control enough to successfully partake of the wine. I was overjoyed. The ritual was done. Jeff, Anna, and I were then able to receive Communion with the rest of the congregation. After Communion, the priest said a few words commending us on raising our girls to follow in the faith. Jeff and I both felt the sting of tears as we listened. We try so hard, but only God knows how much they understand.

At the end of a very heartfelt service, the priest again mentioned Maria and Christina. He invited the congregation to congratulate them on this very special moment in their lives. Everyone began clapping, and a couple of gentlemen came up to shake their hands. The excitement continued with photographs and ongoing attention. Others seemed to understand what a remarkably wonderful day this was for us as a family. There is always so much grace when Maria and Christina are involved, especially during a religious service where their innocence keeps them cradled in God's hands.

About the Author

School

Julie Clark Ames graduated from Georgia Institute of Technology in 1987 with a bachelor's degree in industrial systems engineering, minor in Spanish, and a minor in technical business communications.

Love and Marriage

Julie met her husband, Jeffrey Ames, at Georgia Tech. A West Point graduate, he had just completed five years at Fort Bragg, NC, with the Army's 82nd Airborne Division, and was earning his master's degree in operations research (a branch of industrial engineering) in preparation for his next assignment at the Pentagon. Jeff and Julie were married while at Tech and then moved to Alexandria, Virginia. Jeff was assigned to the army operations staff in the Pentagon; Julie's first career job was as an industrial sales representative for a paper recycling company. Her territory included Maryland, Virginia, and DC.

Professional Career

Julie subsequently was hired as an industrial engineer with Naval Sea (NAVSEA) Systems Command in Arlington, Virginia. She is a graduate of the NAVSEA two-year Cost Intern Program. Julie first served as an analyst for Submarine Combat Systems, then as the lead cost analyst for the Aircraft Carrier Program (USS *Ronald Reagan*), and finally as business analyst for the USS Missouri Battleship Museum.

Motherhood

After many years in the workforce, Julie decided to become a stay-at-home mother with the birth of their first child. Jeff and Julie are the proud parents of three daughters: Maria, Christina, and Anna, twenty-three, twenty-one, and eighteen, respectively. Jeff and Julie moved to Tampa in 2002 after fifteen years in Washington, DC. Soon thereafter, they received diagnoses that their eldest two daughters were atypical autistic, with severe intellectual disabilities. An innate genetic abnormality was theorized to be the cause. Following her daughters' diagnoses, Julie has become a special needs expert and activist. She started writing *A Special Journey* in July 2003 and completed her draft in June of 2013, when the girls were seventeen, fifteen, and twelve. In 2019, she was mentally and emotionally ready to publish.

Moving

In December 2012, Julie and her family moved into a small midcentury modern home that required extensive renovations and an addition to accommodate the family. The addition and major systems in the home were completed by October 2014. Her original plan was to publish the book and have a website. She envisioned a library of podcasts that people could access for free, containing information on special needs topics that would help them with their challenges. The plan was to have friends (doctors, educators, professors, and other professionals in the special needs field) over to her new home office, to record podcasts. Then, an opportunity became available to have the radio show.

Radio Talk Show Host, 2015 to Present

On May 10, Mother's Day 2015, Julie officially started the Special Needs Family Hour Radio Show. Julie has developed an extensive nonprofit business, centered around the radio show, coupled with a website populated with a library of resources. The show airs on Sundays from 1:00 to 2:00 p.m. and is coupled with professionally produced podcasts that listeners can access at any time to get the information they need to be a successful caregiver for individuals with special needs. As the announcer for all of the shows always says, "You are not alone." Julie covers all things educational, financial, legal, medical, psychological, and social. She interviews nationally known personalities, individuals with special needs, and other mothers like herself. For more information on the Special Needs Family Hour and to access podcasts on various subjects, go to the website—specialneedsfamilyhour.com.

Speaker/Contact Information

Julie is a radio show host, author, and speaker. She is completing her Masters Degree in Clinical Mental Health Counseling through Liberty University's accredited program, to become a Licensed Mental Health Counselor. As a trained speaker, Julie regularly gives speeches and provides resources to other special needs parents, and to professionals working with those who have special needs. Contact Julie at julie@specialneedsfamilyresources.com to have her speak to your organization.